BUDE

THROUGH TIME

Dawn Robinson-Walsh

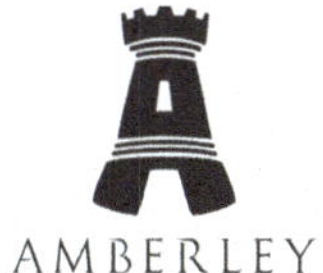
AMBERLEY

First published 2013

Amberley Publishing
The Hill, Stroud
Gloucestershire, GL5 4EP

www.amberley-books.com

ISBN 978 1 4456 1797 8 (PRINT)
ISBN 978 1 4456 1811 1 (EBOOK)

British Library Cataloguing in Publication Data.
A catalogue record for this book is available from the British Library.

Typeset in 9.5pt on 12pt Celeste.
Typesetting by Amberley Publishing.
Printed in the UK.

Appointed GPSR EU Representative: Easy Access System Europe Oü, 16879218
Address: Mustamäe tee 50, 10621, Tallinn, Estonia
Contact Details: gpsr.requests@easproject.com, +358 40 500 3575

Introduction

For the many annual visitors to the wonderfully diverse North Cornwall coastal town of Bude, the superb beaches and Atlantic rollers, offering fine surfing at Summerleaze, Crooklets, Northcott and out to Widemouth Bay, are probably the key attractions. Bude today is generally seen as a welcoming, friendly, safe and small Victorian family holiday resort, compact enough to explore by foot. It was once described by the poet John Betjeman as 'the least rowdy resort in the country'.

Behind the charming seaside exterior, the town, despite its proximity to the River Tamar (Bude is 5 miles from Devon) is very proud of its Cornish heritage. The community is today heavily reliant on tourism, but still retains its own very special historical character. Locals feel that Bude's historical development was determined by the sea canal, railway, beaches and the sea. The sea canal is still a vital part of the town for recreation and tourism purposes, but the railway is sadly long gone, irreversibly damaged, like many others, by Beeching's Axe.

In 2011, the population of Bude was 9,222, but it is said to almost triple in the summer months when the visitors arrive, many by way of the A39, 'the Atlantic Highway', which runs through Devon to reach well into the Duchy of Cornwall. The road name originated because of strong links to Southern Railway's Atlantic Coast Express from Waterloo, which brought visitors from the cities to the seaside. Adopted in the 1990s, the Atlantic Highway encompasses the stretch of A39 from Bideford in North Devon to Fraddon in central Cornwall, providing a scenic route to the West Country that takes visitors to the A3072 turn off to Bude. The town's situation, which is slightly off the main road, is important in terms of its historical development.

Due to its inaccessibility, there is no surviving evidence of very early settlements apart from a handful of Roman coins found nearby. According to the local archives based in the Heritage Centre at Gurney's Castle, in 1800 there was virtually nothing here. Bude would not exist at all if not for the canal, and the later Victorian passion for sea bathing. Without that, after the closure of the canal, Bude would have disintegrated.

Even by 1800, it was neighbouring Civil War market town, Stratton, that was much more important; hence, the local saying, 'Stratton was a market town when Bude was just a furzy down'. Before the coming of the canal, Bude really had little to commend it. In 1897, Arthur Norway wrote in his book *Highways and Byways* that 'The traveller who is wise will give a large berth to Bude with its unsafe harbour and new hotels, and seek out Stratton'. However, within fifty years, after the arrival of the railway in 1898, the Post Office Directory commented on the popularity of the summer sea bathing at Bude.

In the Middle Ages, the only dwelling in Bude was Efford Manor, seat of the Arundell family of Trerice. Bude (or *Porthbud*, to use the Cornish) was known as Bede's Haven, meaning the 'chapel on the rock'; the '*bede*' element referring to the holy man who lived in the chapel on Chapel Rock. But in reality, the origins of the name seem to be unclear. The Cornish word '*budr*', meaning a stream with a muddy bed, is rather similar, as is the sometimes used '*bewd*' version, so there is a good deal of debate about the etymology.

Chapel Rock still exists on the breakwater, and the name, Budehaven, was adopted by the local community secondary school, partly rebuilt after a fire in 1999 and sited in Stratton.

The spectacular sandstone coast here is a Site of Specific Scientific Interest (SSSI). Bude is renowned for its dangerous, jagged reefs, which have wrecked many ships, so the idea of a 'haven' seems heavily ironic, until you look at the rest of the coastline of North Cornwall and North Devon. Towards Morwenstow, Welcombe and Hartland the area is known for 'wrecking', and while tales of locals luring sailors to their deaths may be overstated, they were certainly ready for the pickings when a ship was washed up. The original breakwater, supposed to act as some kind of shelter, was destroyed in 1838 by a terrible storm and the new version, less steeply pitched and still there today, was constructed in 1839. It makes for a stunning walk and provides access to other lesser beaches, plus wonderful views to Summerleaze Beach.

In an area known for storm damage and destruction, the most famous Bude wreck was the *Bencoolen*, a 1,415-ton cargo ship wrecked during gale-force winds in 1862, leaving most of the crew of thirty-three drowned; six sailors survived. Despite being close to Summerleaze Beach, the sea was too rough to launch the lifeboat, leaving the rocket brigade, whose apparatus swiftly broke in the huge waves, to attempt rescue. The name *Bencoolen* lives on in Bude, not least because many parts of the broken ship were used in building houses and workshops, with the figurehead held in the Heritage Centre. Many structures in Bude have been named after the ship, including the bridge over the Neet and several houses.

This area of coast is inhospitable at best, and treacherous at worst. There are few places of refuge from winter storms and a continual heavy swell for shipping to contend with. Atlantic gales and high tides regularly wash over the Bude breakwater, taking no prisoners. Yet, compared to the rest of the coast, Bude did provide something of a 'haven' for the many schooners, ketches and barges that had worked the waters since the Middle Ages, until the last sailing ketch, the *Traly*, purchased by the Petherick family to replace the sunken *Ceres*, sank in 1936. With the shipping trade expanding over the centuries, the number of ships coming to grief on the Cornish coast increased, with many wrecked off Bude itself. The saying was 'from Padstow Point to Lundy Light, is a watery grave by day or night'. Over eighty vessels were said to be wrecked off the coast here in the fifty years prior to 1874, so generally locals have a healthy respect for the might of the sea.

Alongside the sea and the canal, Bude also has a river running through it – the River Neet (sometimes called the Strat). The two halves of the town are connected by a small bridge over the river, known as Nanny Moore's Bridge. Beyond this lay the quay, rebuilt in 1577 with funds from the Blanchminster charity, a legacy from local landowner Sir Ranulph Blanchminster of Binhamy (now the name for a proposed large housing development in Stratton).

The river acted as a historical dividing line for land owned by two Cornish families. Land to the south of the river was owned by Sir John Arundell, master of Trerice, while the land to the north was owned by Sir Richard Grenville of Stowe Barton, Kilkhampton. During the 1700s and into the 1800s, Bude was a thriving port used by smaller vessels, with goods shipped to and from the west, and the photographs in this book demonstrate the extent of the shipping. Lime kilns on Summerleaze were also used to burn lime shipped in from Wales. In the town itself, the land of Bede's Haven eventually changed hands: Grenville's land passed on to the Carterets, while the south side of Bude passed to the Aclands, the different families shaping the areas they owned.

Today, Bude looks very different in many ways but remains unchanged in others, and the sea canal remains a key feature. The Victorian passion for sea bathing helped Bude to stay in vogue. Sea bathing was then a constitutional or natural pastime inspired by the Romantic movement. Previously, it was perceived as unhealthy, but a sea dip developed into a growth area as doctors believed it to be a cure for all manner of diseases like scurvy and gout, as well as promoting general health. The ladies, with the appropriate decorum of beach huts and cover-all bathing costumes, used Crooklets Beach for their dips in the sea, with the gentlemen segregated and confined to Summerleaze for theirs. Beach holidays maintained their attraction long after the demise of the canal, and eventually the sexes were allowed to mingle.

Nonetheless, it was the coming of the canal that was vital to Bude's fortunes, bringing the area to people's attention in the first place. In 1800, Bude would have been lucky to have a hundred people living here, but people flocked when the canal opened as it provided economic activity, work and income. It could take vessels of 40–50 tons and, at the sea lock, could allow sailing vessels of 70–100 tons, according to the Bude Canal & Harbour Society, which keeps some fascinating historic records of the canal's development.

The original rationale for Bude Canal was simple. The passage around Land's End for coal had always been a very difficult and treacherous one, with many ships lost *en route*. The River Tamar, the dividing line between Cornwall and Devon, could in theory cut that journey short if it was connected to the coast. This was the dream of Cornishman John Edyvean, in 1774, pioneer of the St Columb Canal, near Newquay.

Various ideas for the canal fell by the wayside, but by 1814/15, after the Napoleonic Wars, when labour was very cheap and widely available, a group of entrepreneurs revived the concept. In 1811, when the Acland inheritance fell to Sir Thomas Acland, various people in his circle, including Lord Stanhope, invested in the idea of a canal, primarily to serve inland farms with sand from the beach. In the fourteenth century, a charter had been granted for people to take lime-rich sand from beaches for agricultural purposes. The soil inland from Bude is very acidic and full of clay. Conversely, the beach sand is very alkaline, with high shell content, so makes good fertiliser. Local entrepreneurs thus saw a business opportunity. They could take huge quantities of sand inland and, moreover, carry other goods in and out. This was at a time when communications were isolated and roads were mere tracks, as some of the photographs illustrate. It was not, however, until 1819 that the Bude Harbour & Canal Company was formed with 330 shareholders. The work on the canal lasted until 1823, at a final cost of around £120,000. The combination of a sea lock and inclined planes made it an important canal in heritage terms, and it retains its historical interest today.

The canal, of course, changed the topography in Bude. Victorian engineers built the breakwater and changed the course of the river to scour out a channel and create a makeshift harbour. They also built the big sea lock and, of course, the canal itself. One of the key features of the canal was the series of six inclined planes, upon which to haul tubs, an idea first used by the Egyptians on the Nile. Instead of locks (there was not enough water and the land was too steep) the planes were designed by James Green and surveyor Thomas Shearn, using Acland family money. Green was a civil engineer born in Birmingham. He worked on the canal from 1819 to 1825. The plan was to build a breakwater to connect Chapel Rock with the mainland, a sea lock, and alteration of the River Neet, all of which came to fruition.

The planes had rail tracks that accommodated the wheels on the boats to tackle the steep inclines (and they *are* steep). The sea lock is still in working order (despite several attempts by the weather to destroy it). In 2008, for example, powerful storms wrenched one of the lock gates off and all but drained the canal, which then had to be dredged and repaired by Cornwall Council.

It seems the quality of the materials available for these innovative engineers was sadly not really up to the task they were asked to do, so there were frequent breakdowns, breakages and problems, which were expensive to repair. Most profits made were actually used to simply keep the canal going until, eventually, the coming of the railway effectively ended the reign of the canal, which had become expensive in upkeep and maintenance. The railway had reached neighbouring Holsworthy by 1879, and opened in Bude in 1898, which brought sea bathers to Bude. Launceston families also visited regularly, which perhaps explains modern-day links between the two distinct towns. This infrastructure was axed in 1966. The railway, sited on the outskirts of Bude, near what is now the rugby club, served Stratton too. The Atlantic Coast Express would leave Waterloo at 10.35 a.m., arriving in Bude at 15.25. Most people now drive to Exeter to catch a main line train, something in the region of 70 miles away. There are now few signs that the railway ever existed, though there is a bridge over the marshlands near the rugby club. Progress? Perhaps not, but Beeching's cuts did not stop the visitors who simply came by car instead.

With trade growing fast during the mid-eighteenth century, so Bude grew. Warehouses were built to hold cargo, and many cottages sprang up to house merchants, workers and captains. As the railway became more efficient, and artificial chemical fertilisers reduced the need for sand in agriculture, the Bude Harbour & Canal Company finally wound up in 1901, by which time the population of the town itself was 2,308. The local Bude-Stratton Council, however, wanted a water supply for the town, as Bude was rather behind the times in 1901, still only having a parish pump. So, in 1902, the council assumed responsibility for the harbour and shipping trades, and the canal area was used to improve the public health of the area.

However, by the turn of the twentieth century, trade began to diminish. The invention of steam engines and the coming of the World Wars proved fatal. The small fishing fleet was not enough to keep all men at work and Bude was forced to find a new future. When the canal closed (although over 2 miles are still open to the public for leisure purposes) Bude focused on the emergent and developing tourist trade. Interestingly, women forged themselves a new economic role as they began to let out rooms and run guesthouses; still caught up in the private, traditional domestic sphere, but now making money from it at last.

By 1926, there were fifty-nine boarding houses and five hotels: the Falcon, Grenville, Globe, Norfolk and Commercial. Bude was connected to the national railway grid and with that, thousands of well-to-do holidaymakers arrived for their summer holidays. The prestigiously large and grand Grenville Hotel was built in 1909, and with it many a guesthouse opened its doors to the influx of people at the start of the tourist haven that Bude has become today. The guest houses on Summerleaze Crescent, Downs View and others were sizeable because large families came down to Bude for weeks or even months, bringing servants with them, and preferred to rent apartments rather than rooms.

To uncover more about the history of Bude, a visit to Goldsworthy Gurney's castellated mansion, Bude Castle, is essential. Built in 1830 on sand, following a challenge from local people who said it could never be done, the castle now houses the town's Heritage Centre, and is a mine of information. Built on a concrete raft, it is still standing. Gurney also invented the Bude Light, a bright oil lamp that used manganese, and was employed to light the Houses of Parliament.

In its honour, Bude now has *The Light* statue, created for the Millennium by local artist Carol Vincent.

During the twentieth century, Bude's population continued to grow. The town developed its own newspaper in 1924, *The Bude and Stratton Post,* which still sells well today, and in 1953, the first Surf Life Saving Club in the UK was established in Bude. Still incredibly popular today is the Bude Sea Pool, which opened in 1930, situated in a corner of the gentlemen's bathing beach, Summerleaze (for the sexes definitely did not bathe together in the 1920s). Bathing in the sea at Bude is not without its dangers (rips are common) so the original Sea Pool also had a paddling pool for children, and promoted safe bathing, actively promoting Bude as a resort.

The Sea Pool was previously administered by Cornwall Council but, during the funding crisis in the winter of 2010/11, the pool's public funding was withdrawn. Local councillors, pool users, businesses and supporters fought a vigorous campaign to keep the Sea Pool open for the 2011 season. The Friends of Bude Sea Pool was formed in early 2011 to secure the pool's future, and the FoBSP took on its day-to-day management in April 2012. The campaigners, supported by local people and tourists, have continued to run a high-profile campaign to maintain the old pool, and aim to restore it to its former glory. While the foreign package holiday became the vogue in the 1970s, Bude has now once again rebuilt its reputation, this time as a great centre for surfing and other outdoor activities, with the added attraction of one of Britain's few Sea Pools.

So, let's take a tour of beautiful Bude, and drink in the history, starting with the sea and the canal.

Acknowledgements

I wish to acknowledge the contribution made to this book by Ray Boyd. Without his impressive and extensive collection of catalogued old photographs and postcards, combined with his detailed historical knowledge of Bude, it would not have been possible to produce it. Several of the older images are reproduced from original F. Frith & Co. postcards.

Also, thanks to Christine Kett of Bude-Stratton Town Council, who was very helpful in providing some key information and dates/sources.

Finally, to my family, for those days I shut myself away to do the work, and especially to my daughter, Rosie, who loves Bude, and who accompanied me on the photography sessions around the town.

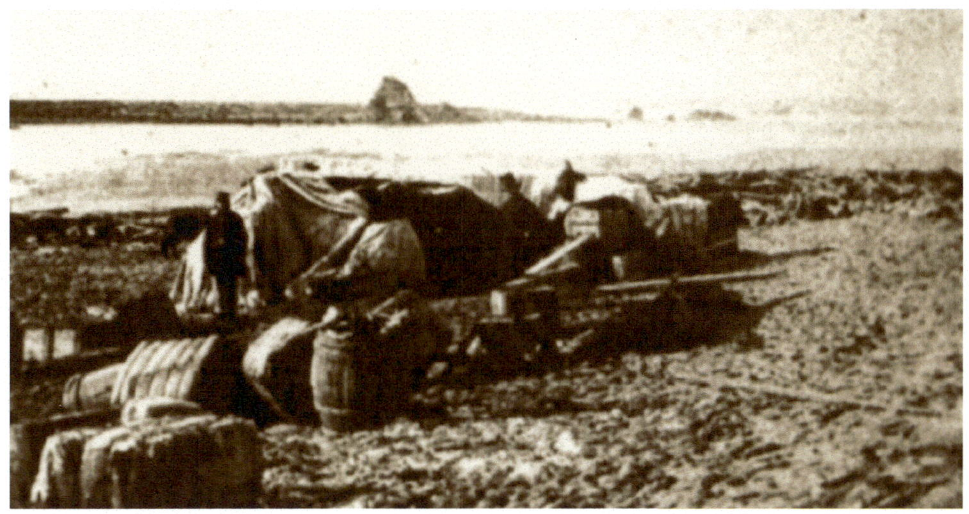

Wreck of the *Bencoolen*

These pictures show the wreck of Bude's most famous sinking, the barque *Bencoolen*, lost off the coast of Bude on 21 October 1862. The stricken crew (thirty-two men and one boy) constructed a raft out of fallen debris on the wreck, desperately attempting to reach shore. The ship, captained by William Chambers, was carrying general cargo for Bombay, including iron telegraph poles and wire ropes. In atrocious weather, the ship lost her masts, steering and lifeboats. Two crew members were lost overboard. Only six of the thirty-three were rescued alive. The cargo of hollow telegraph poles was reputed to have found its way into the plumbing and sanitation systems of many houses in the area; there is a suggestion that some of these may still be in use! The timbers of the vessel also proved useful in the local construction trade. One of the wire ropes found a good home later, in transforming the riverbank from a gently shelving slope (covered in huge baulks of timber) into the well-defined bank we know today. Before the building – in 1961 – of the present wall, the river edge was protected by a line of posts, painted green with white tops, with the wire strung between them. It feels strange that a relic of that tragedy was still in use, and an everyday sight, nearly 100 years after the actual wreck, but people did make use of whatever came their way – for reasons of thrift perhaps, but hopefully to preserve history too.

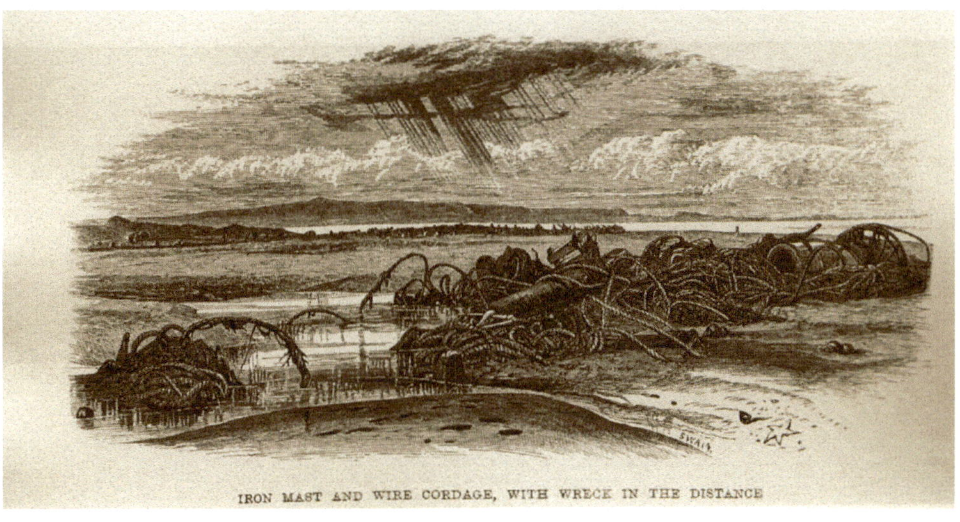

IRON MAST AND WIRE CORDAGE, WITH WRECK IN THE DISTANCE

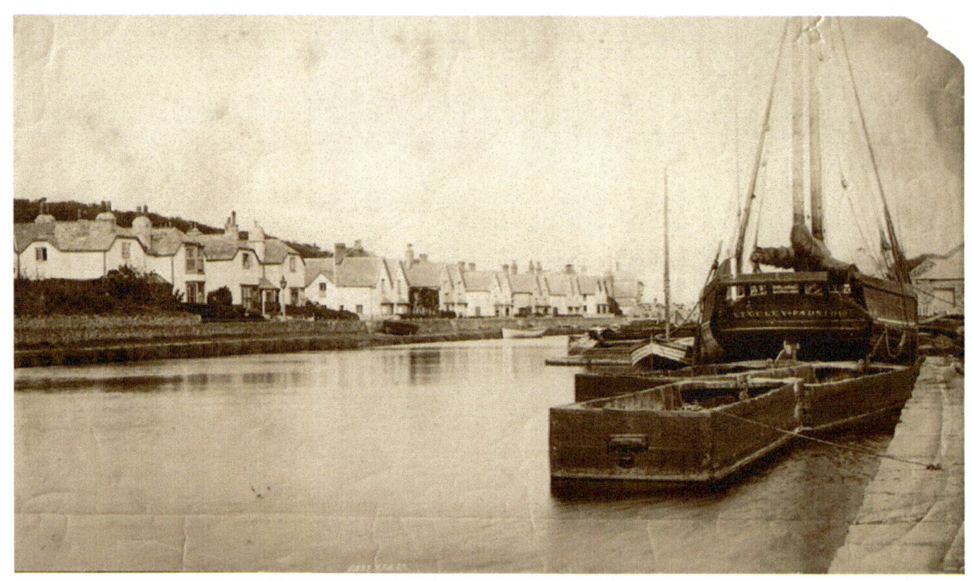

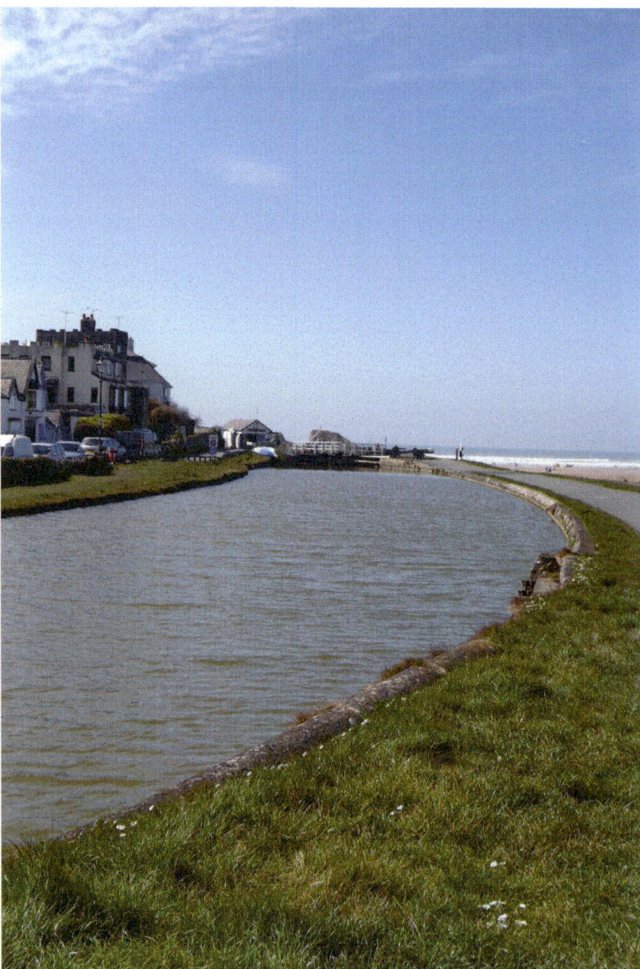

Bude Sea Canal

The canal is the main reason for Bude's existence as a town at all. Here, all is looking calm on the Bude Sea Canal in this Francis Frith original postcard showing the *Stucley of Padstow*, 1893. Also, in the foreground are some of the special tub boats, with wheels, used to transport sand inland along the Bude Canal with its series of inclined planes. The housing does not look very different today, though it used to be largely canal cottages, popular with retired sea captains who named them after their ships. The Breakwater Road cottages are part of the mid- to late nineteenth-century growth and development of Bude. To the left is a view of the Bude Canal down towards the lock gates and the sea, with a noticeably castellated house, originally fashioned on Goldsworthy Gurney's Bude Castle.

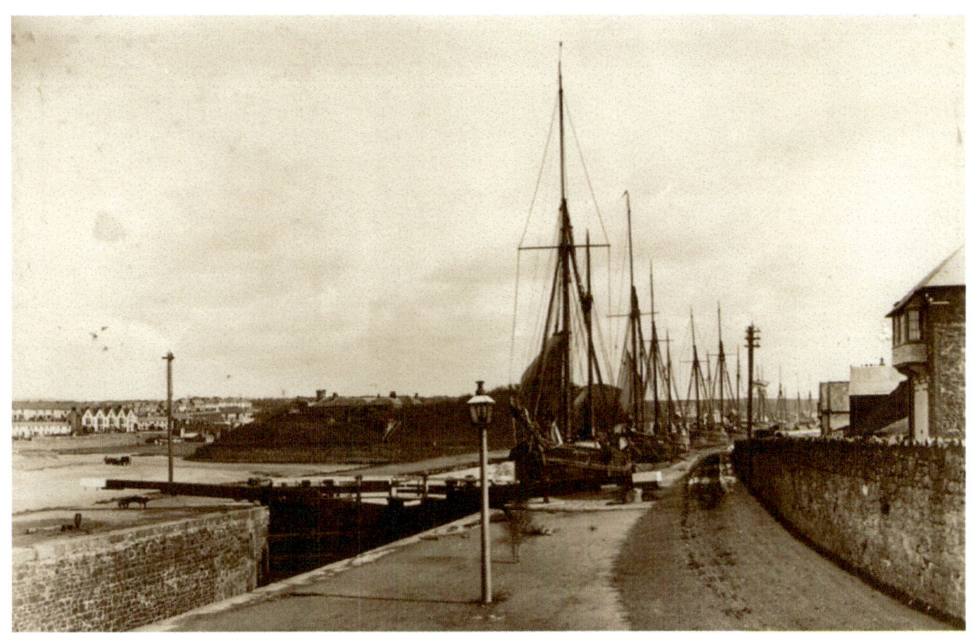

The Shipping News

Shipping in Bude Sea Canal in the 1890s must have been glorious sight. Here, the two-masted ketch *President Garfield* is the nearest vessel. The ships are waiting for the tide, which might take days if it were neap tides or the wind was in the wrong quarter. The *President Garfield* was sadly wrecked upon leaving Bude for Newport, when a heavy swell grounded her off Coach Rock, Summerleaze, in March 1906. Her crew of three was rescued. Below, Bude Canal today is a popular area and a vital part of the leisure and tourism industry, with the Wharf area home to bustling farmers' markets on Fridays during the summer.

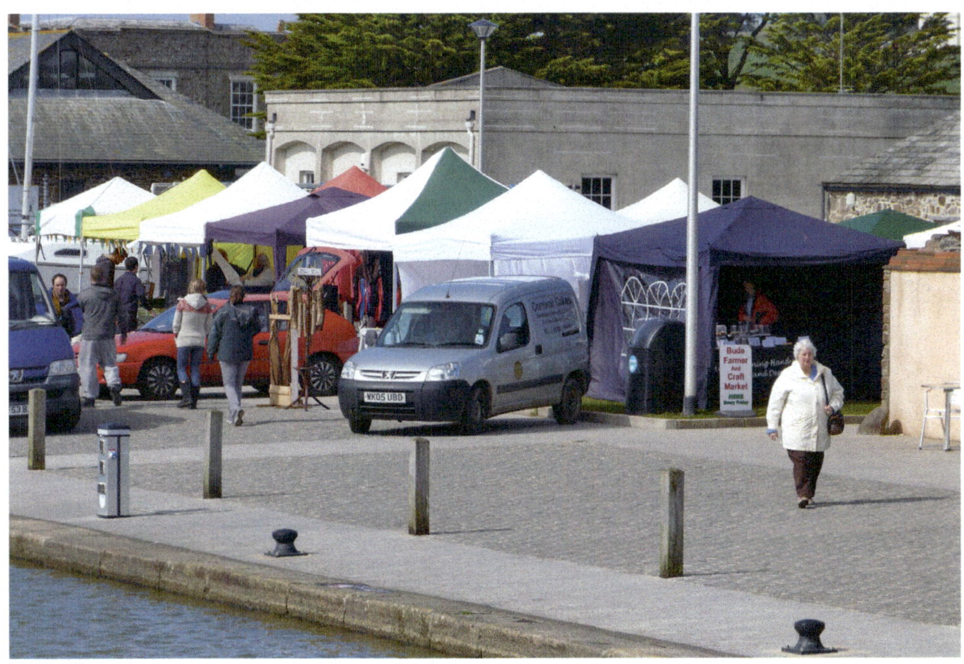

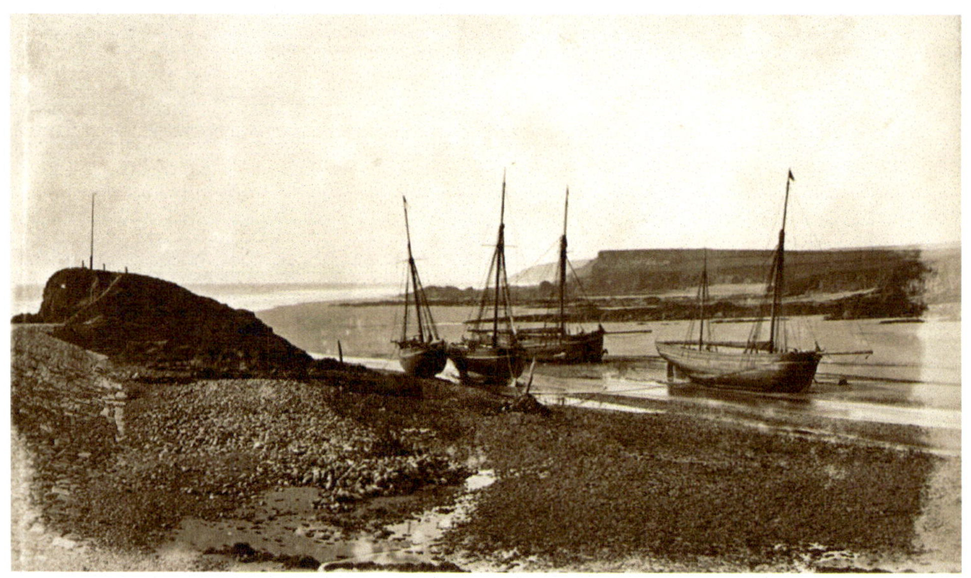

Bude Harbour

Above, the harbour in 1875 with three single-masted smacks (traditional fishing boats, small coasting vessels), *Nimrod, Hawk* and *Bee,* and the two-masted ketch *Ceres.* Back in the eighteenth century, the harbour was small and unprotected, but naturally sited between the treacherous sandstone cliffs, it was still a haven for shipping. The building of the breakwater offered greater shelter, although the tides would often wash over it. Modern 'shipping' is mainly comprised of sailing boats, dinghies and small fishing boats. The present breakwater is much more substantial, and a popular place for walking, enjoying the scenery and fishing at low tide, as well as offering marvellous views to Summerleaze, the cliffs and the South West Coastal Path beyond.

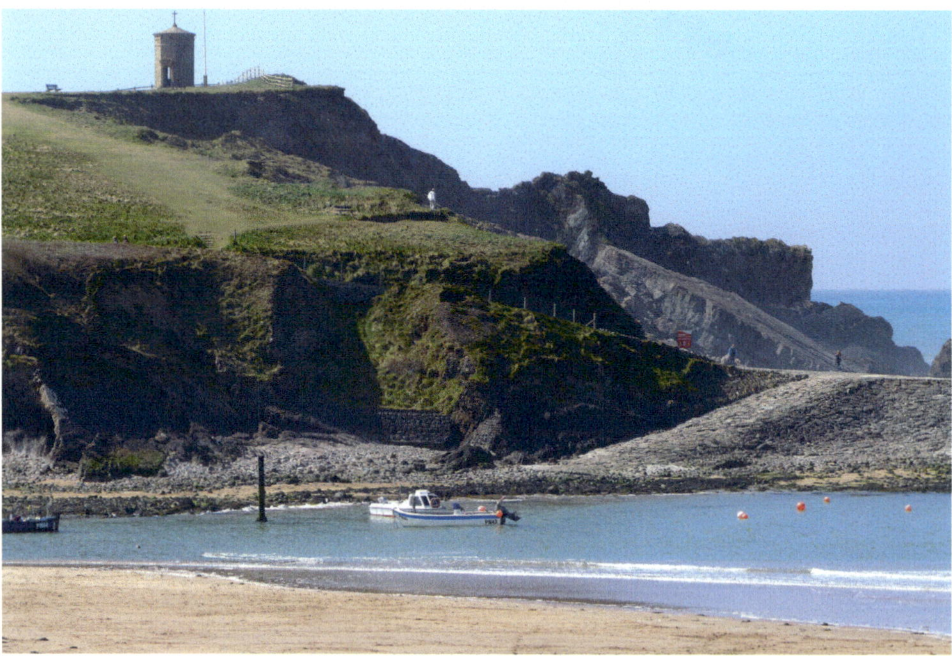

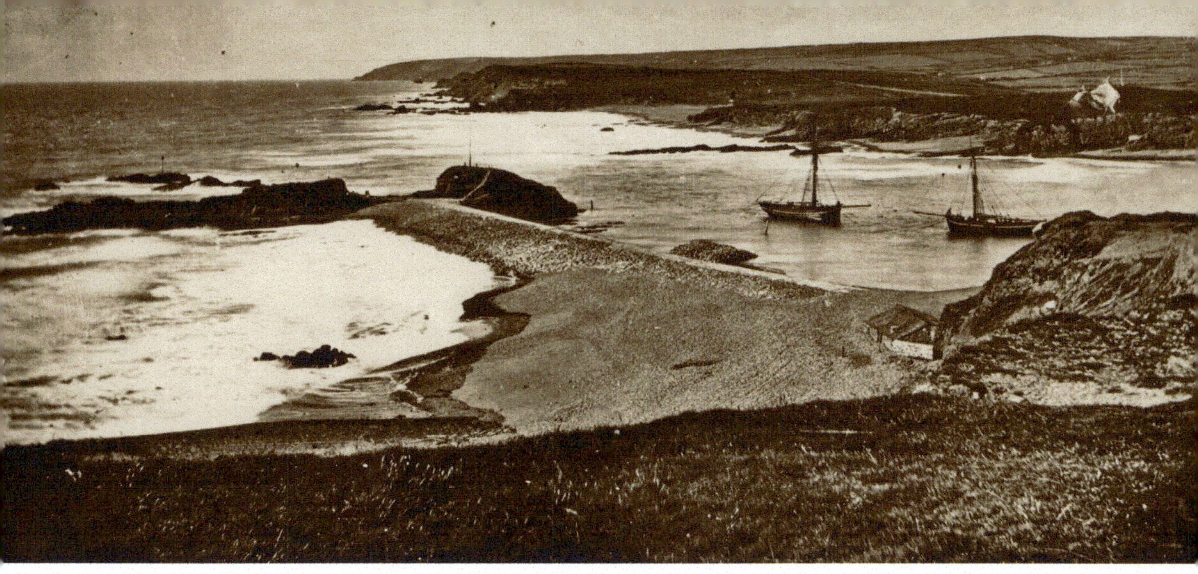

Breakwater

The Bude breakwater was built between 1839 and 1843 and this photograph was taken *c.* 1880. This is the second breakwater, as the first one was washed away a few years after it was built. The breakwater is now Grade II listed. There are two single-mast smacks in the harbour in this photograph; one is probably the *Bee*. The unknown building at the base of the breakwater is likely a store or a shelter, and is no longer in existence. Today, the breakwater is a popular place to walk during low tide, but it is easy to be taken by surprise as the waves wash over it. There has been more than one rescue from the breakwater in recent years.

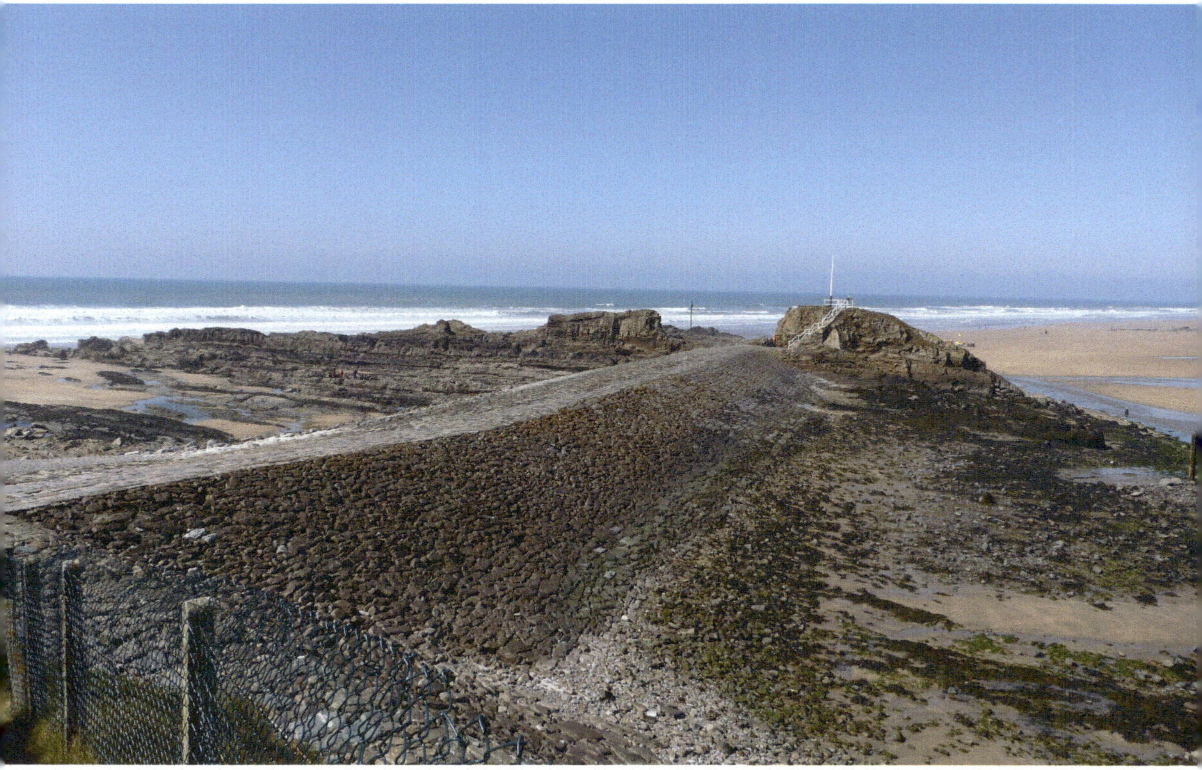

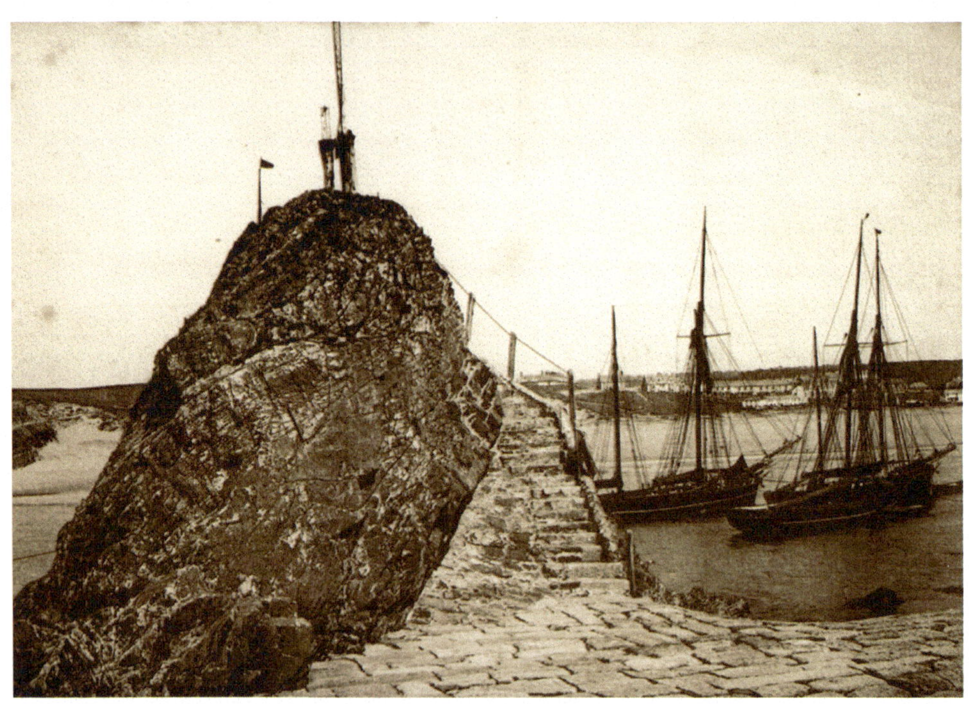

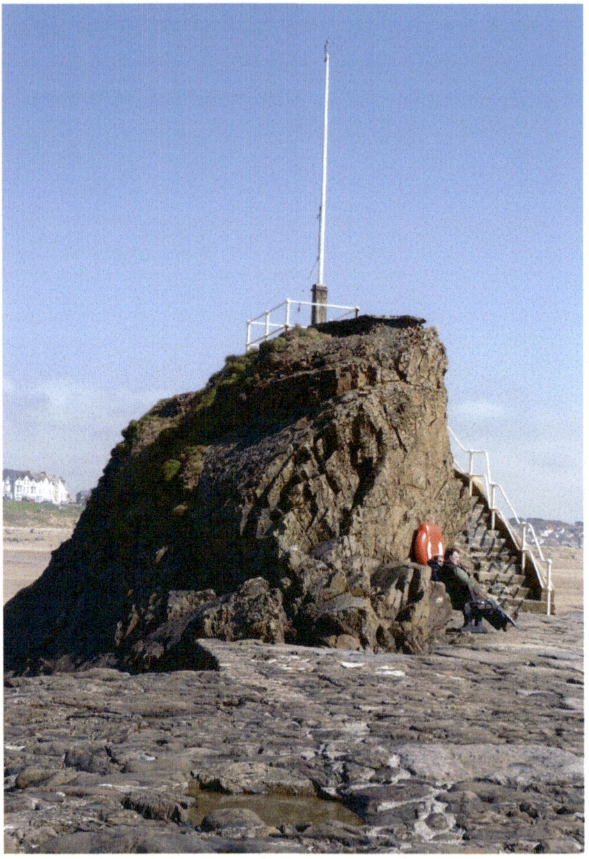

Chapel Rock

Shipping by Chapel Rock, at the breakwater in 1896, with the ketch, *Friendship*, and the smack, *Boconnoc*. Chapel Rock is supposed to date from the days when Bude was really just a 'chapel on a rock', with a holy man (or Bede, thus Bede's Haven) *in situ*. In the background is Marine Terrace, sixteen years before it disappeared. Othello Terrace, Tapsons Terrace and Garden Terrace are also all long gone, some physically and some by change of name. Richard Carew in his *Survey of Cornwall* (dated 1602) described Bude (of which you get a wonderful view from Chapel Rock) as 'an open sandy bay, in whose mouth riseth a little hill, by every sea flood made an island and theron a decayed chapel: it (the haven) spareth road only to such small shipping as bring their tide with them, leaving them dry when the ebb hath carried away the salt.'

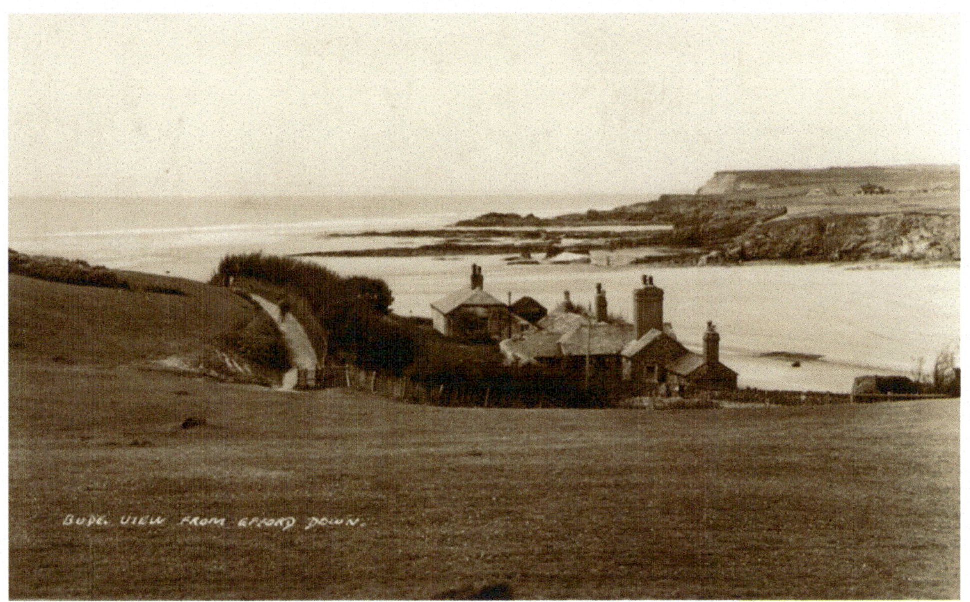

Efford Down

A view from the 1930s of the harbour from Efford Down, known as a wonderful place for horse riding, and which still rises above the harbour. There is little evidence of the overgrown brambles and gorse hedging that is behind Efford Cottage today (*see below*). Sir Thomas Acland built the house as a summer home in 1823. It is now out of alignment, but originally was intended to match the cardinal and sub-cardinal points of a compass. What a lovely site Sir Thomas chose! Originally a fish cellar for storing mackerel when there was a good catch, the residence was later called Ivy Cottage, and then the more location-appropriate Efford Cottage.

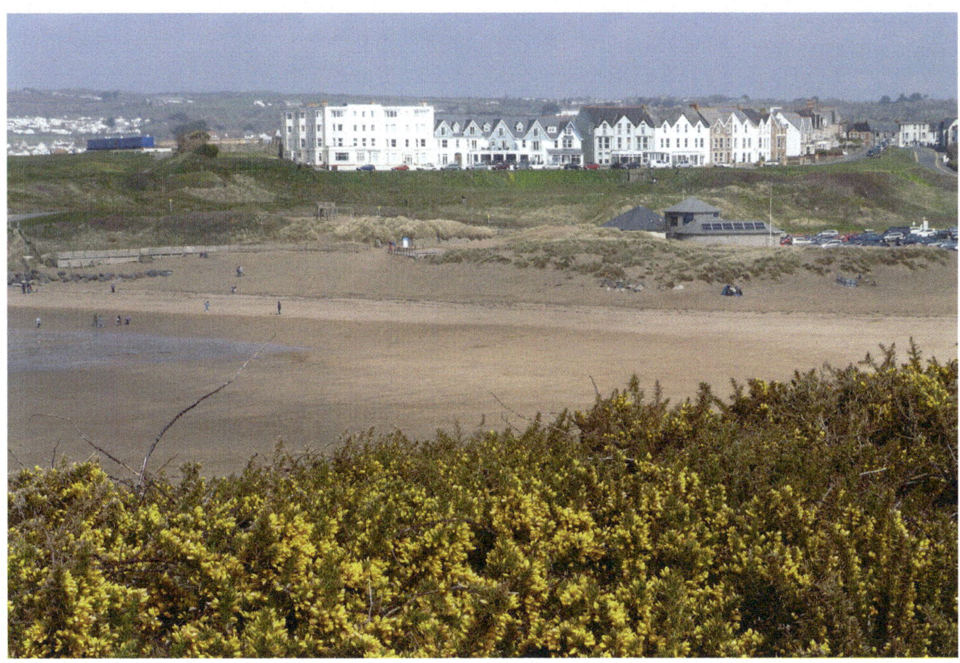

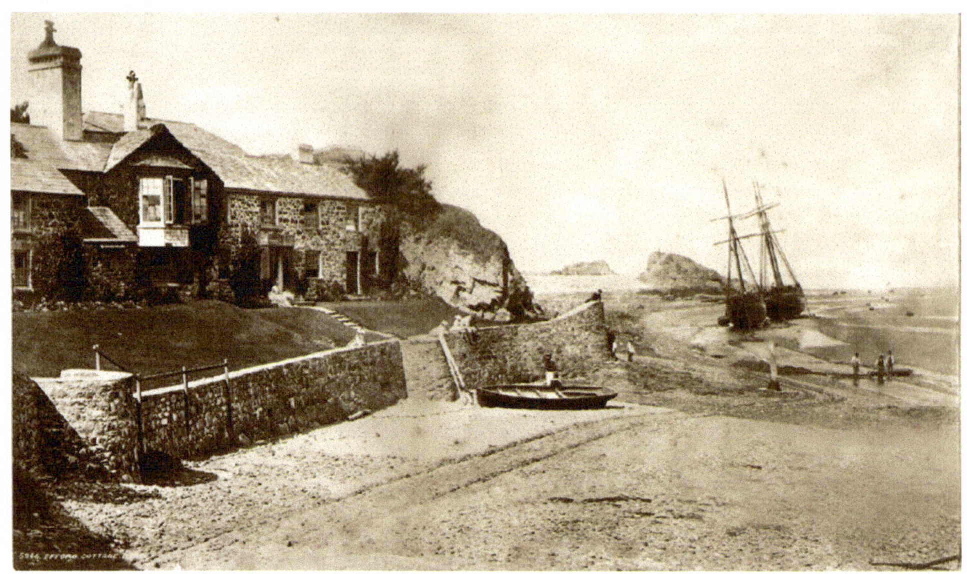

Efford Cottage

The Harbour in 1871 showing Efford Cottage, the last building beyond the lock gate. This is an original Francis Frith photograph. A schooner and a ketch lie in the harbour. Efford Cottage is seen with the wall lower than it is at present – it was increased in height to prevent waters overtopping it. Something of a local landmark, the cottage is now prettily painted pink. The lawn was then also much steeper. Efford (or Ebbingford) is the site of the earliest recorded development in the area during the late 1100s, but no buildings survive from this period.

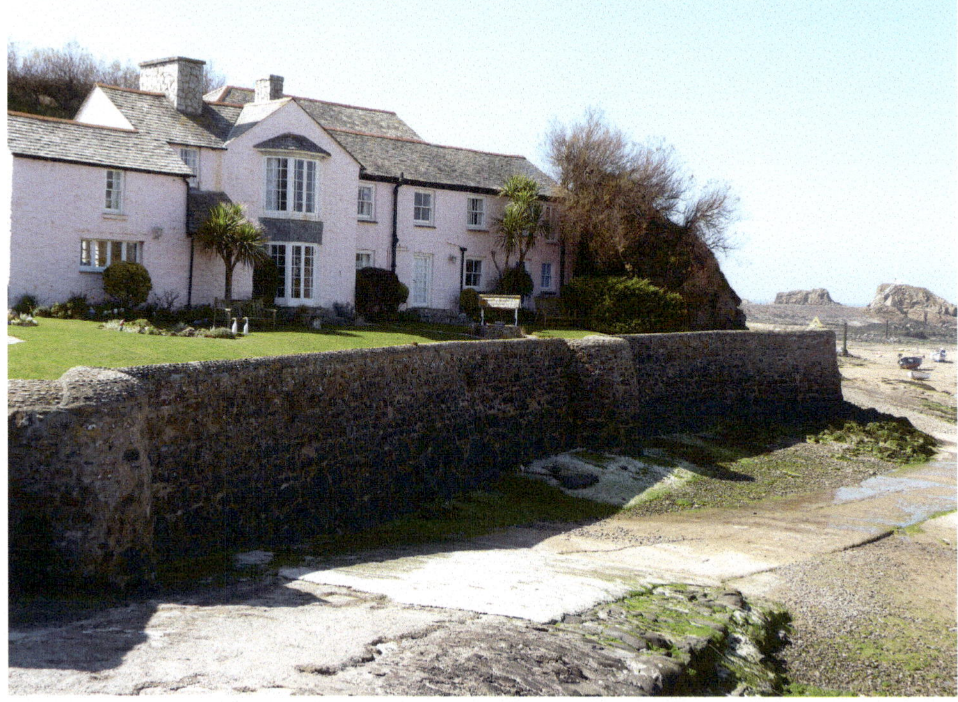

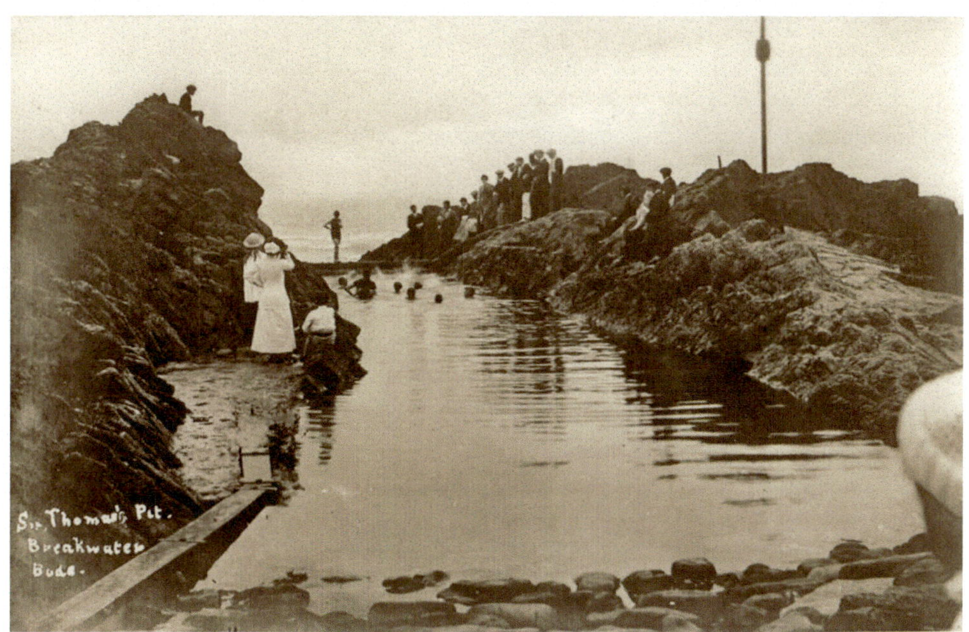

Tommy's Pit

At the end of the breakwater lies Tommy's Pit, Bude's first 'swimming pool'. This photograph is from the early 1900s. Sir Thomas Acland built the eponymous Sir Thomas ('Tommy's') Pit into the breakwater. It was the gentlemen's pool before the building of the Bude Sea Pool. Certainly, the ladies would have struggled on the slippery rocks and seaweed in their long skirts, even if mixed bathing had been acceptable. The pool is still there today (*right*) right at the end of the breakwater; not looking terribly enticing on a chilly March day, but still well used, most recently by the hardy trainees at Adventure International. At high tide, the pool is not usable, and it would be easy to be swept out to sea.

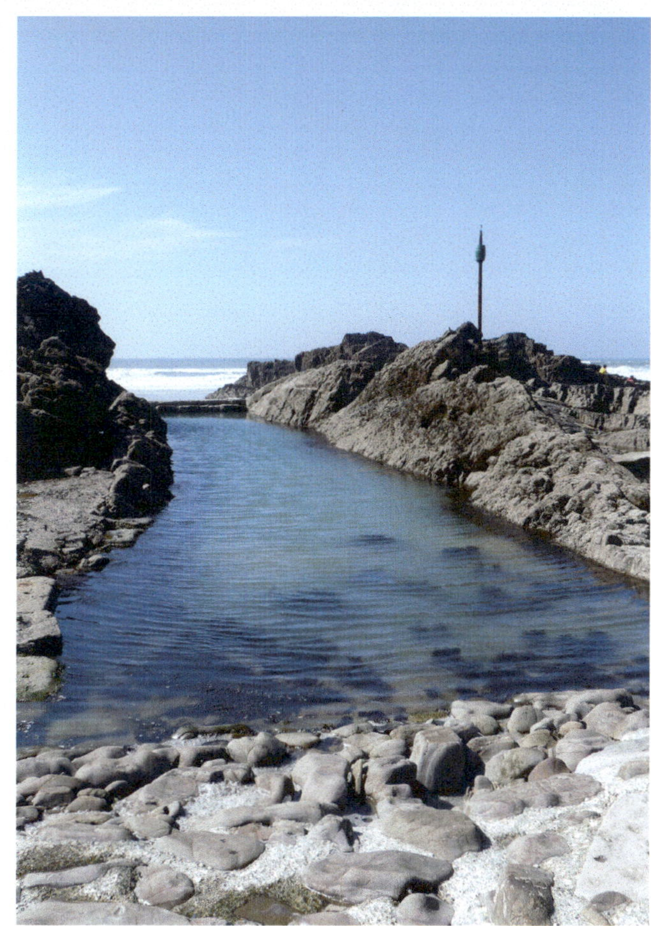

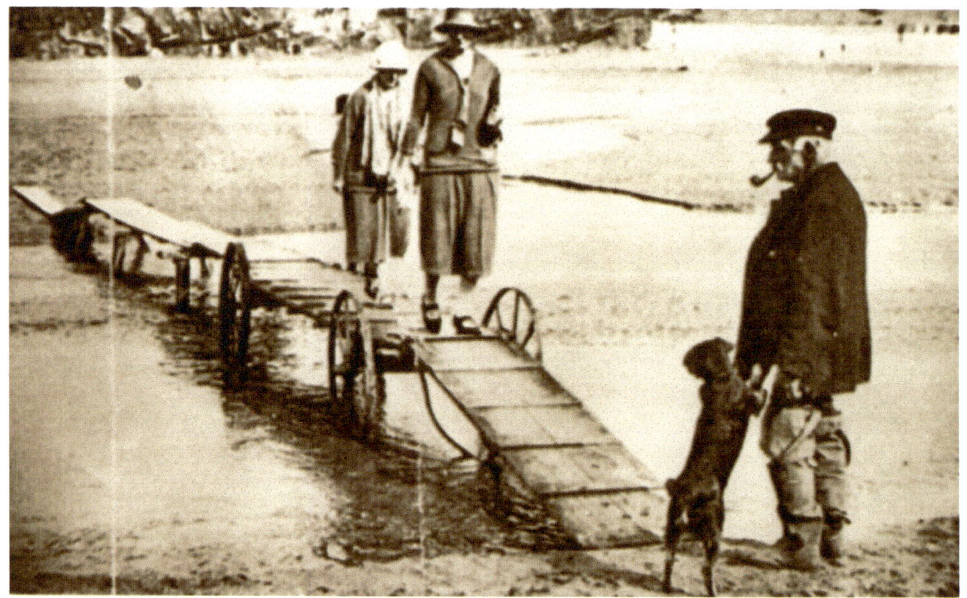

Captain Brinton's Bridge

Above we see Captain Brinton's footbridge, which linked Summerleaze Beach to the Breakwater. Captain Bill Brinton was a small-scale entrepreneur and retired sea captain. At low water he charged 1*d* to cross the river by the pontoon bridge to the breakwater, thus keeping people's feet dry. The footbridge was wheeled away and parked in the Ocean Caves during winter. Now there is the permanent bridge most people use today, though it often floods at high tide. Below, the view over the Neet shows the more modern bridge to the left of the imposing canal lock gates. The permanent bridge existed then, but it saved a walk to use Brinton's footbridge. The bridge had rails running over it. It has been resurfaced and had new railings added in recent years, but it was built around 1900.

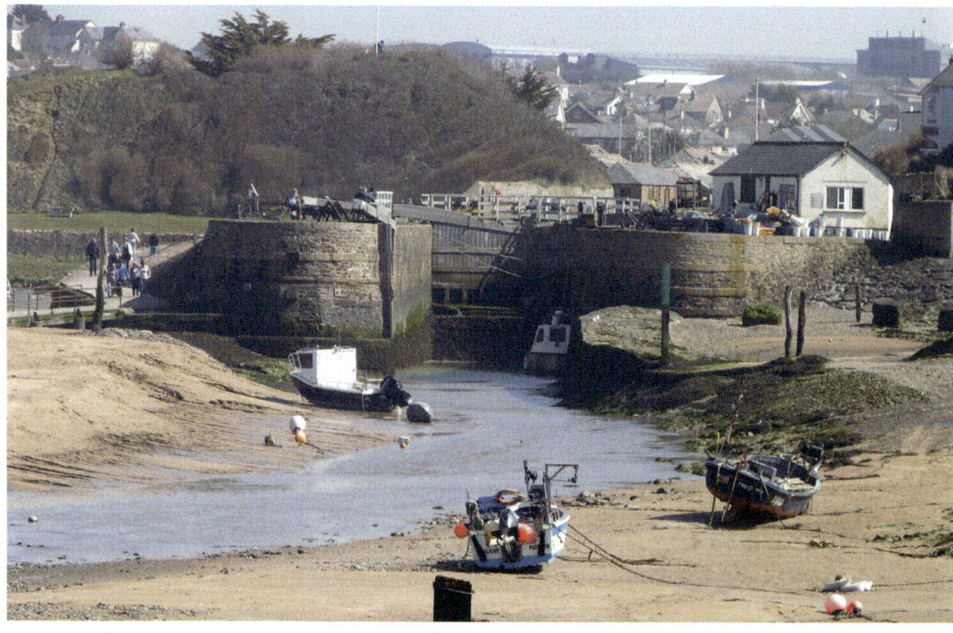

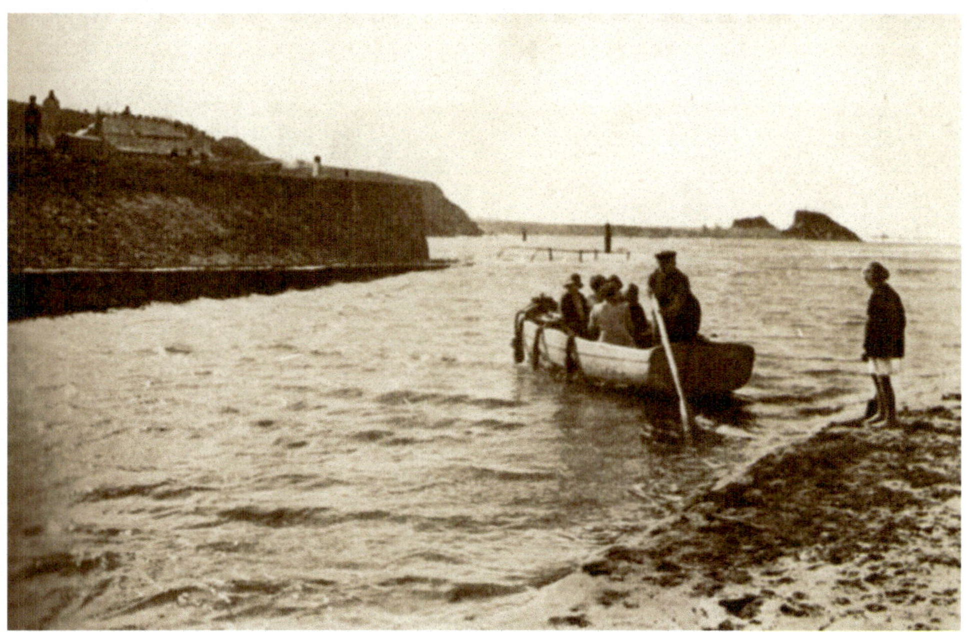

Brinton's Ferry

The above image of the harbour in 1926, with Captain Brinton's ferry in action, is another Francis Frith original. Captain Brinton operated a ferry at high tide during the season, situated by Iron Bridge (the one that is there now). According to Bude Canal & Harbour Society, a lifeboat called *Alcide* was washed ashore during the First World War and was used by Captain Brinton as the ferry for his 1*d* crossings. Bill Brinton had previously skippered a boat called *Elizabeth*, which ran aground at Summerleaze Point in February 1912. The river can still pose a wet crossing, but there is no gallant Captain Brinton waiting there to help now.

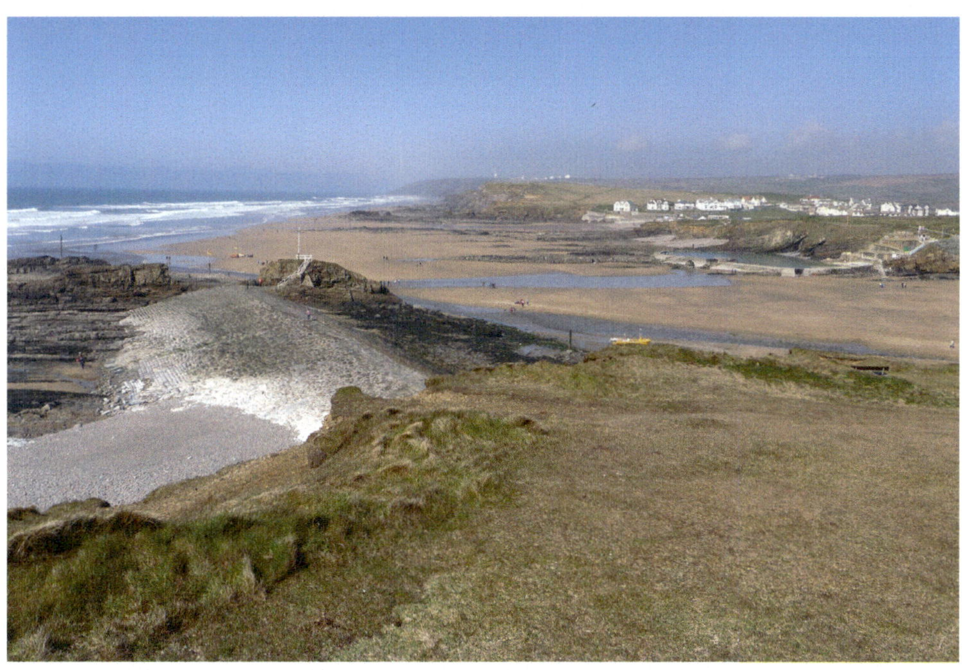

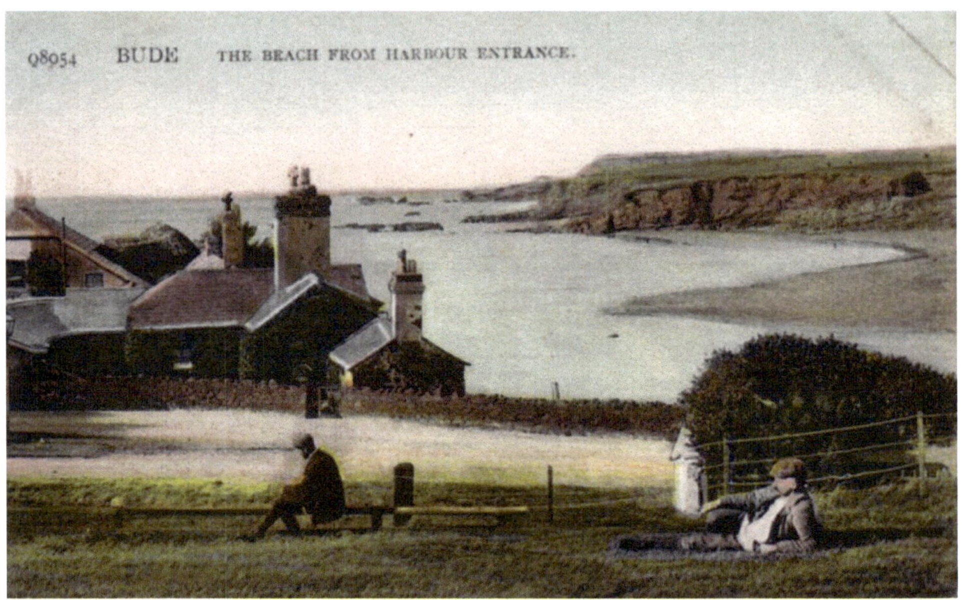

Smile, Please

This image of the beach from the harbour entrance and Efford Cottage is carefully arranged and coloured, as they often were in 1906. This image is included to show how postcards were constructed around this time, with posed figures and careful shading. The figures are more relaxed in 1906 than those during the 1880s, depicting different fashions in photography. Colour photography was not widely available until the 1940s or 1950s. Below, Bude Harbour in the 1880s; another posed shot but in sepia. Efford Cottage, before its enlargement, can be seen with a smack near the lock gates and shipping coming and going in the background. Efford Down looks very tidy, too!

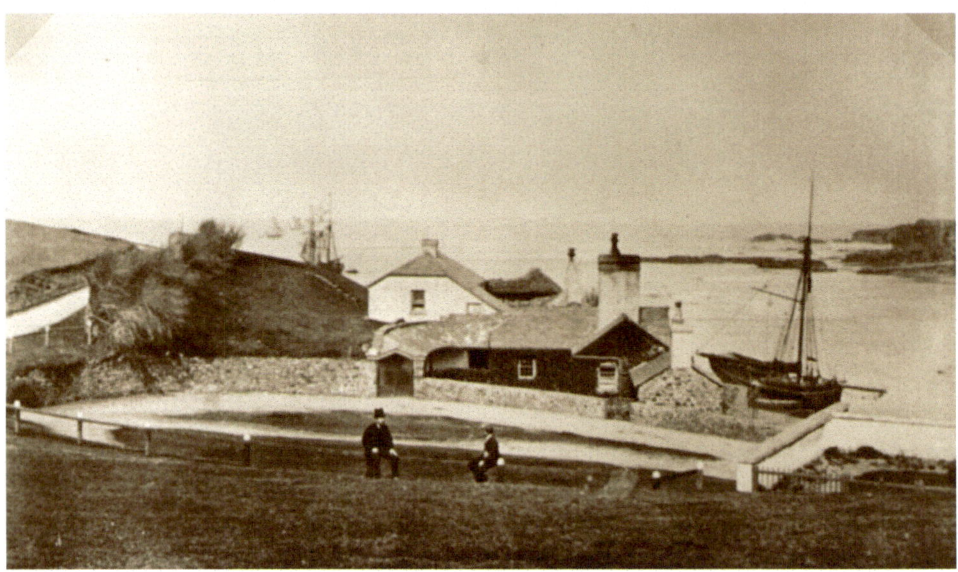

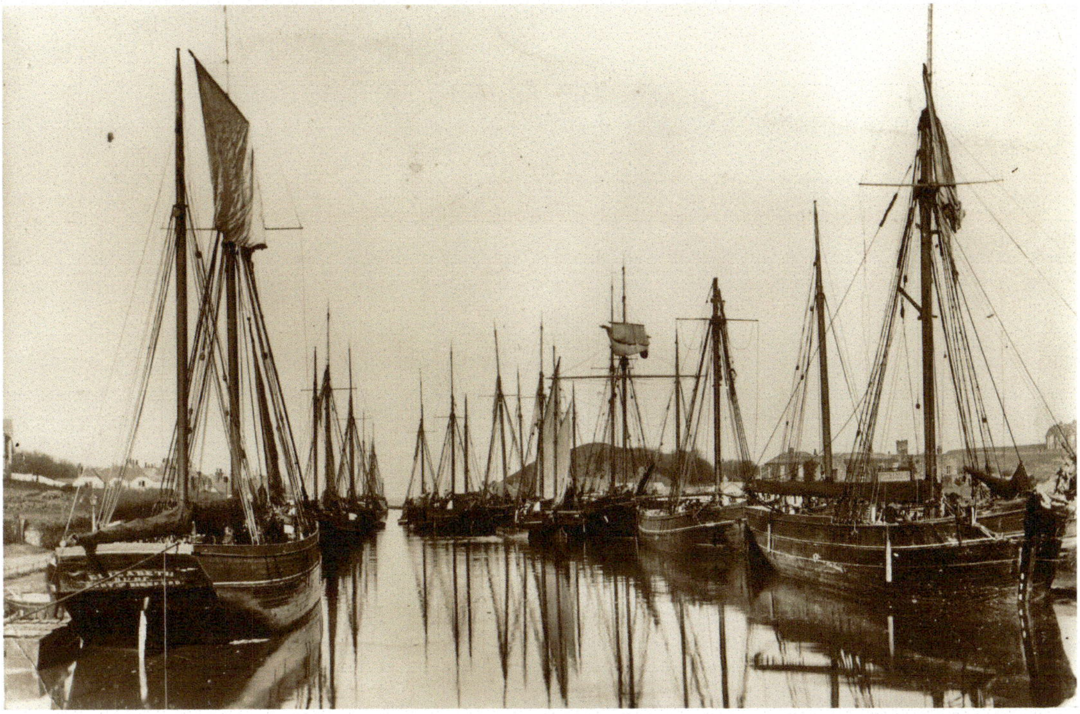

Bude Shipping

The Bude Canal, alive with shipping in 1897. Watching boats arrive is always exciting, so how vibrant and bustling this display must have felt. This is a well-known shot of the canal, bringing it to life and showing the actual scale of the shipping that once used the port. Schooners and ketches line both banks here; on the left is the *Elizabeth*, wrecked some years later on Summerleaze Beach when skippered by Captain Brinton. There is nothing like this quantity of shipping now, and traffic consists mainly tourists' pleasure boats and kayaks used by the activity centres.

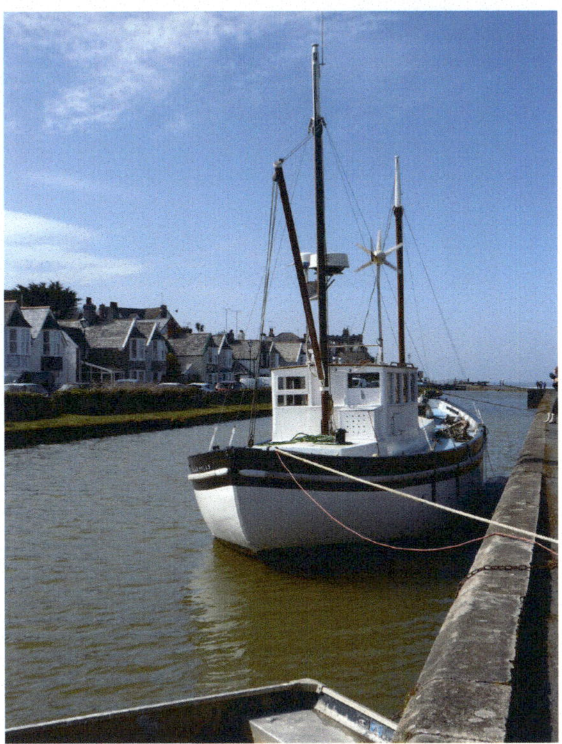

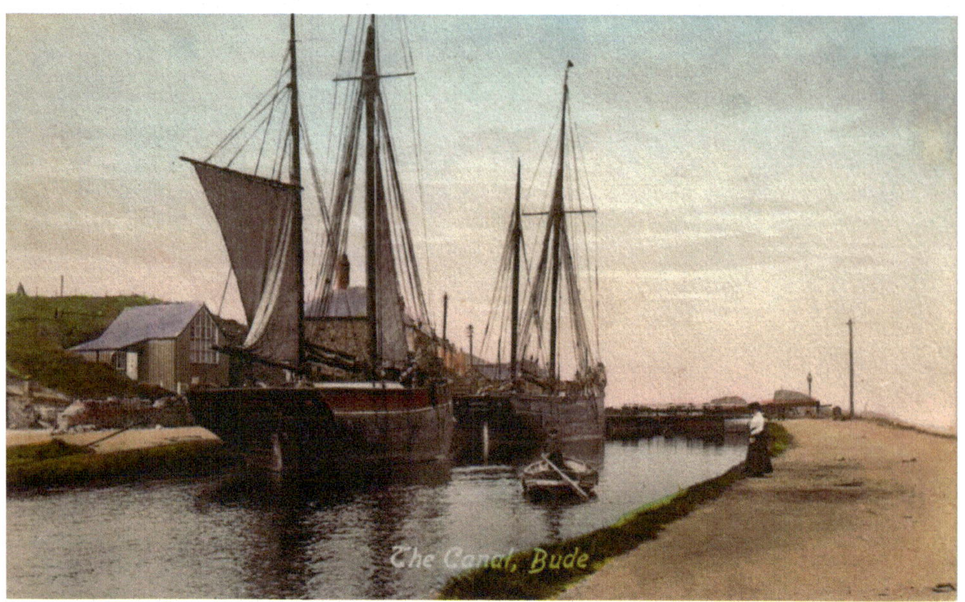

Bristol Packet and *Susanna*

At the Bude Canal in 1911, two ketches really dominate the scene – the *Bristol Packet* (used to carry fertiliser) on the left and *Susanna* in front – as they await the tide. This gives some idea of the size of ships that used the port; some schooners, which could be multi-masted, were too large to fit into the locks and discharged their cargoes into carts in the harbour. There are still some large boats, but they are few and far between.

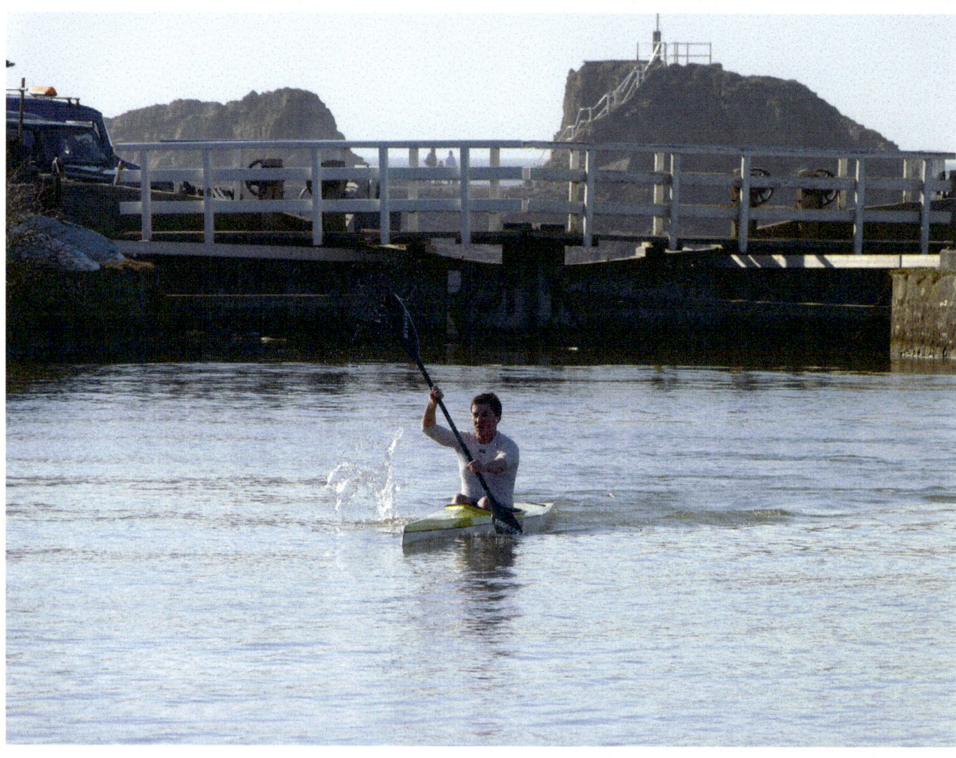

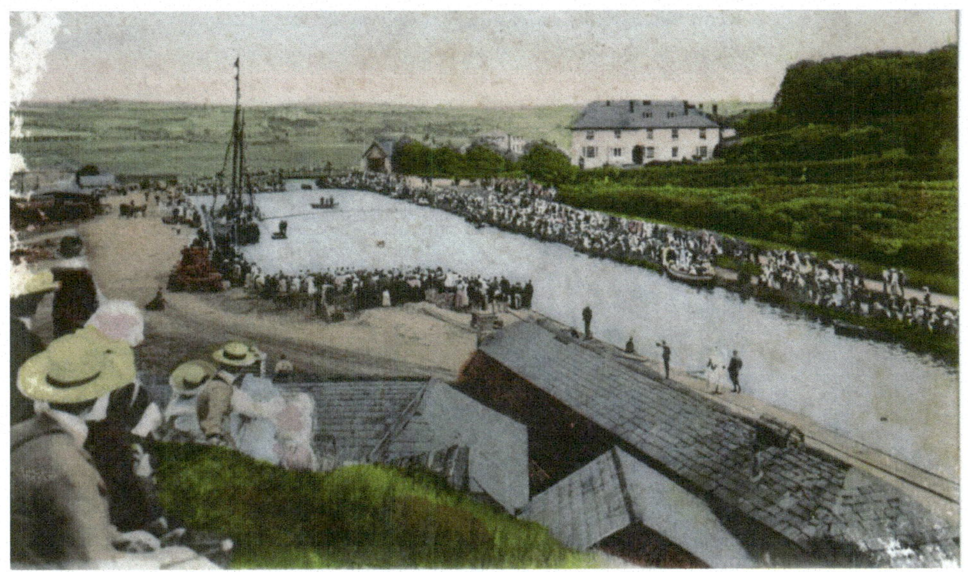

Lifeboats

Above, the canal on Lifeboat Day during the 1890s. The absence of the railway spur places it before 1898; the bridge was replaced in 1906. Bude lifeboat station was established in 1837 and was closed in 1923, but reopened in 1966. The boat could launch within two hours of high water, or with the aid of ten horses from either Summerleaze or Crooklets Beach. It was nevertheless closed for many years from 1923, when a motorised lifeboat was stationed at Padstow. In 2002, a new D class boathouse was completed at a cost of £516,000. This now lies on Summerleaze car park. Bude has a great deal of pride in its lifeboat crew and boat, which is a class D inshore vessel; useful for the rocky inlets around this part of the coast. Lifeboat Day, held every August, remains popular, as Bude RNLI remains well-loved in the town. Below, they have a presence in the procession on Carnival Day. On Lifeboat Day, the RNLI volunteers usually perform a Search and Rescue (SAR) demonstration, sometimes assisted by the emergency helicopter from RAF Chivenor.

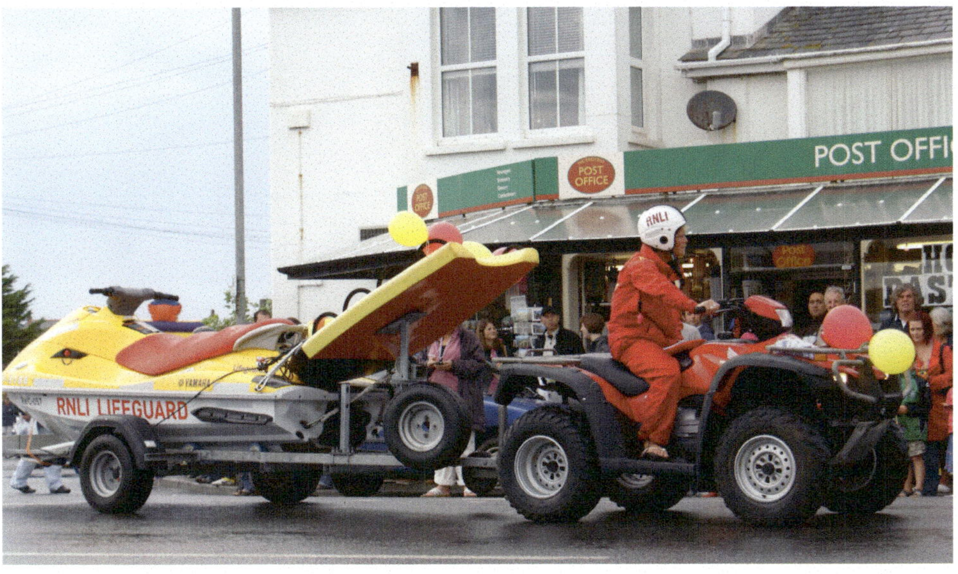

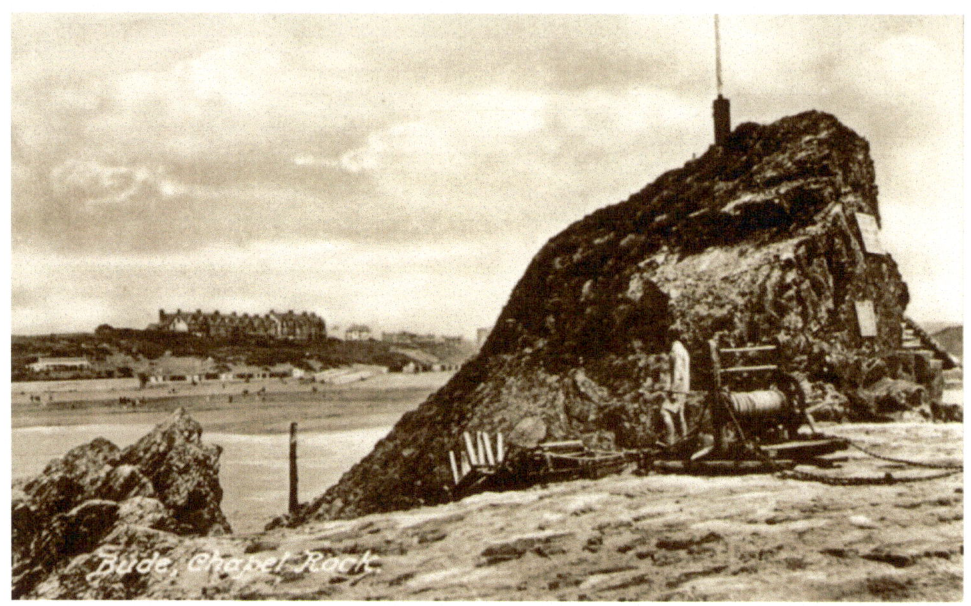

Chapel Rock

The Breakwater, 1928, with Captain Brinton's bridge in place. Captain Brinton's pontoon bridge is pulled up here, as the tide has come in; in the background Westcliff House has not yet been converted to the Westcliff Hotel. Today, Chapel Rock offers a good vantage point to enjoy fabulous views over Summerleaze, to the cliffs and dramatic South West Coastal Path beyond, and to the satellites of GCHQ Bude. It remains a popular spot with locals for walking, fishing and relaxing.

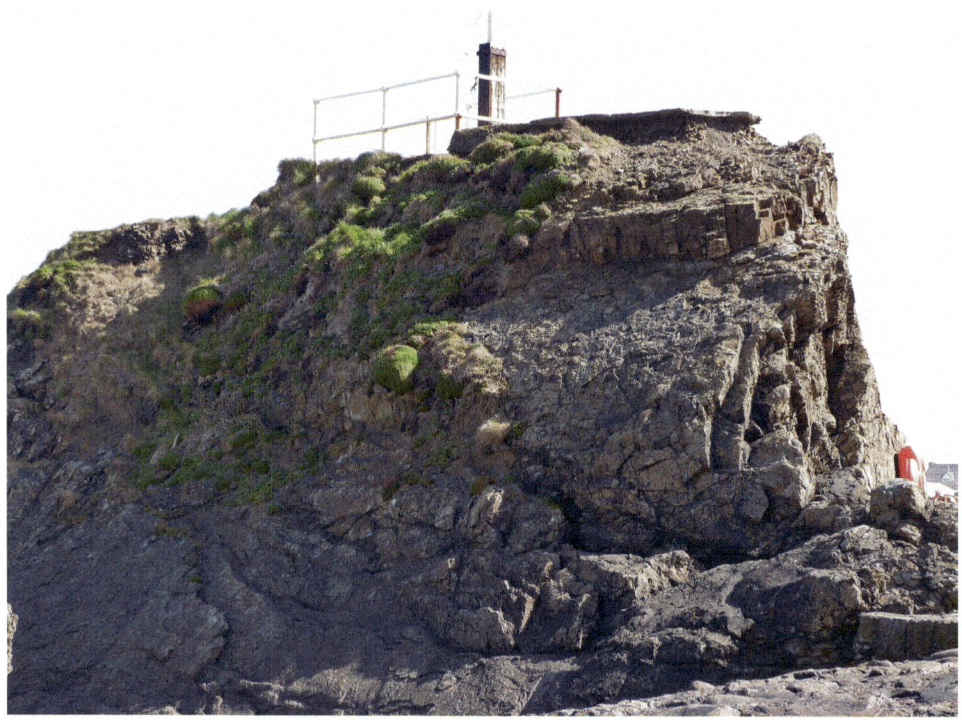

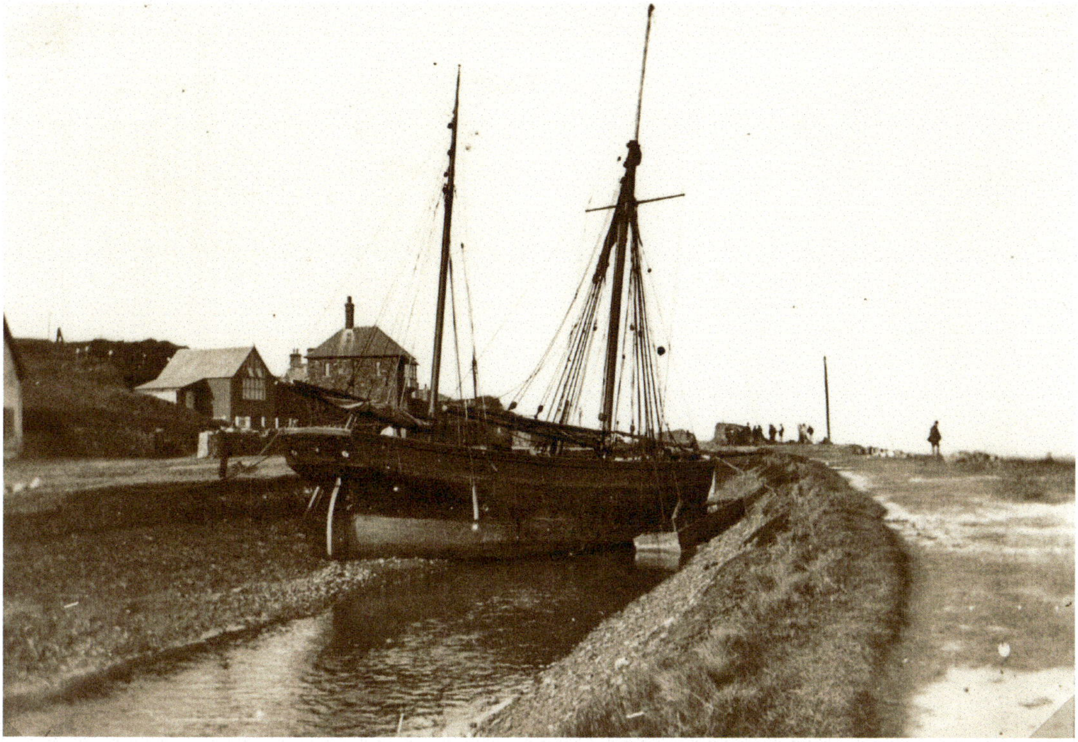

Storm Damage

The canal where the ketch *Jessie* was stuck after the lock gates were carried away in 1904, seemingly by a freak 20-foot wave. This happened on 16 February, when a storm damaged the lock gates, emptying the canal, which you can see semi-drained here. *Jessie* stayed broadside on to the canal, caught on mud, but the ketch *Wild Pigeon* was swept out of the canal and wrecked under Summerleaze cliffs, despite attempts to save her. Luckily, the crewmembers were alerted and leapt to safety before she was swept off to sea. The repair of the lock gates cost £430 in 1904. The drained canal yielded many items, apparently including a sawn-off shotgun! The lock gates were again wrenched away by stormy seas in March 2008, requiring more major repairs. Cornwall Council took the opportunity this time round to repair the canal walls and dredge the basin.

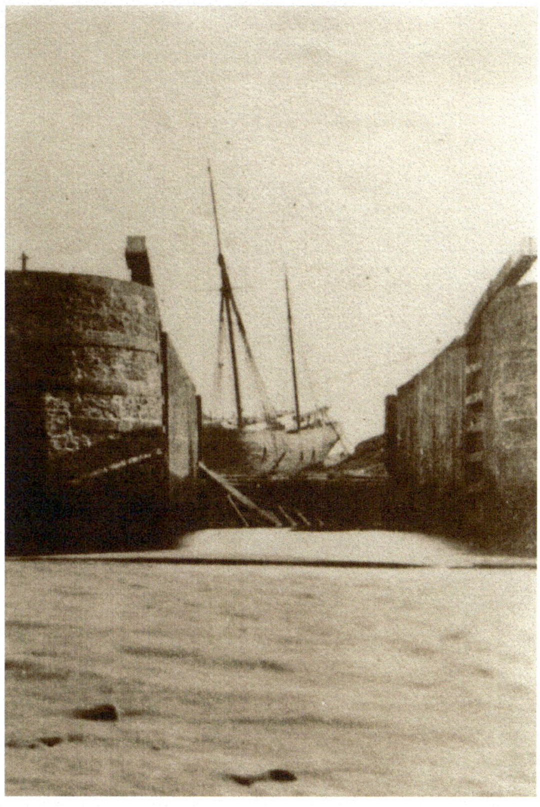

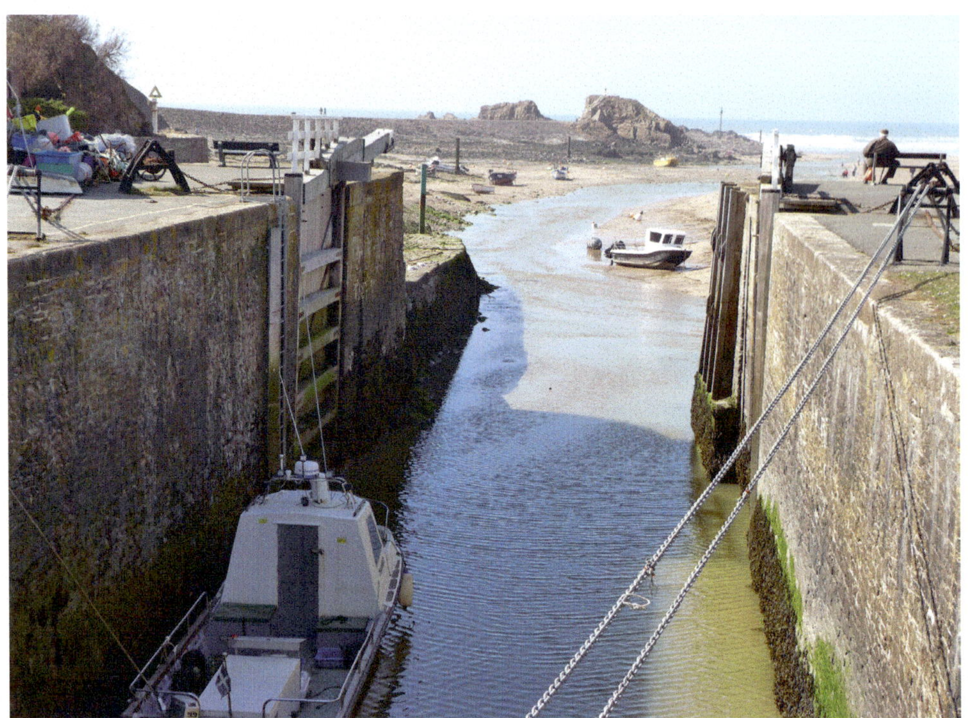

The Lock Gates

This 2011 photograph shows the locks gates open and functional. Rocket apparatus was kept at the end of Breakwater Road (in Rocket House, which was built for the purpose) for sea rescues. Bude Heritage Centre displays figureheads from wrecked ships, but also a Rocket Brigade pistol and Breeches Buoy. Meanwhile, the sea can be temperamental here, and even when it looks calm, there are often rip currents.

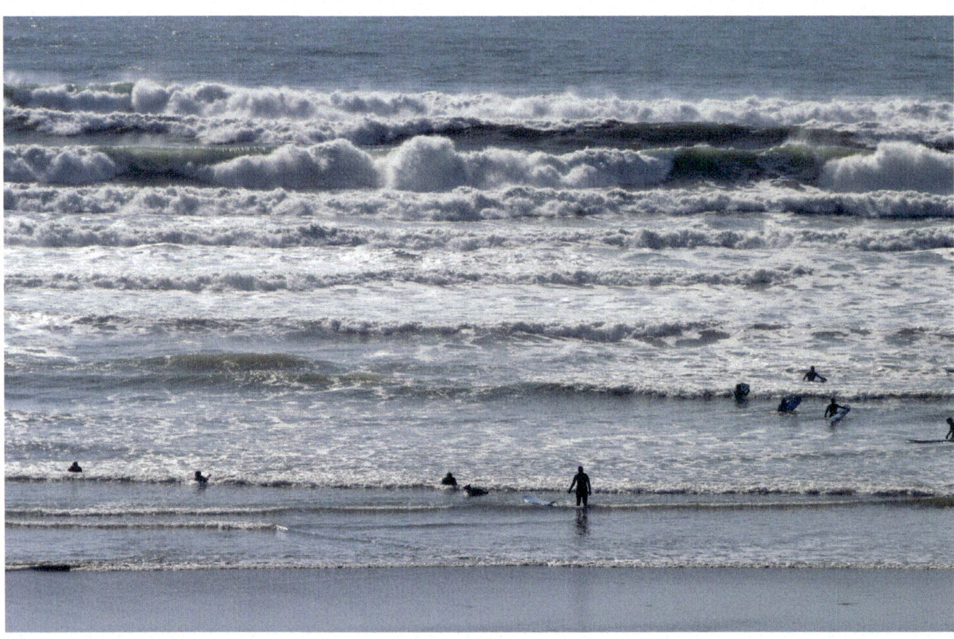

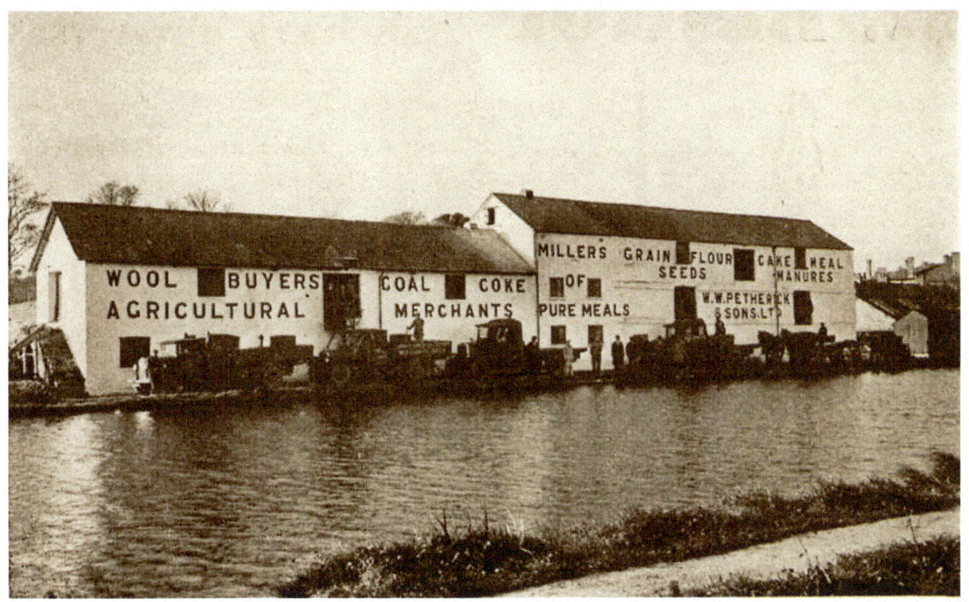

Canal Upper Basin, 1920s

This is the canal upper basin with lorries and one horse-drawn vehicle. To the right is the area now known as Pethericks Mill, as the warehouse contained flour, animal meal, fertiliser and other items needing milling. Coal and wool was also stored here in the warehouse to the left. Further along near the Bencoolen Bridge at Lower Wharf now lies the Olive Tree brasserie, housed in a sympathetically converted warehouse in a picturesque location almost opposite the Falcon Hotel.

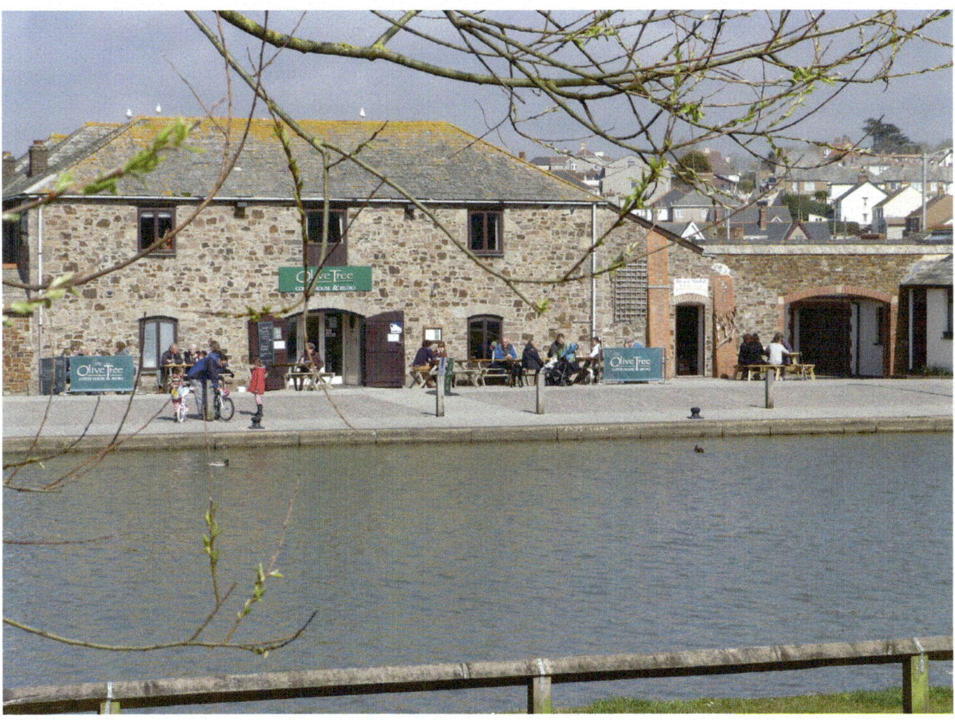

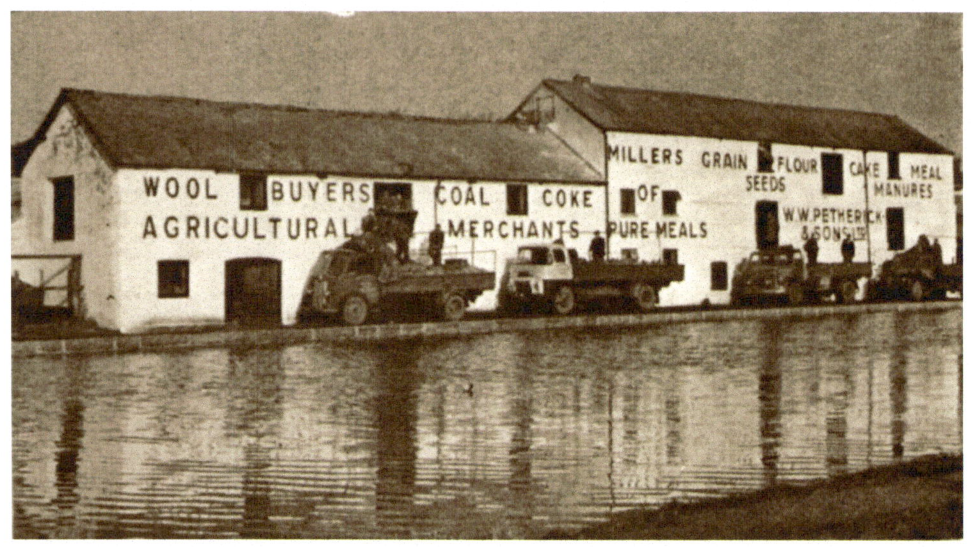

Canal, 1960s

Above, the canal, still showing the upper basin, including lorries, but now set in the 1960s. No huge changes in many respects, though the vehicles are larger. However, the left-hand warehouse was demolished (rumour has it just before a preservation order was issued) and replaced by retirement flats. Now, flats overlooking the canal are the order of the day, along with water-based recreations that are increasingly popular. In this photograph, the kayakers are from Outdoor Adventure, based at nearby Widemouth Bay.

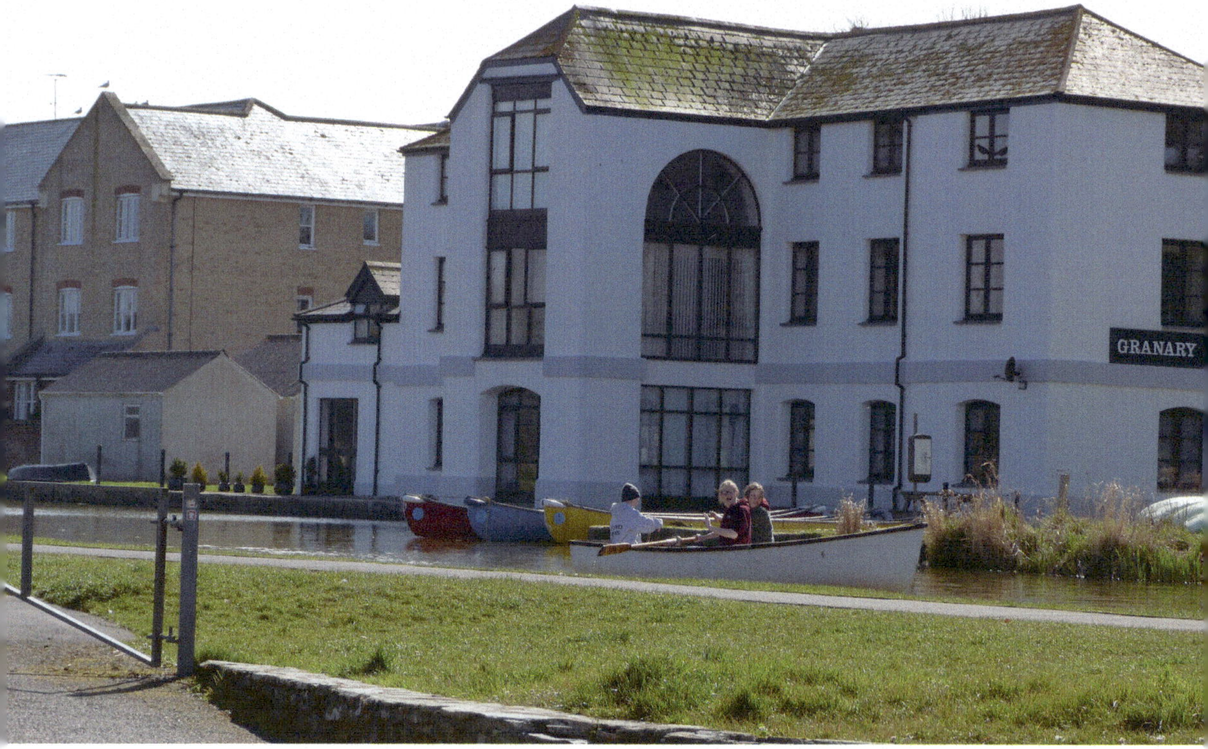

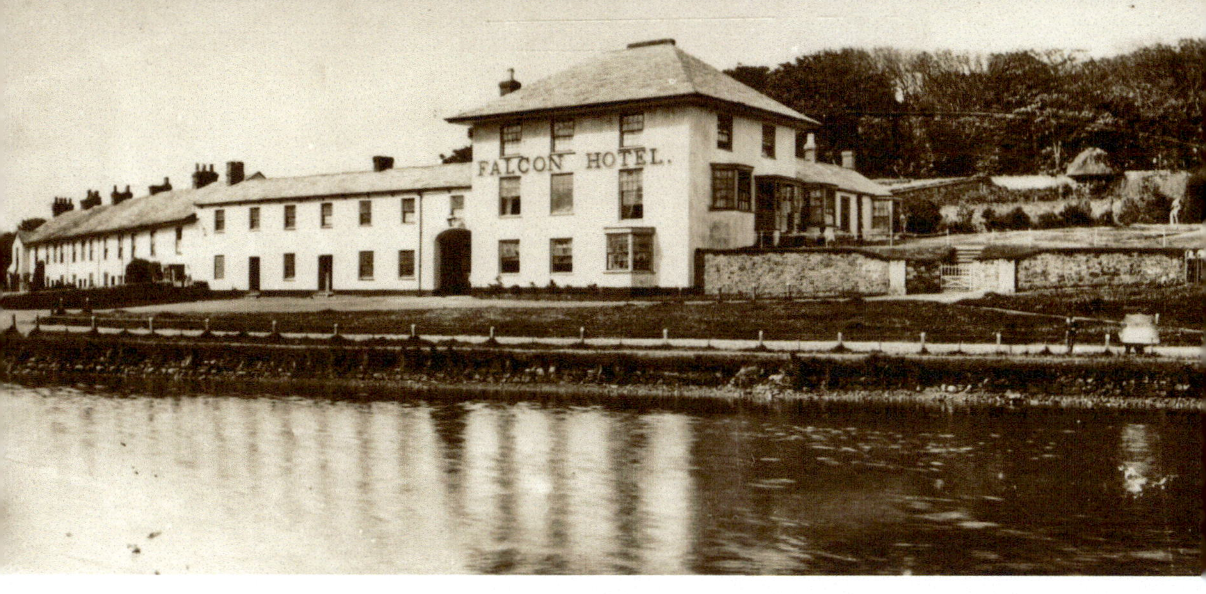

The Falcon Hotel

The Falcon was established in 1798, providing accommodation for the ships' captains of merchant vessels carrying goods to and from the town. It started life as a lodging house, but was extended to become an inn and later a hotel (the latter taking place in 1826). The hotel was also a stopping place for the many coaches from Exeter. Perhaps the hotel's most famous visitor is the Victorian poet, Alfred, Lord Tennyson, who is said to have broken his leg there in 1848 after falling over a garden wall. As he was a known heavy drinker, a likely cause may be posited but this is difficult to ascertain. He seemed to enjoy his convalescence, and local opinion has it that here he was inspired to write his twelve Arthurian narratives, *Idylls of the Kings*, published between 1856 and 1885. Tintagel may also make the same claim, of course!

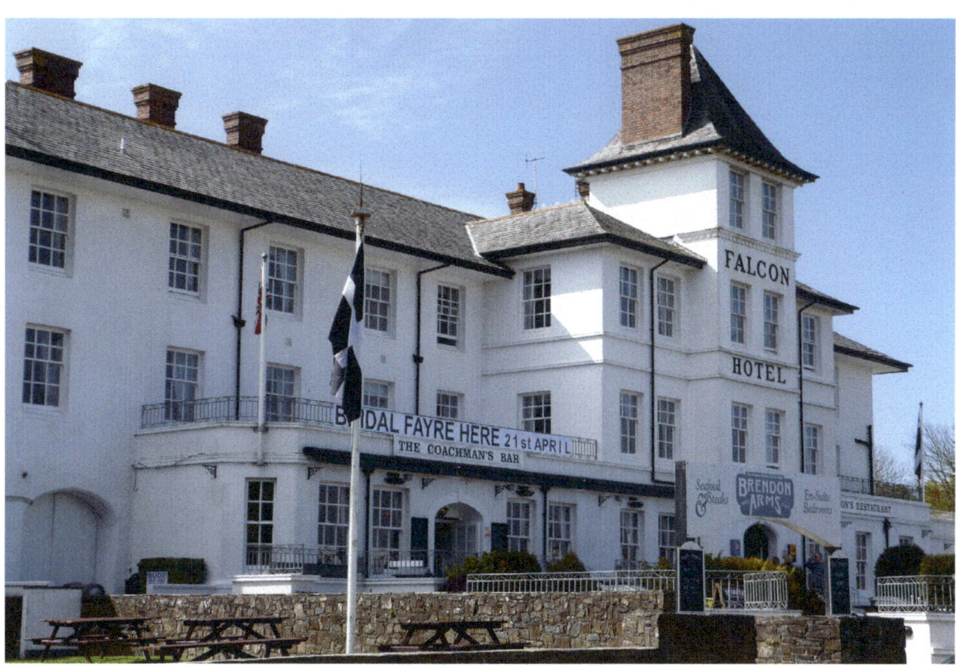

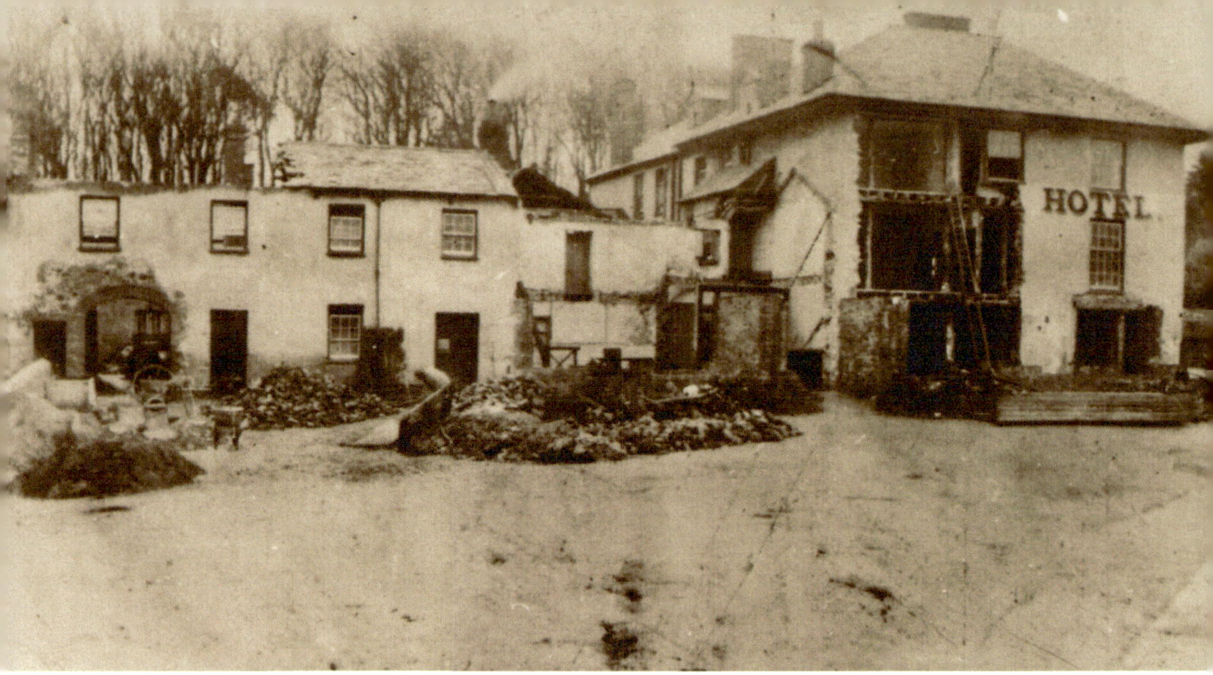

The Extension of the Brendon

Although this looks like a fire has occurred, it is believed that this image actually shows the Brendon Arms merely being enlarged and extended in 1912. Now, the Brendon Arms is a popular local public house with a great deal of history. The hospitality trade started here in 1872 with a four-horse coach service to the neighbouring towns of Boscastle, Tintagel and, over the border into North Devon, Clovelly. George Brendon started serving welcome refreshments to his coach customers and the trade has continued ever since.

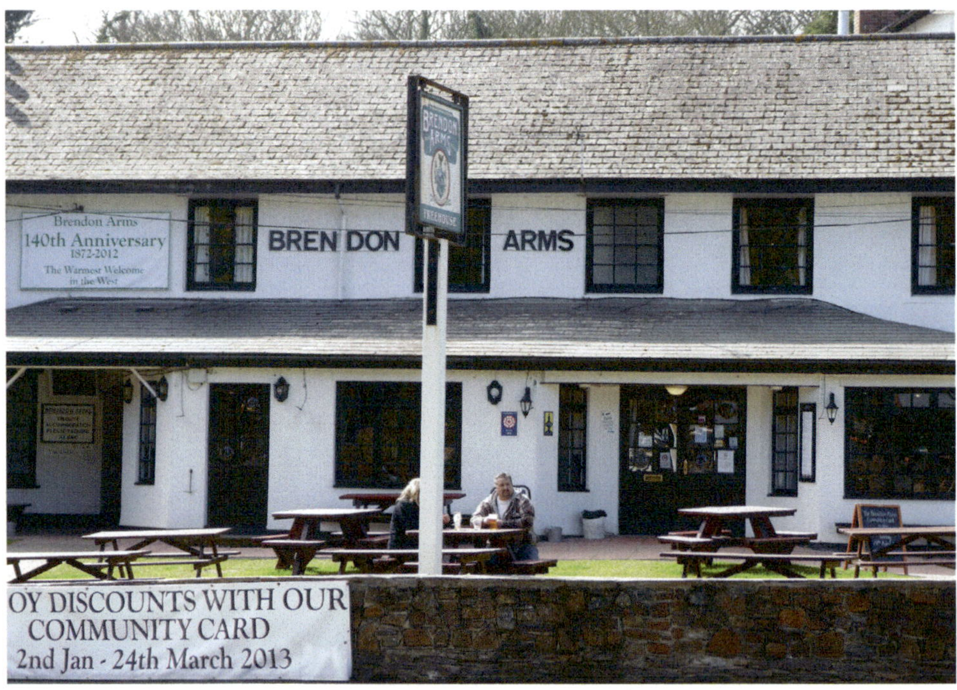

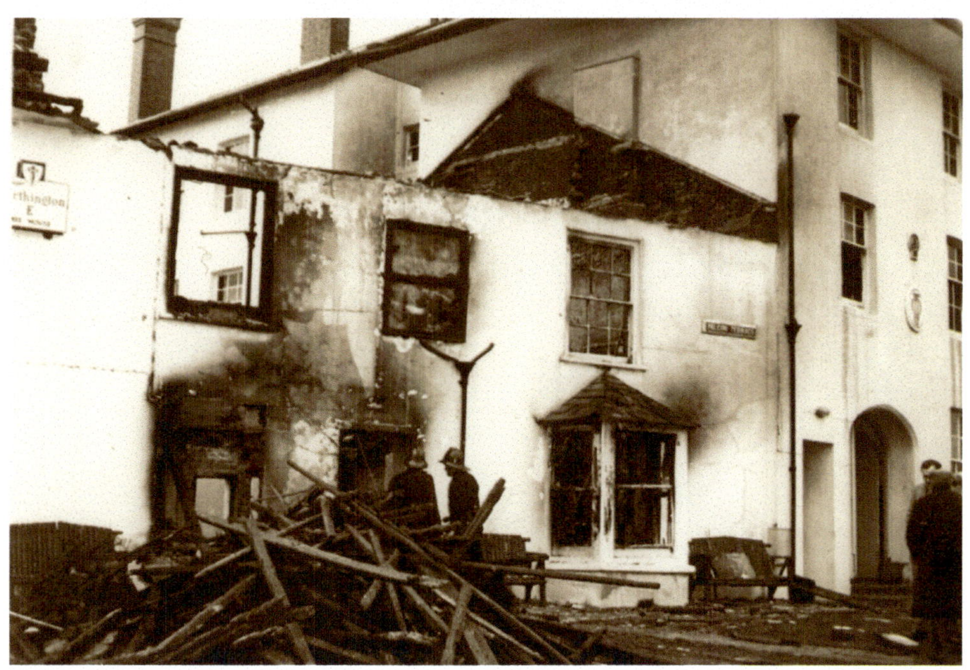

A Fire at the Falcon

The Falcon Hotel, after a fire in 1961, with all that was left of the Falcon Inn (now the Brendon Arms). The only thing salvaged was a post horn. For a point of contrast, the 1860 image of a steam tug, owned by a member of the Canal Company, gives a different view of the Falcon. To the right appears to be St Michael's and All Angels church, which looks remarkably – and inaccurately – close in this picture.

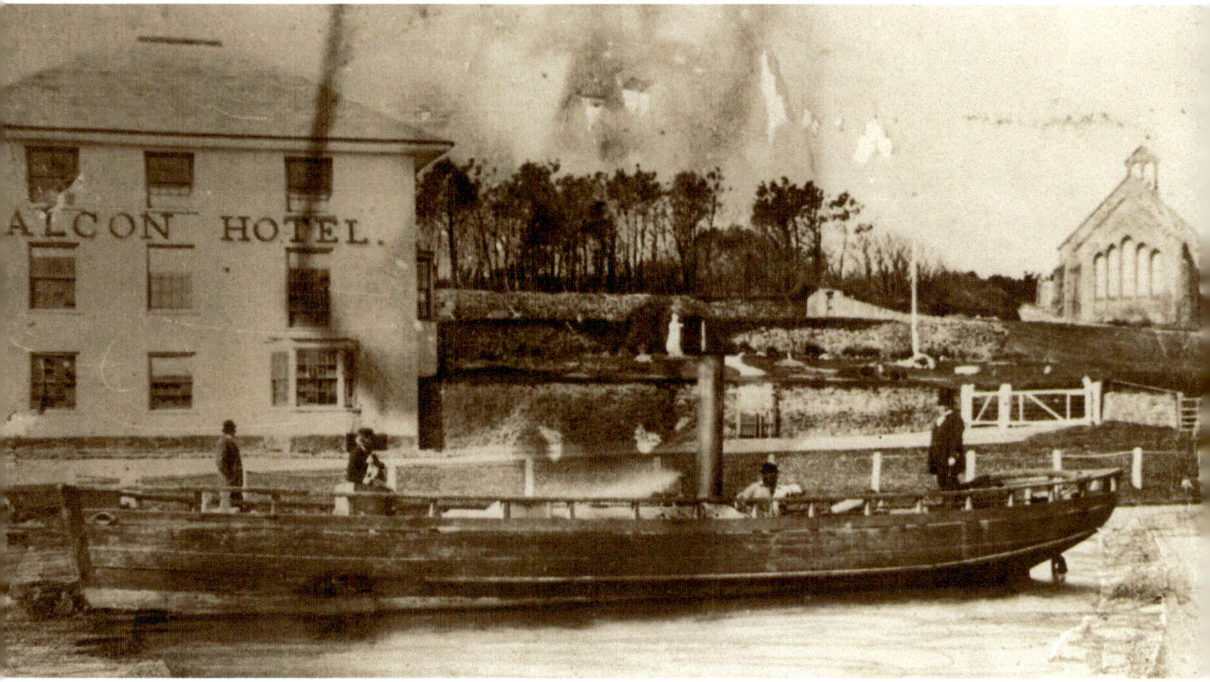

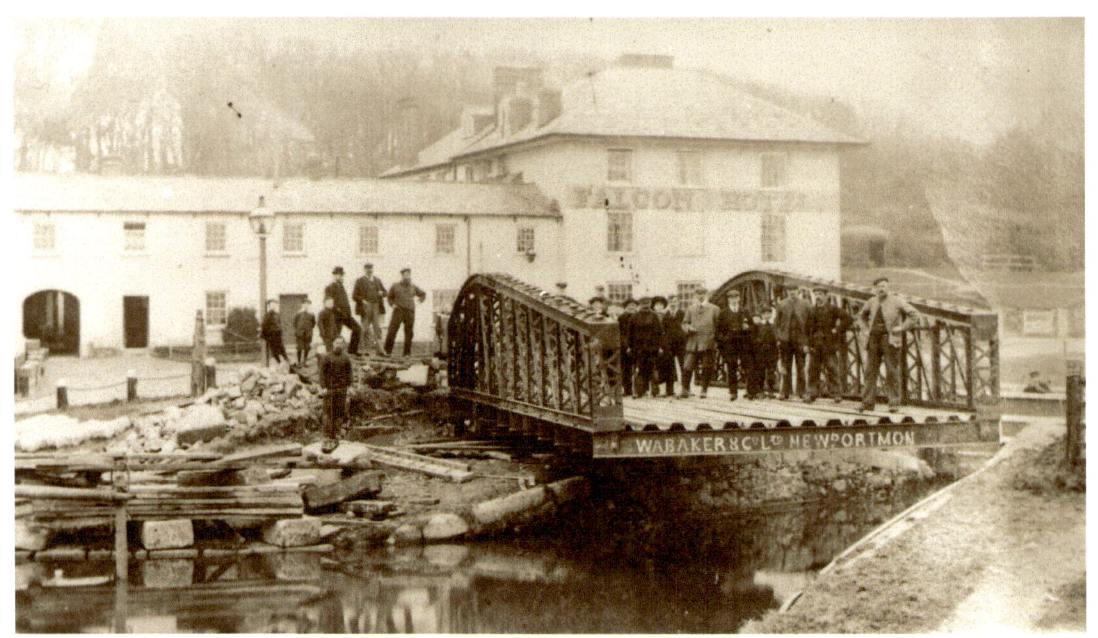

Bude Swing Bridge

The rather imposing Falcon Hotel in 1906, with a new, impressive-looking swing-tailed bridge being installed, the last one that opened for shipping. Lots of people born and bred in Bude remember walking across the swing bridge, which is much more spectacular in appearance than the current low bridge. The Falcon here is seen pre-extension. The postcard shows Bude Canal, in the early 1900s, with Falcon Bridge. This was the second Falcon Bridge, which opened to permit shipping to pass; it was replaced in 1906 by the swing bridge in the previous image, and then in 1962 by the present fixed bridge.

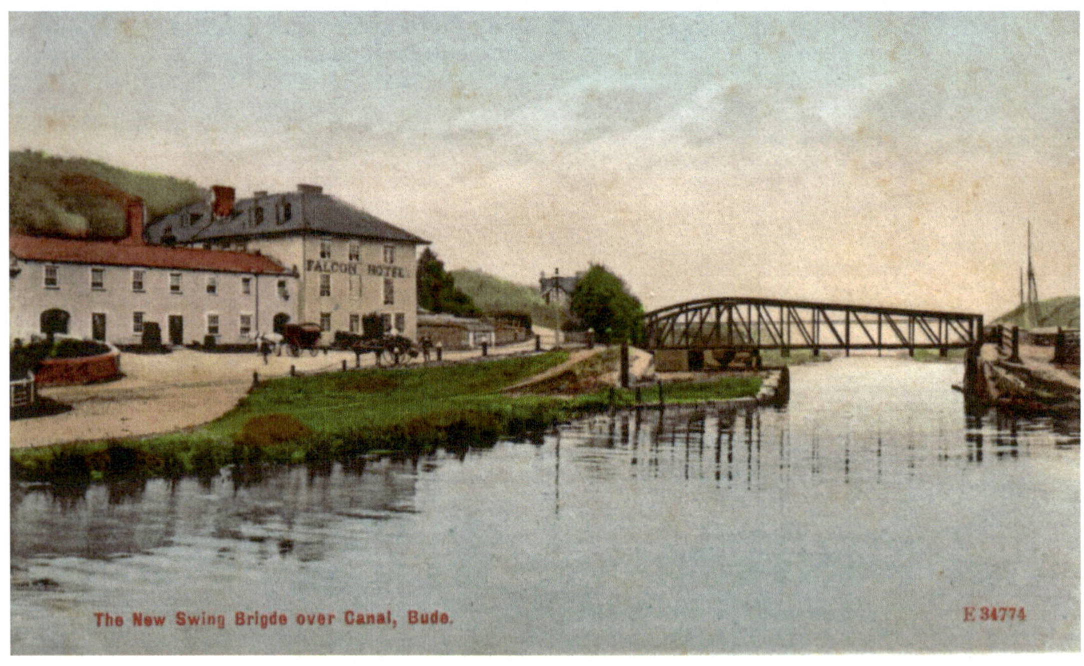

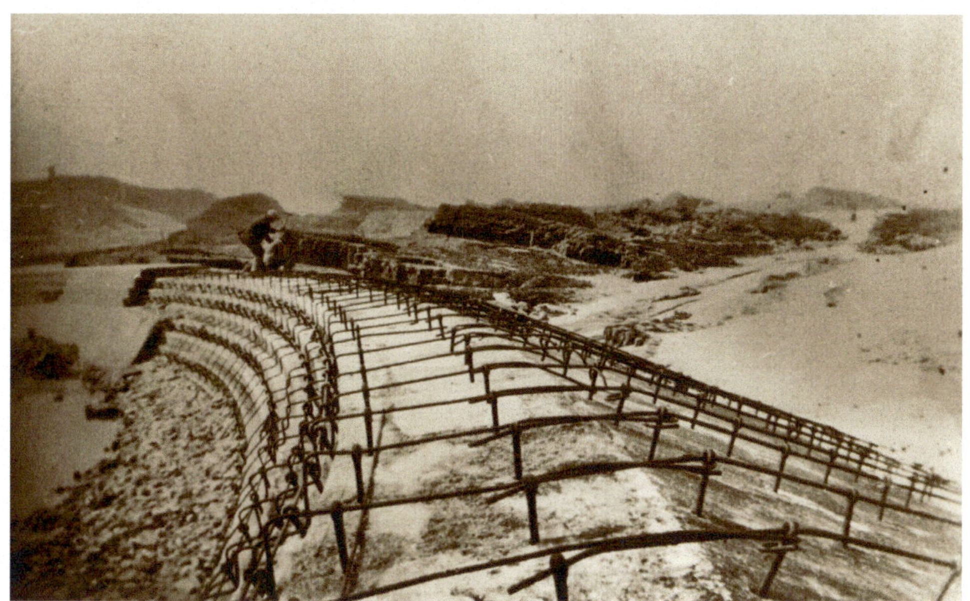

Bude Sea Pool

This photograph shows the iconic swimming pool's construction in 1929, at Summerleaze Beach. Here we have the construction of the wall of the pool, which was made of concrete. Steel reinforcement was added in 1933 to bolster the original construction. The pool was built with the help of money donated by the Thynne family and continues to be a real asset to the town and much loved. Below, the 2012 beach huts on the concrete terracing of the pool, as an attempt to recreate the original feel and reduce some of the starkness of the concrete. It works!

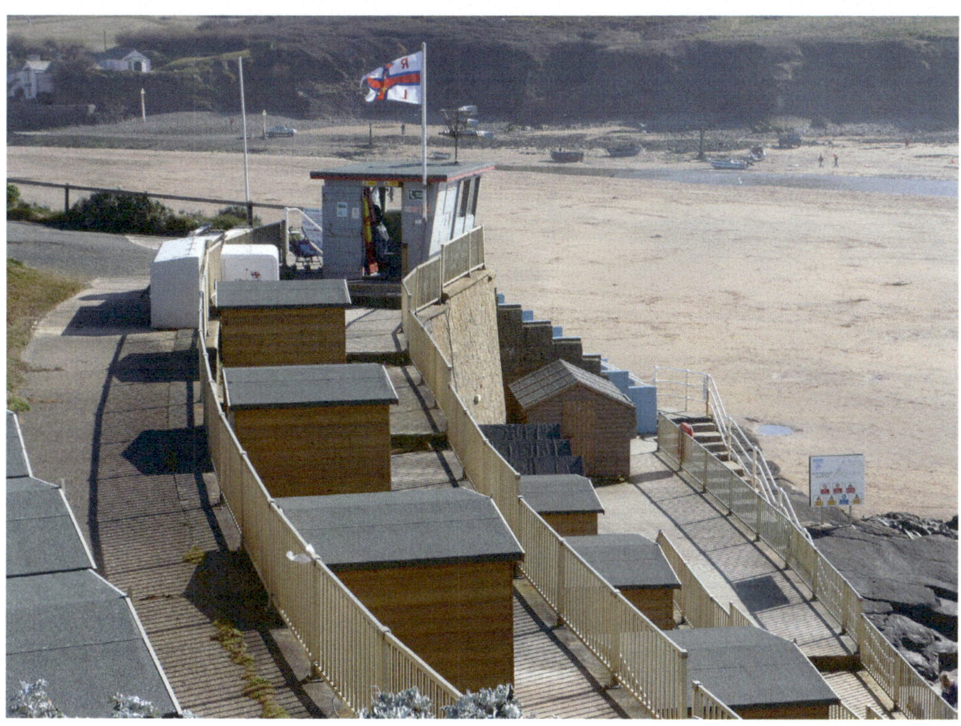

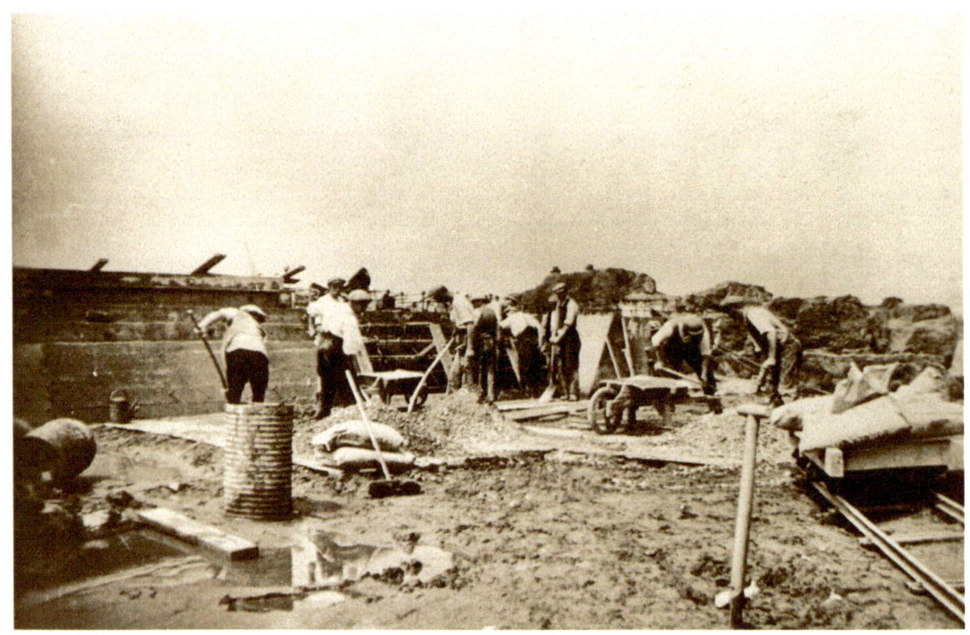

Bude Sea Pool Construction, 1929

Here, the men are hard at work, labouring within the pool. A huge amount of work and pride went into the venture. The Sea Pool is now a major part of Bude's historic landscape, and there have been suggestions that it should be made part of a conservation area. Below you can see the Sea Pool, the terracing and the sluice gates (replaced in 2013), which used to be the site of the old paddling pool that accompanied the main Sea Pool. Now the 'shallow end' has the same effect.

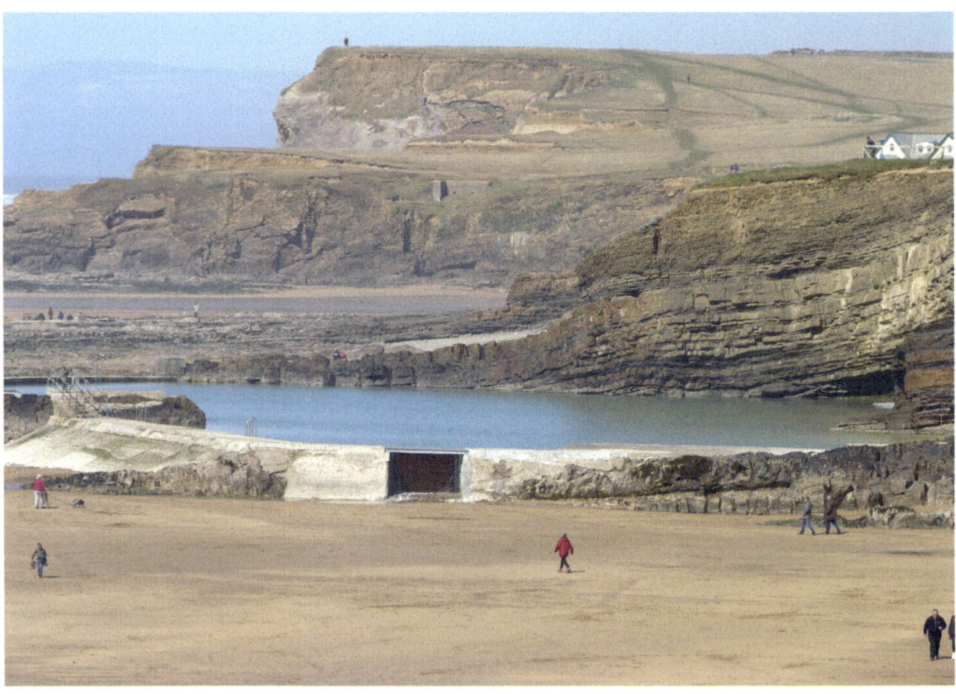

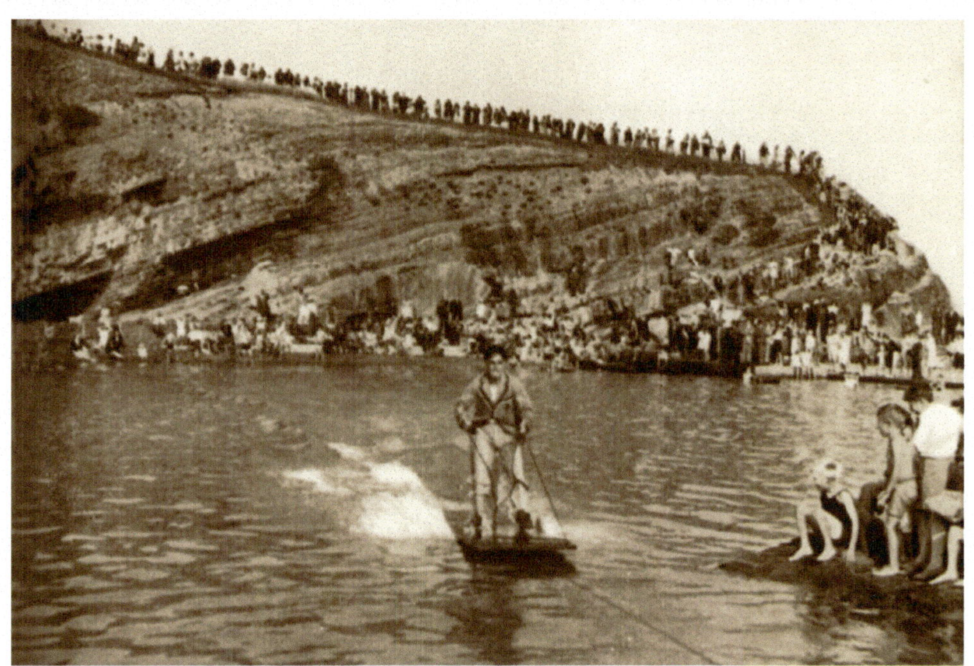

Watersports

Clifton College Sports, at the Sea Pool, 1940s, during the school boarders' evacuation in Bude. Today, the pool, which refreshes itself each high tide with sea-water, is used for lifesaving training by Bude Surf Life Saving Club, teaching surfing basics, kayaking and, of course, swimming, with many a child earning their water wings here. Bude was actively promoted as a resort once the Sea Pool was built. The pool is semi-natural and one of the few remaining tidal pools in the UK. Below, the sun glistening on the Sea Pool as a hardy swimmer takes to the water. There is an ongoing campaign to save the Bude Sea Pool after the pool's public funding was cut by Cornwall Council in 2010/11.

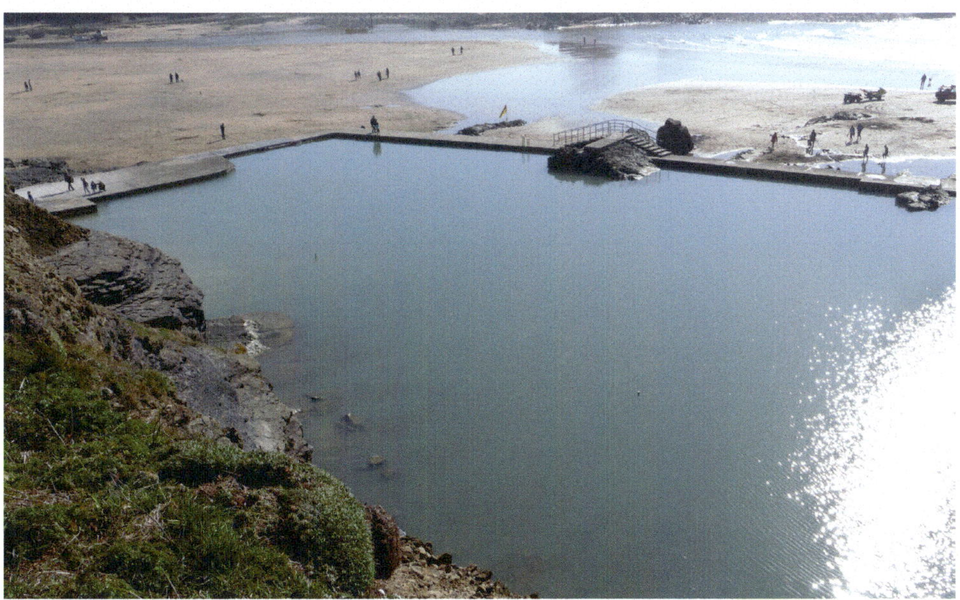

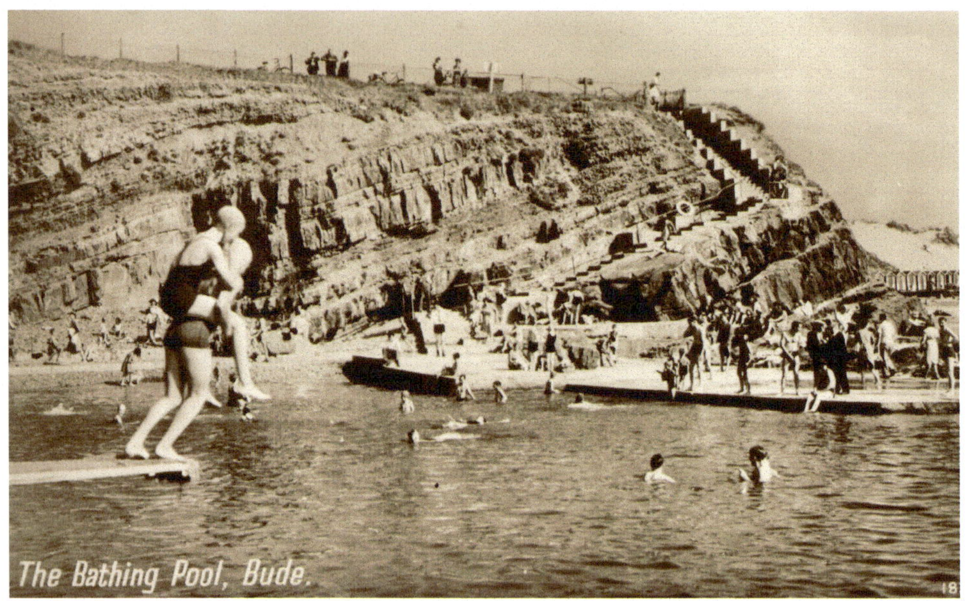

Diving Practice

In 1949, diving was allowed and indeed, there had been diving competitions at the Sea Pool during the 1930s and '40s. However, it was always a bit risky, given the constantly shifting sands and unknown water depth; there was also no terracing at the back. Diving is no longer allowed in the pool for health and safety reasons and an accumulation of sand and rocks in the pool. Below, the pool looking out onto Summerleaze in January 2011, with its safer bathing, makes a splendid scene, especially when the sea roars in behind. This is a relatively calm day and the view is simply beautiful.

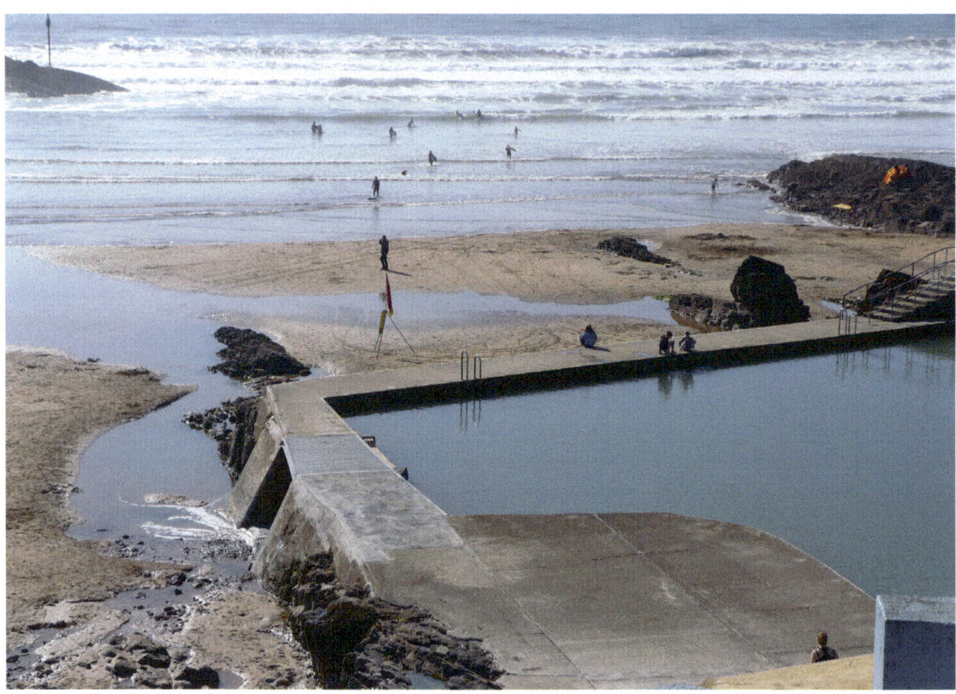

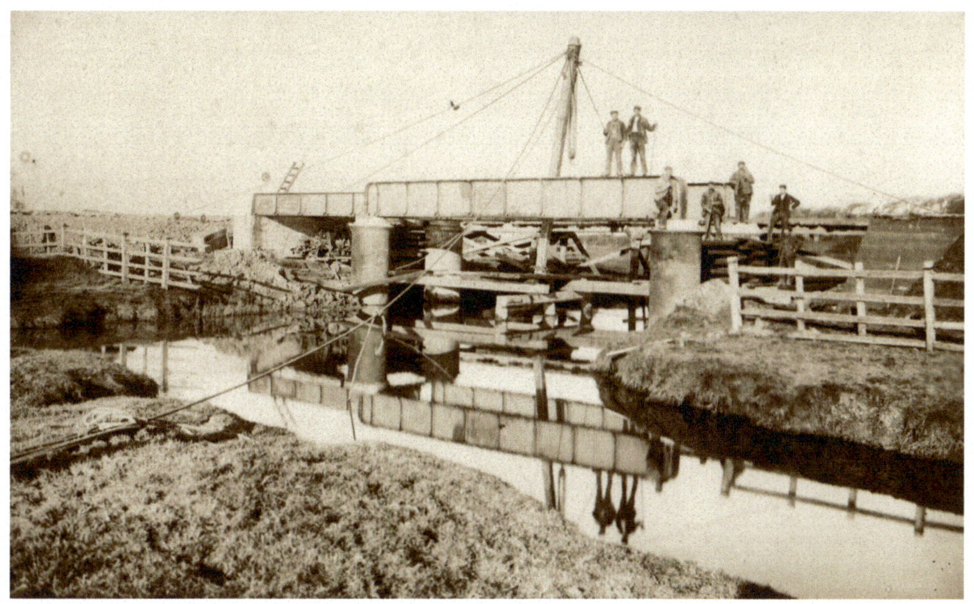

Railway Construction, 1898

This is the building of the railway bridge for the spur to the Wharf. It was built at same time as the rest of the local lines, and carried traffic to and from the Wharf spur. The bridge is one of only a few relics of the railway still in existence. The railway brought people for seaside holidays to Bude, but visitors from the neighbouring inland towns of Holsworthy and Launceston would also come for a trip to the seaside. The arrival of the railway must have been a very exciting time for the people of the town. The bridge, below, situated behind River Life and Pethericks Mill, is all that is really left of the old railway.

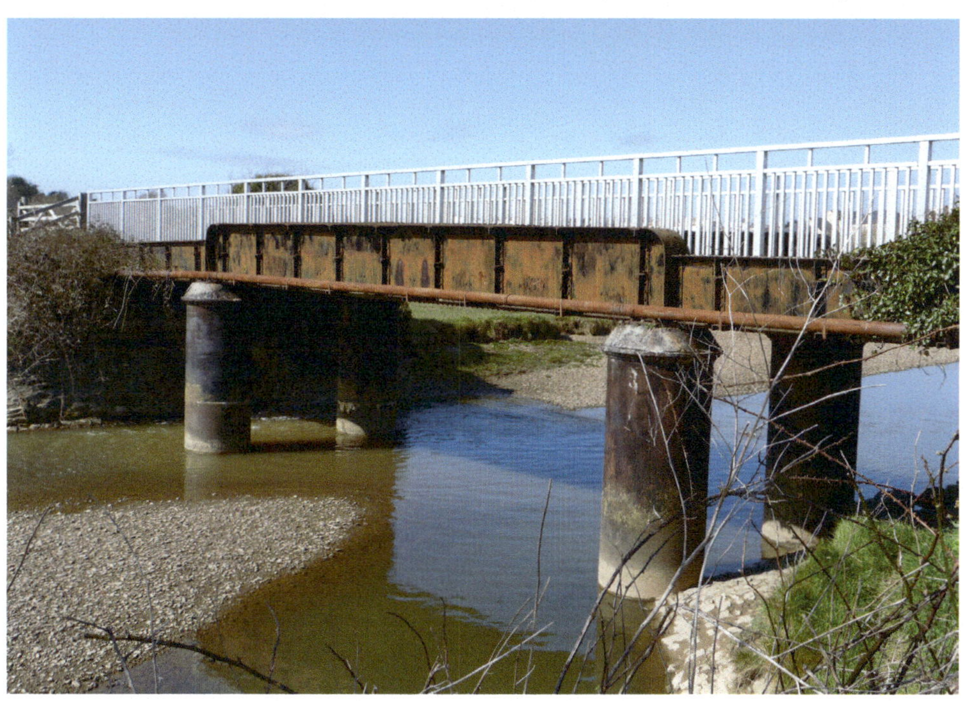

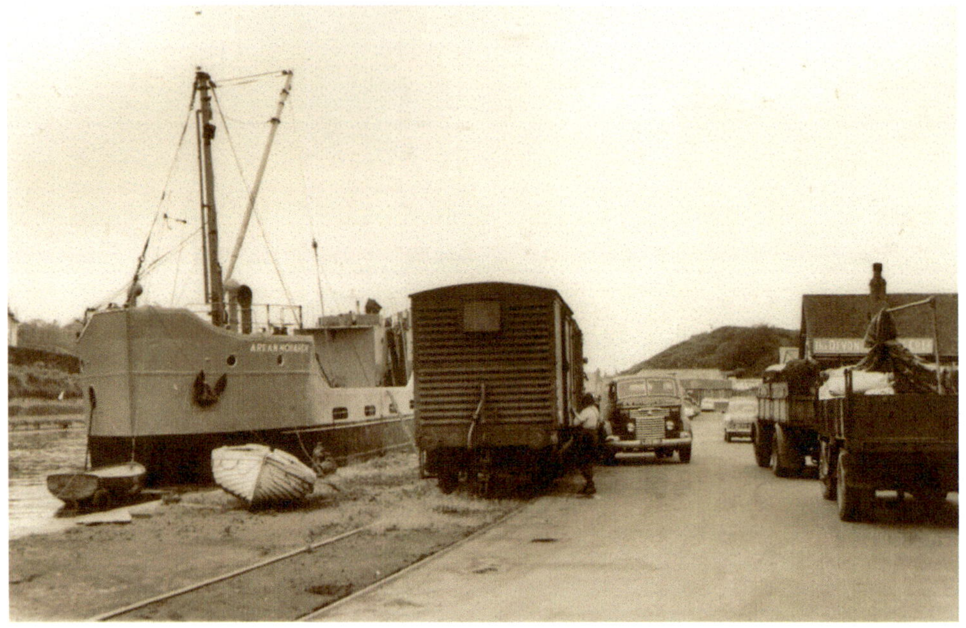

Arran Monarch

Down at the Wharf, the *Arran Monarch* was being unloaded onto the railway and trucks. The *Arran Monarch* had provided bulk cargo services in Scotland, until she was brought in 1960 by a Mr P. Herbert of Bude and continued to carry coal. By 1964, she was renamed *Coedmor* and used for sand dredging at Hayle. Finally, in 1985 she was sold to D. C. Williams of Llanelli, South Wales, to be dismantled in 2003. Below, with a triumphal arch built at the bridge end of Bencoolen Road to celebrate the arrival of the railway in 1898, the town was very excited by the extension of the railway links. They really knew how to celebrate in those days, too!

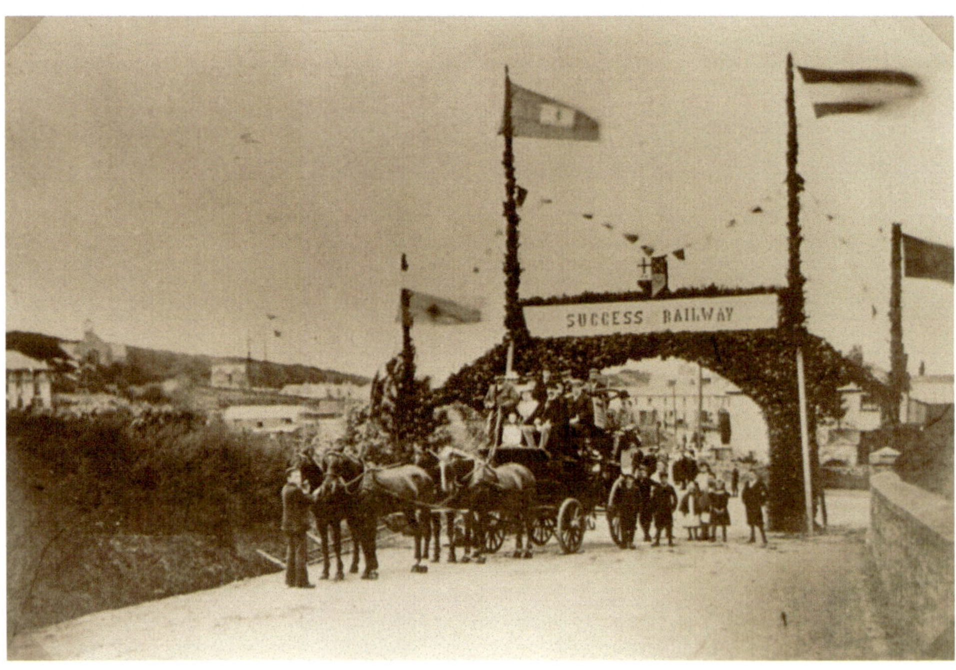

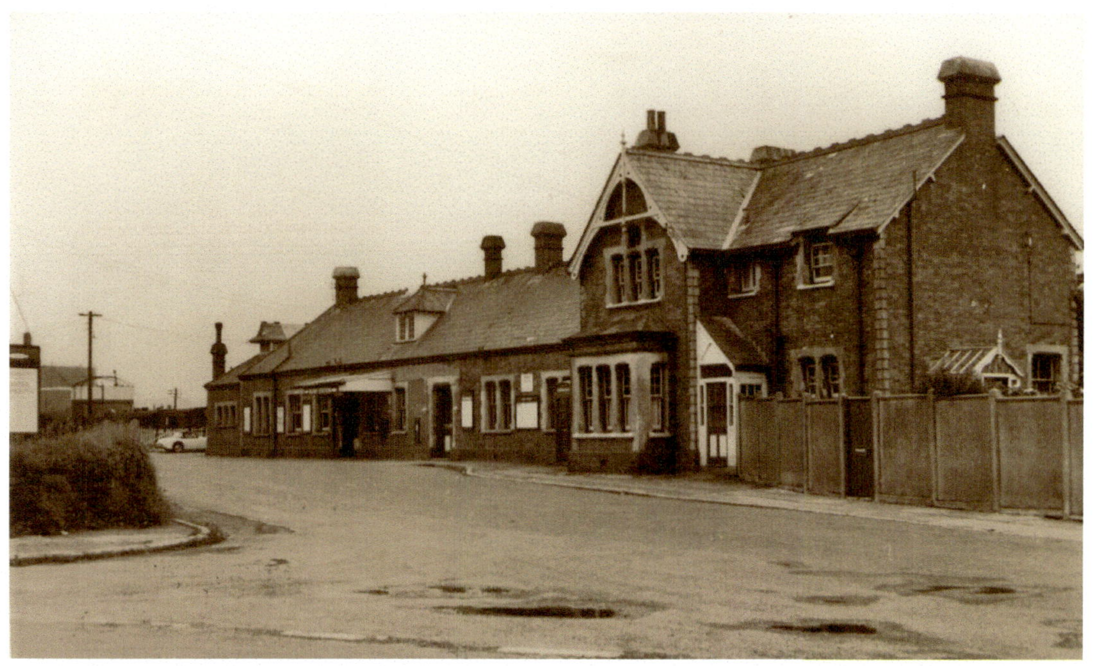

Bude Railway Station

Bude was the terminus for the LSWR branch line from Okehampton. It was placed on the outskirts of Bude to serve both Bude and Stratton residents. While busy in the early days, it was felt to be underused, and the last direct link with London ended in the summer of 1965. Okehampton station, the next nearest link, also closed later. Bude is now out on a public transport limb where the railway infrastructure is concerned, with the nearest railhead now being Exeter. The station, which was a vital part of Bude's development as a seaside resort, sadly leaves few remains. Neighbouring Bideford station in Devon was also closed.

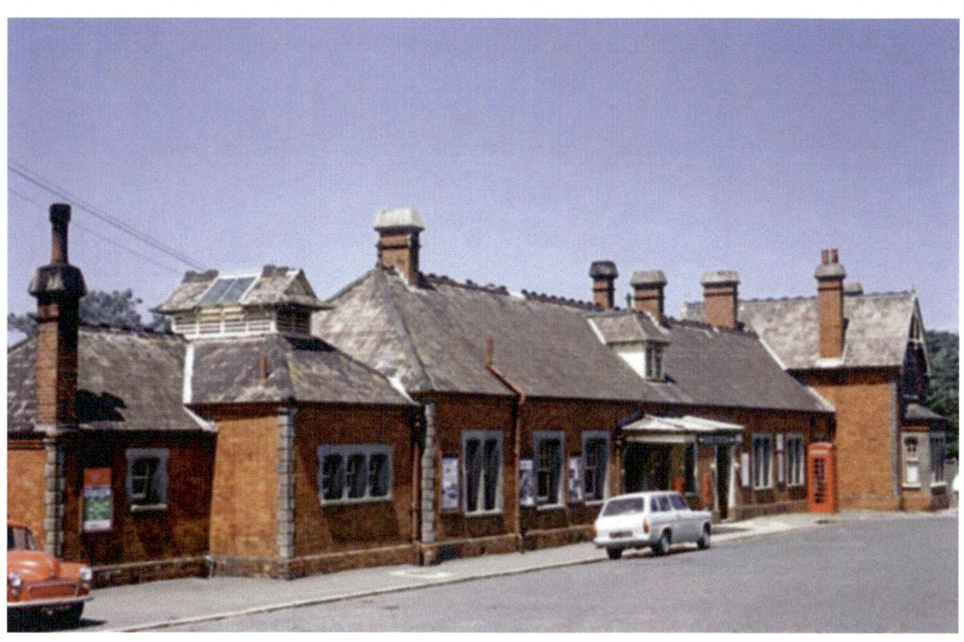

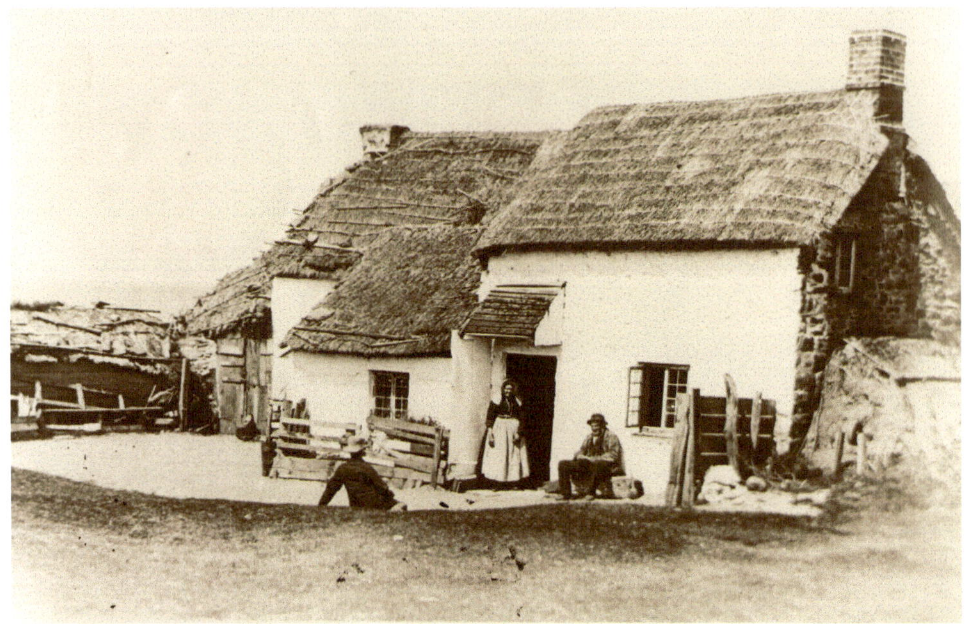

Northcott Mouth Cottage, 1890s

The old fisherman's cottage is partly incorporated into the present dwelling by the beach at Northcott Mouth. Northcott is a rocky cove, quite difficult to reach and approached, if by car, via the village of Poughill. At low tide, it may be visited via a beach walk from Crooklets Beach, but there are tricky rocks that can become cut off by tide quite quickly. Northcott is now a National Trust beach. At low tide, the wreck of the SS *Belem* may be seen. It was wrecked in 1917, and thirty-three men were rescued. The propeller shaft became the metal support for the barrel on Barrel Rock at the end of the breakwater.

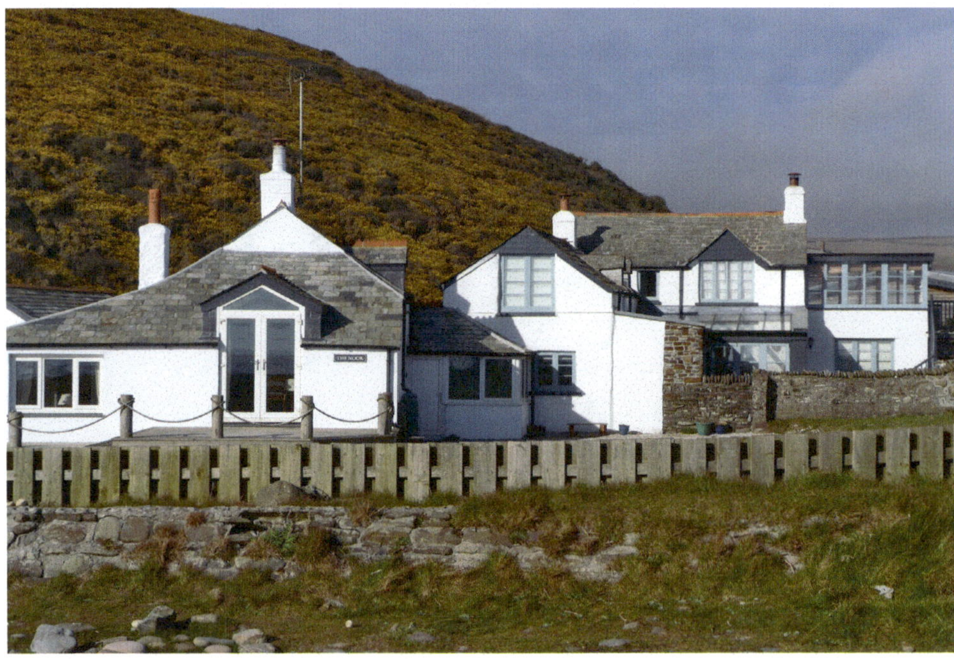

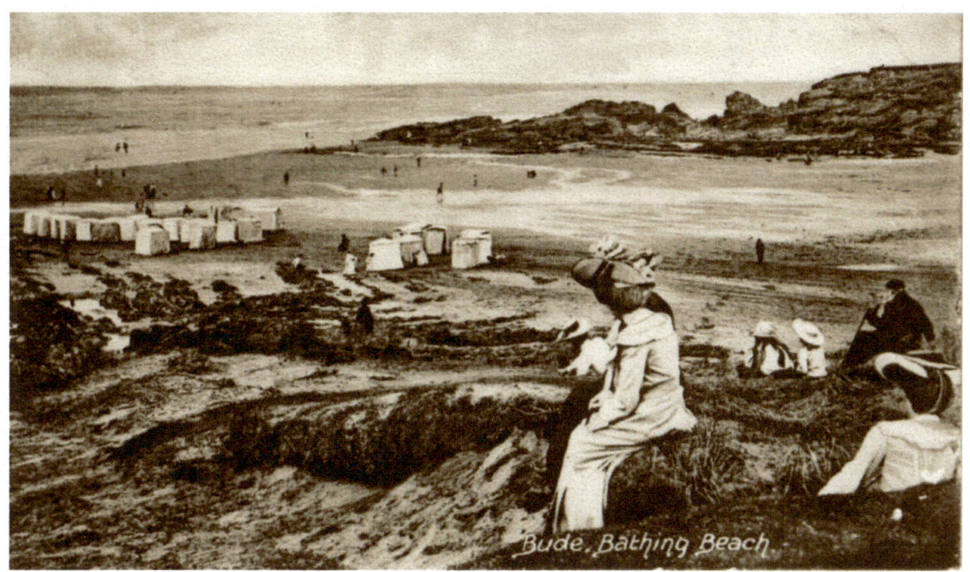

Crooklets Beach, Early 1900s

During the early twentieth century Crooklets was the ladies' bathing beach. An outing would involve changing tents and full dress for attending the beach. The discomforts must surely have outweighed all the benefits of 'taking the air', but at least these seem to be merely changing huts, rather than the wheeled bathing machines used to actually take women into the sea during the late nineteenth century. The Victorians popularised holidays away from the towns and cities, whether the seaside or countryside, so sea bathing really took off – especially once the working classes were able to access holidays from the factories and visit the coast via the railway. This denoted a huge change in fashion, as sea bathing was previously considered to be unhealthy and even risky. Below, a view of Crooklets Beach from the path above shows that the beach is rocky and pebbly despite the sand, so it is surprising that this was the one chosen for ladies. That being said, it was less obviously overlooked, except from Maer Cliff. The beach is much stonier now than previously.

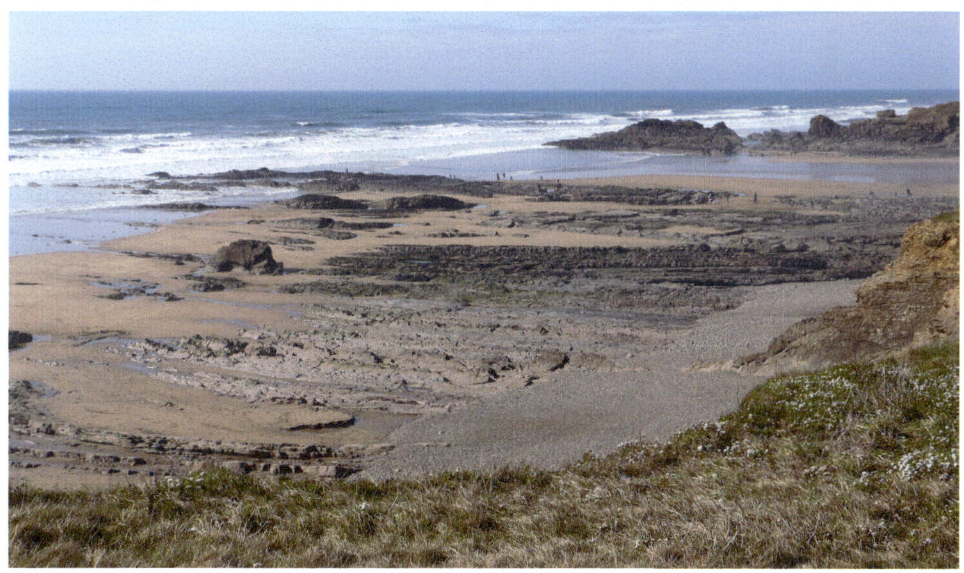

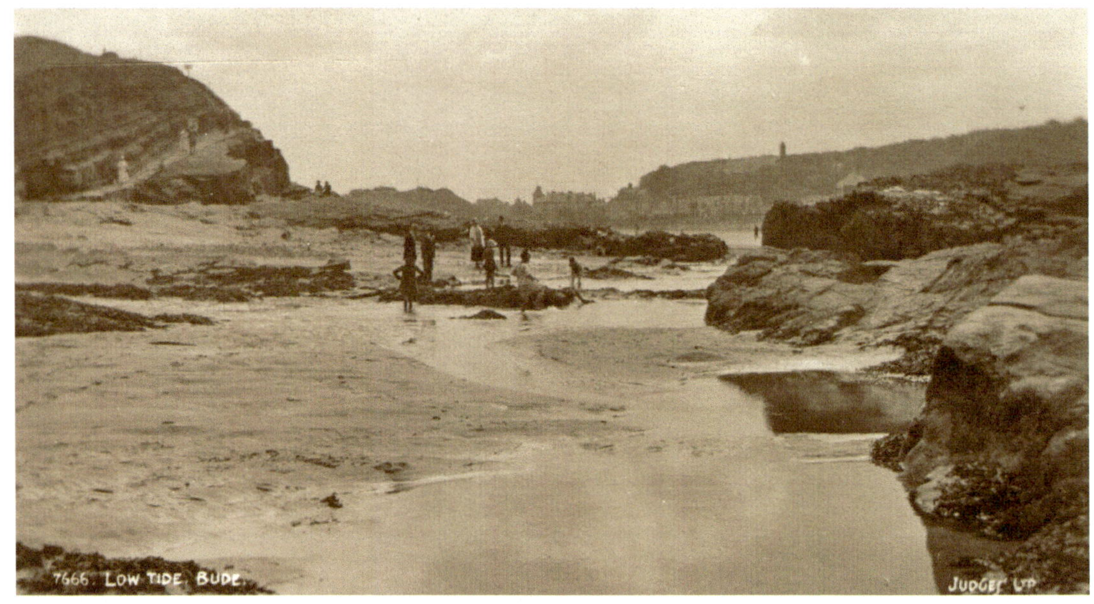

Summerleaze Beach, Monday's Pit

This was where the new pool would be built for safer sea bathing. There was always a natural pool where the sluice gate is now, called Monday's Pit, whereas the nearby pool with the half-tide cross at its end was called Saturday's Pit. It is uncertain where the names originate. Tidal pools were specifically built to keep people away from treacherous sea-bathing conditions. The 90-metre pool provides a saltwater alternative for anyone who does not want to face the risks of the sea. Many locals in the area learned to swim in the Sea Pool. Certainly, the Sea Pool is considered by locals to be one of the safest forms of local bathing; much safer, for example, than Tommy's Pit by the breakwater, which is unregulated.

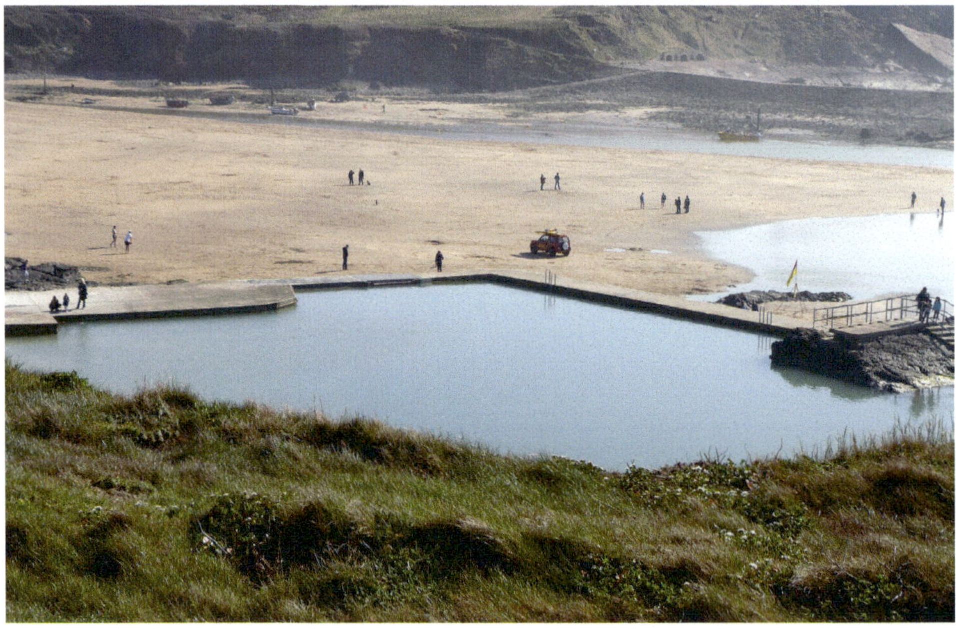

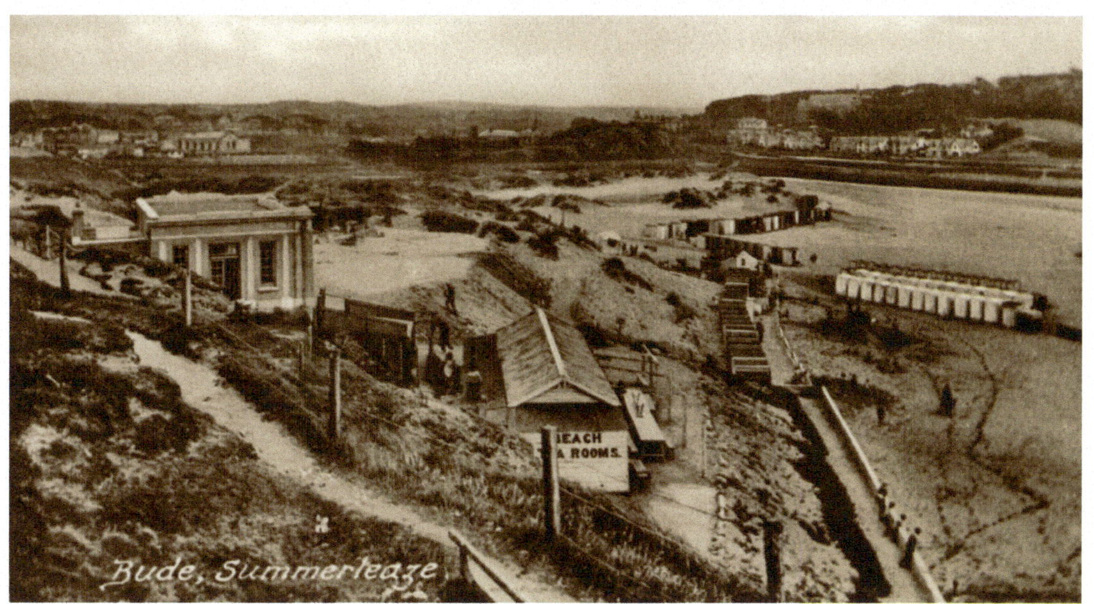

Summerleaze, 1929

Bude has been called 'the liveliest peace of Cornwall' and Summerleaze perhaps best encapsulates this paradox. Off-season, the beach is stunningly peaceful, yet with major facilities nearby including a café. If you walk fairly quickly, it is possible to beach walk to Sandymouth and back at low tide. Photographer Francis Frith, in an original image, captured a view of the beach cafés, nestled in the cliffs and very handily situated for the gentlemen's bathing huts. The second beach café, closest to the sea, was called Beach Tea Rooms. The second beach café was replaced in 1929 by a third, which was then replaced by Life's a Beach in the 1980s, which is still there; very popular with tourists and locals, it has spectacular views. During the day, it acts as a beach café, and during the evenings it is transformed into a seafood bistro.

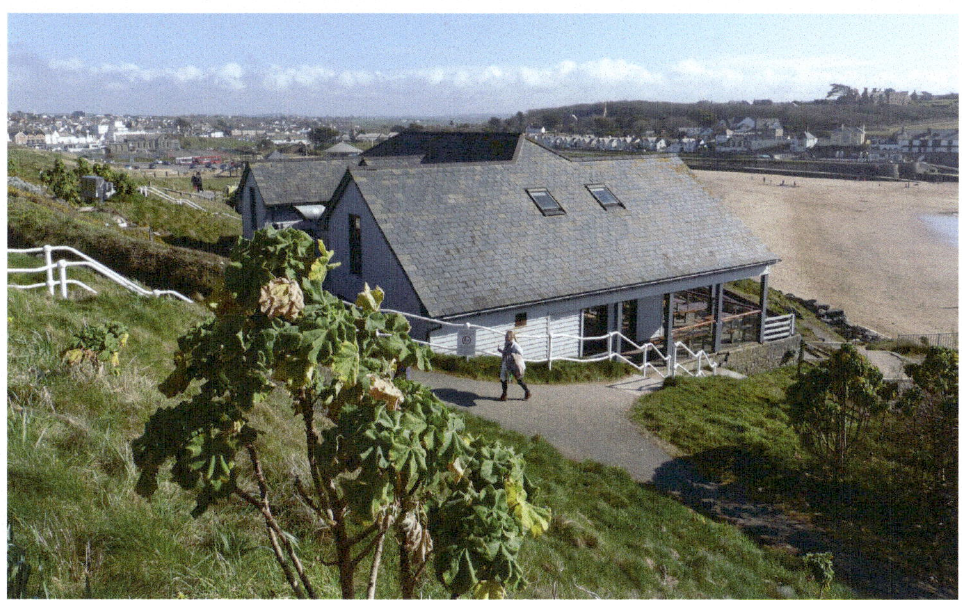

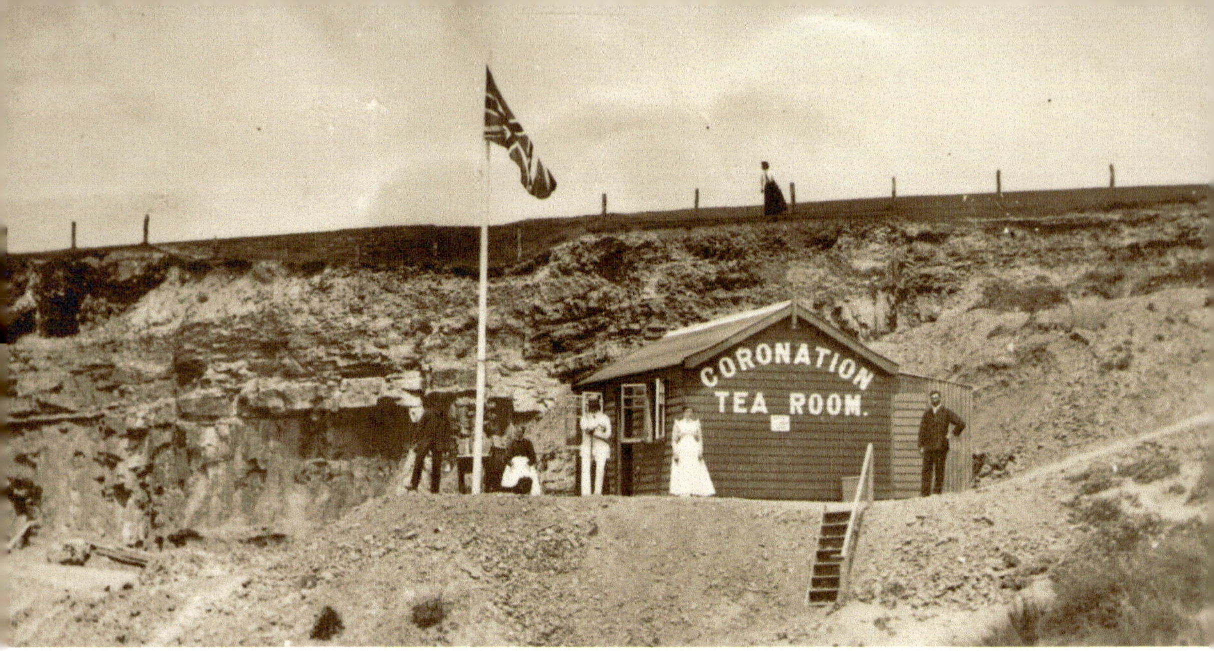

Time for Tea

The Beach Tea Rooms replaced the Coronation Tea Rooms, which looked to be little more than a hut with some wooden steps up to it. Most of the dunes have now gone, as the area has been developed. Below, a view towards Life's a Beach, overlooking Summerleaze Beach, with outdoor seating and parking. Catering for holidaymakers is now done on a much grander scale but, of course, parking was not an issue for those travelling by train. As seen in this photograph, Summerleaze has large beach huts set on wooden decking just below the café.

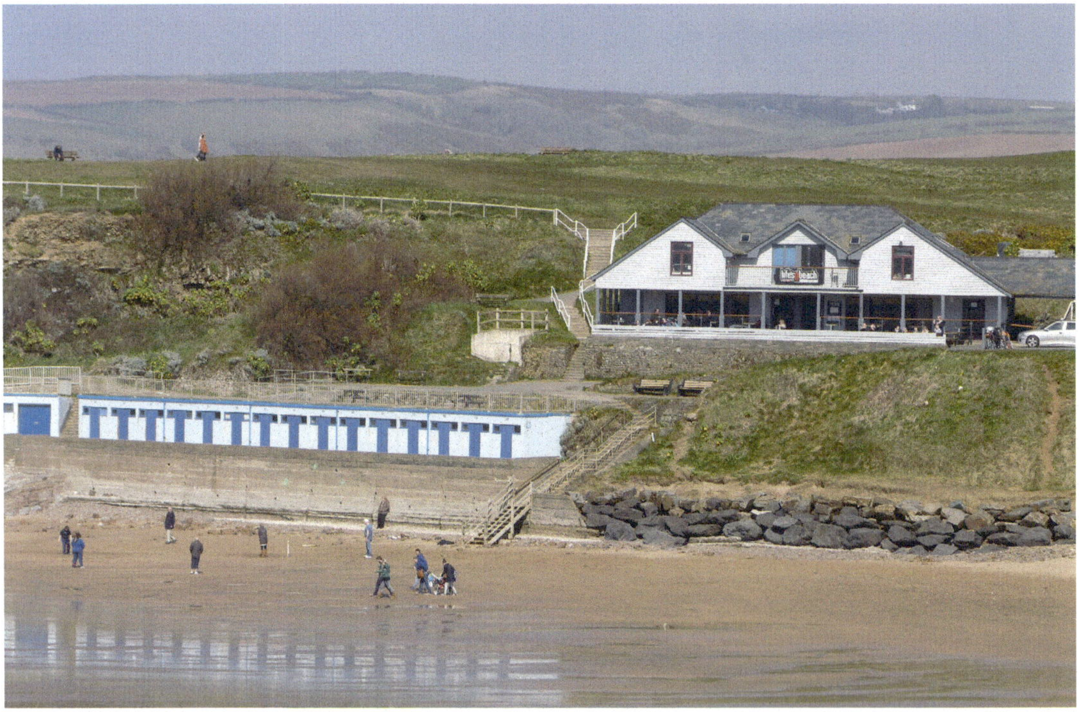

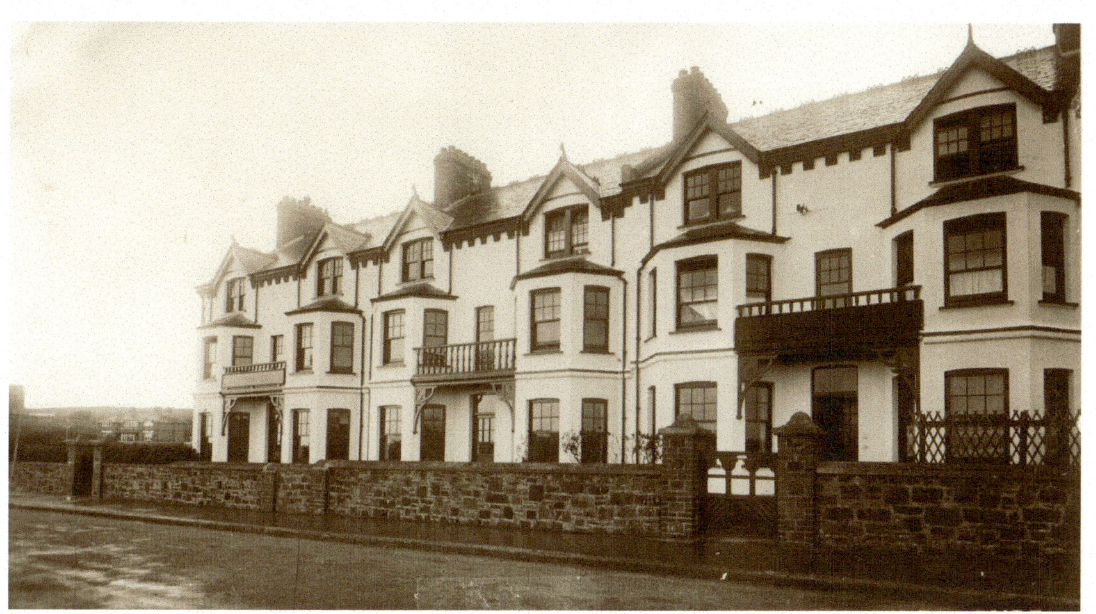

St Catharine's, Bude

St Catharine's was a girls' school on Down Views, created from three terraced houses. Nearby Ocean View had direct views to the sea, for there were no buildings. Part of the sea wall was there, with a groyne to stop sand movement, but only two beach huts had arrived by then. The Crooklets Beach huts have grown spectacularly in number, though many are now in need of some attention. There are traditional beach huts on the south side, with wonderful views over the beach. Larger family huts are near to the café. At low tide, Crooklets offers a wide expanse of sand with rocky outcrops for rock pooling. It is also the home of the Bude Surf Life Saving Club, formed in 1953, which holds an annual Christmas Day dip for the hardy at Crooklets Beach. Below, Rosie's Café (refurbished in 2012) and retro amusements at Crooklets, next to the car park and Bude Surf Life Saving Club, is a very popular haunt.

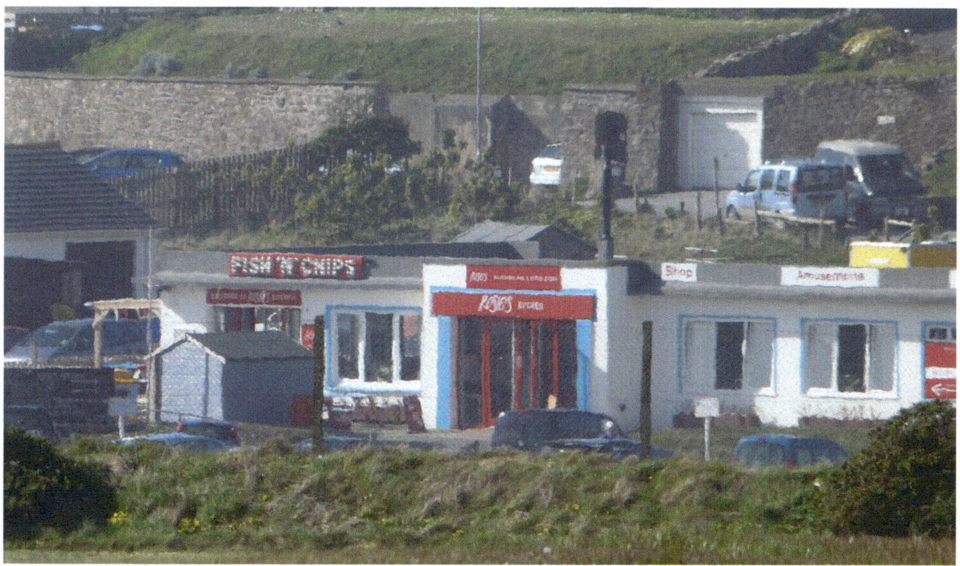

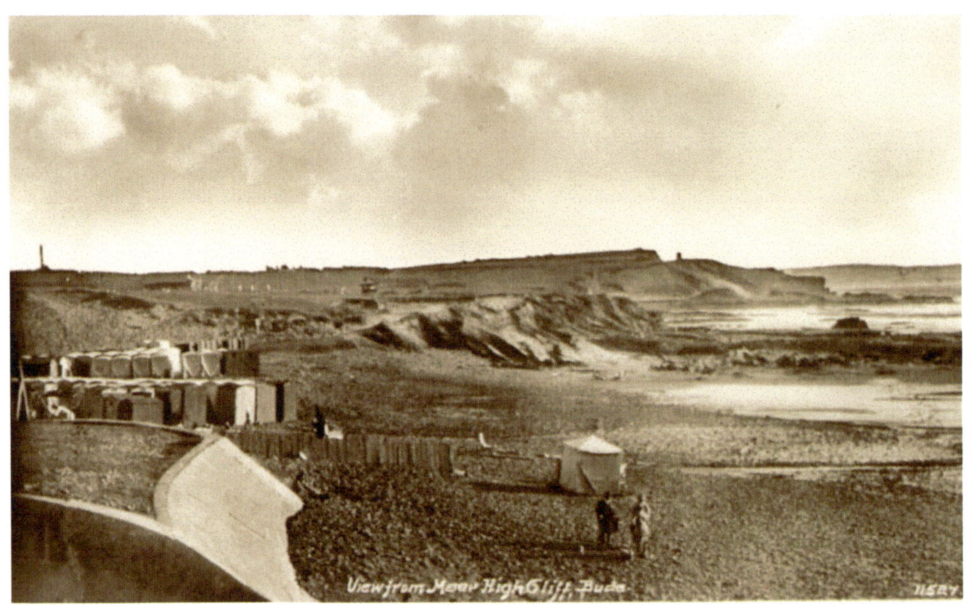

Maer High Cliffs, 1920

This view over Crooklets Beach towards the Pepperpot (or Compass Point) shows there are changing huts, but no fixed beach huts, while the slope on the left has the date 1911 still visible in the concrete. Below is the view towards the Pepperpot from Crooklets. Bude is very fortunate to have Summerleaze Downs and Efford Downs, which, as you can see from the photograph, are popular with walkers because of the stunning views.

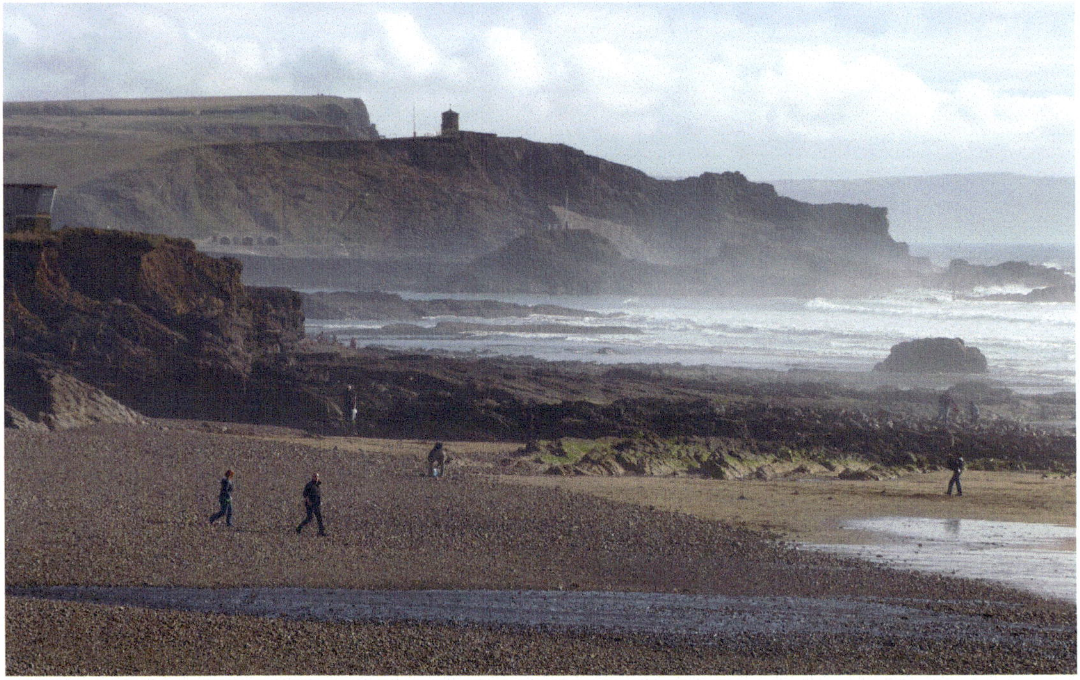

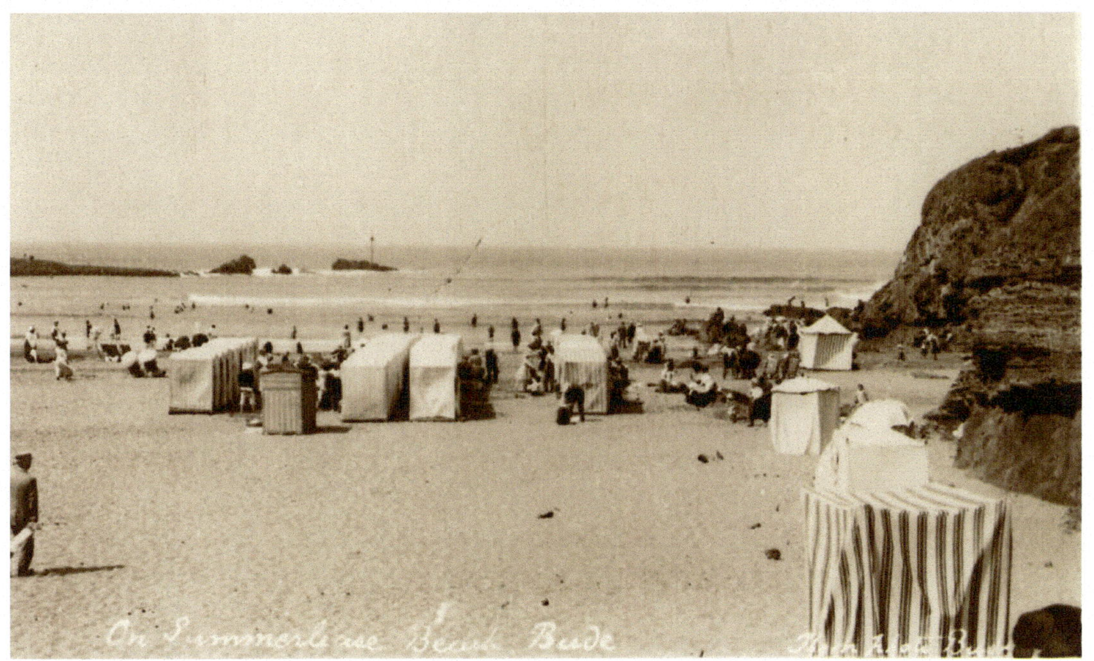

Summerleaze

The portable changing huts still left plenty of space for visitors in 1910; they are well wrapped up – as was the fashion – despite the apparent sunshine. The beach is surrounded by marram grass dunes and the canal runs to the other side. Summerleaze is a popular beach for families due to the proximity of car parking, cafés and beach huts, and because it has RNLI lifeguards in peak season. This view is taken from Efford Down. Summerleaze Beach leads directly to the river, canal and harbour areas, with the added advantage of access to Bude Sea Pool. Popular with surf schools and experienced surfers, it is also a short walk to Middle Beach and Crooklets Beach at low tide.

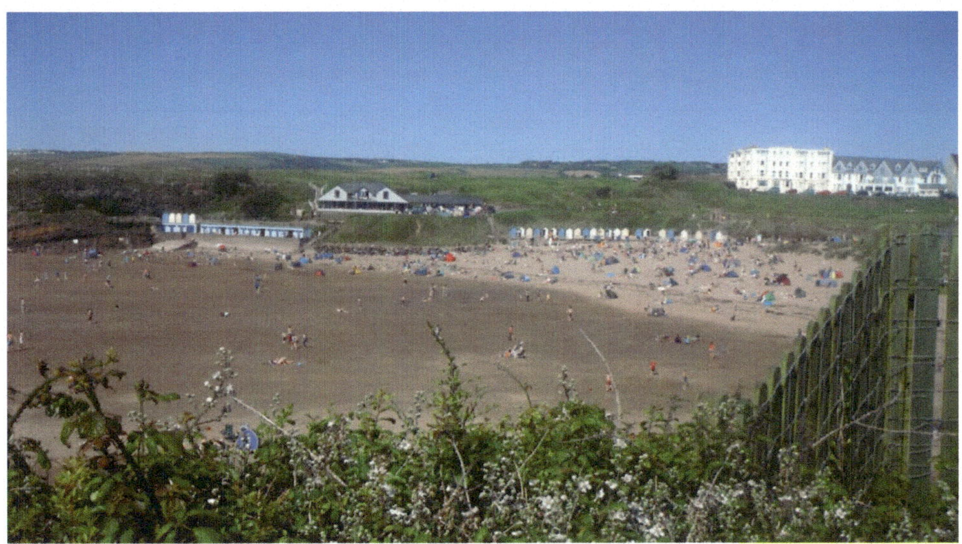

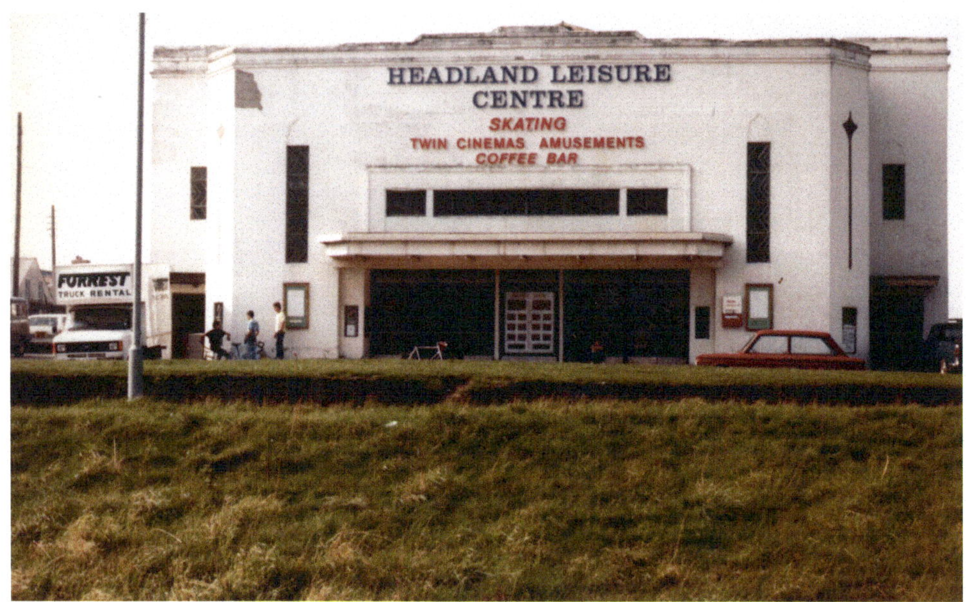

Cinema Demolition, 1986

The Headland Leisure Centre was a popular place, but it was financially unsuccessful as a rather luxurious (for its time and given the small population) twin-screen cinema and skating rink. The cinema (which became the leisure centre) was exactly where Sainsbury's is now. It was built in 1935/36 and held 999 people, with a balcony (stairs to the left of entrance hall) and stalls (to the right). Now, the nearest ice rink is in Plymouth, but Bude once again has a cinema, in the shape of The Rebel independent cinema at Poundstock, about 5 miles south of the town off the A39. Bude also has a community cinema that shows films at the Parkhouse Centre and Budehaven School. Sainsbury's now sits on the site of the old leisure centre, and many people regret the demise of town centre cinema and skating facilities.

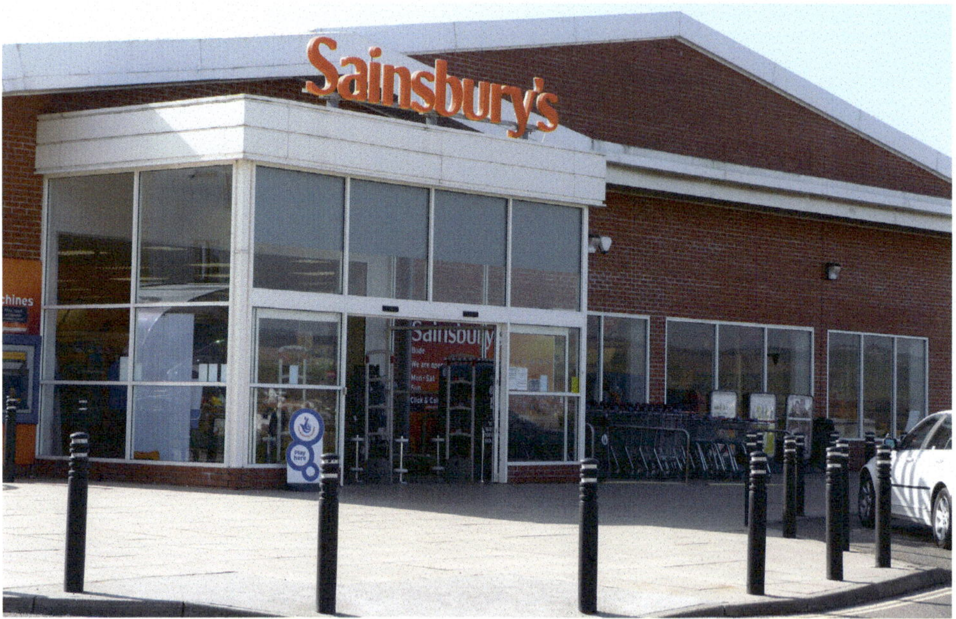

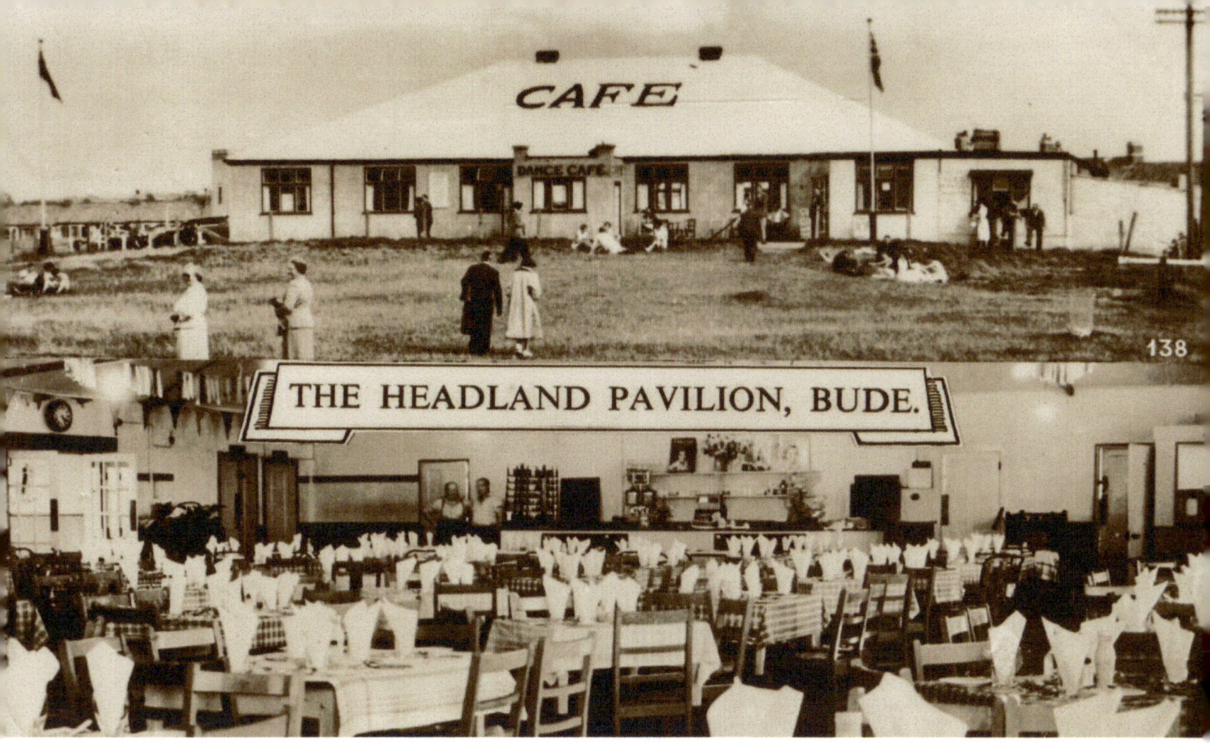

CAFE

DANCE CAFE

138

THE HEADLAND PAVILION, BUDE.

Headland Pavilion, 1930s

Later demolished to make way for retirement flats, this was originally a dance café and then a nightclub with a casino – sophisticated indeed. Situated at the other end of Sainsbury's car park, next to the downs, building is ongoing in 2013.

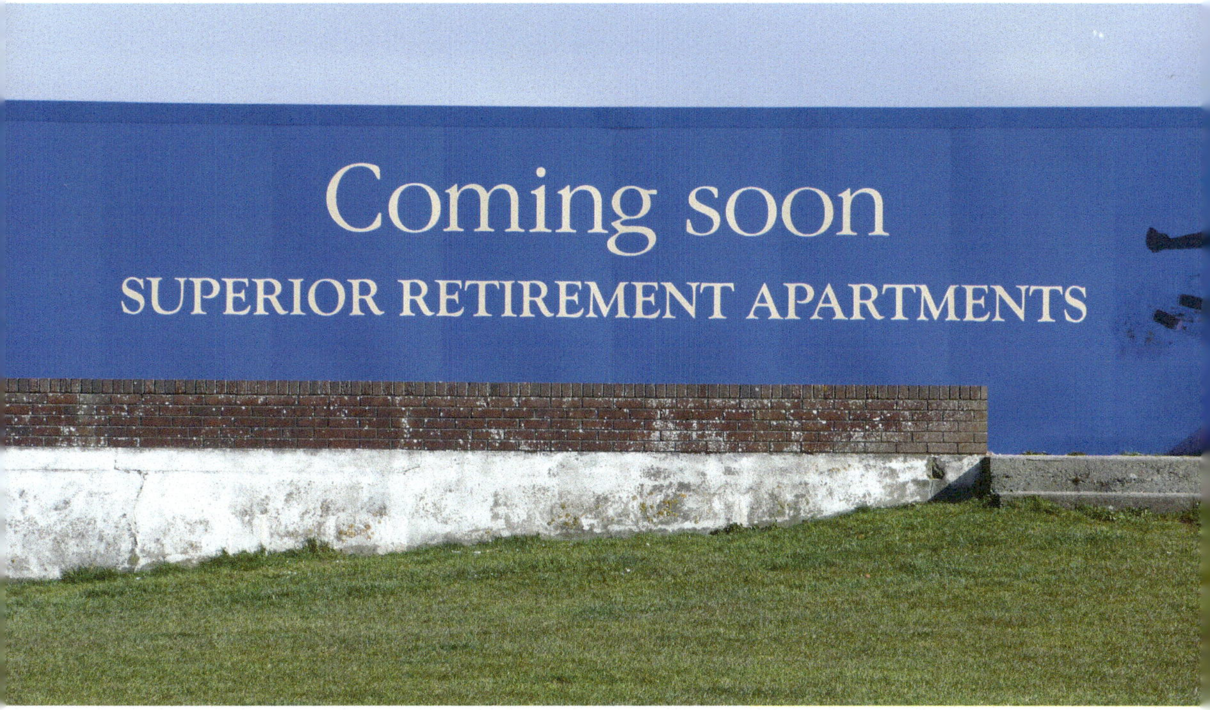

Coming soon

SUPERIOR RETIREMENT APARTMENTS

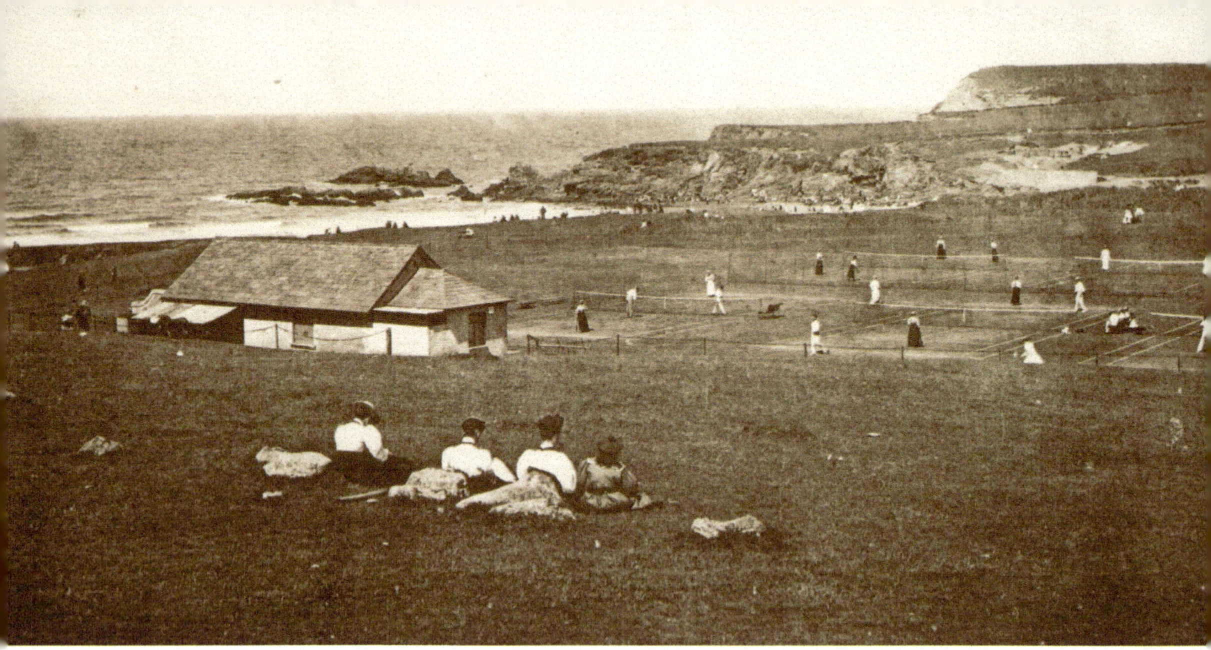

Crooklets

The cricket ground served for many years as tennis courts. In the background Penarvor, home of Sir George Croydon MP, is being built. In 1906, Marks was elected as MP for Launceston Division of Cornwall in the Liberal landslide of that year. Summerleaze Downs were originally used for grazing rights and form an important part of the protected green expanses in the town that help retain its special character. Below, the cricket ground in July 2012. In 2013, Bude-Stratton Town Council heard it had been awarded lottery funding of £50,000 to build a new pavilion, leaving a sporting legacy resulting from Inspired Facilities funding. Bude is widely considered to be one of the most attractively situated cricket grounds in the world, and it certainly is, with a sea view across the downs.

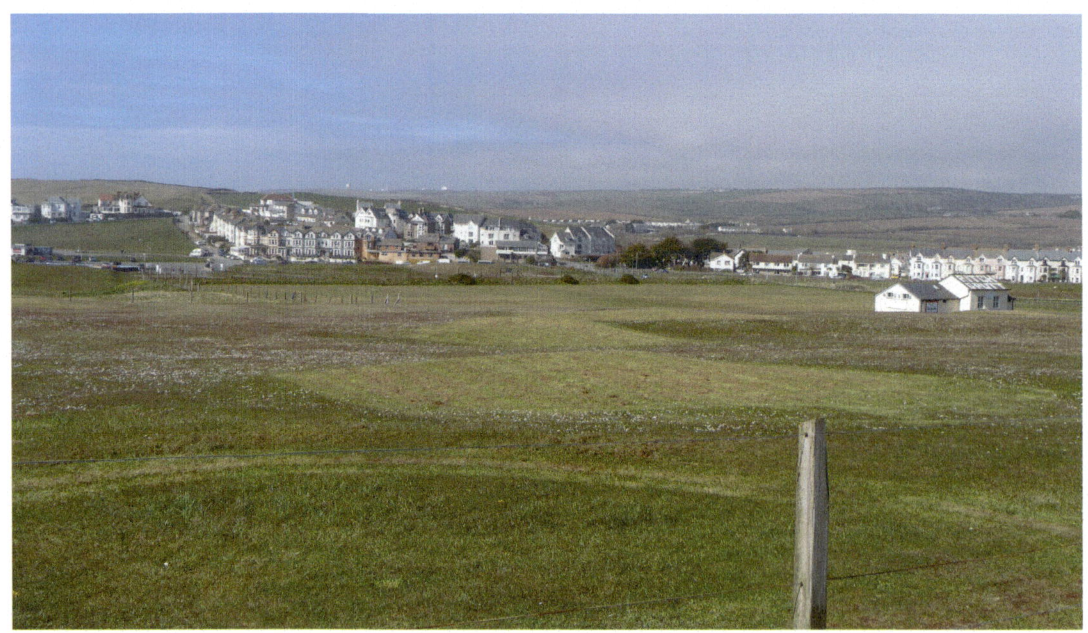

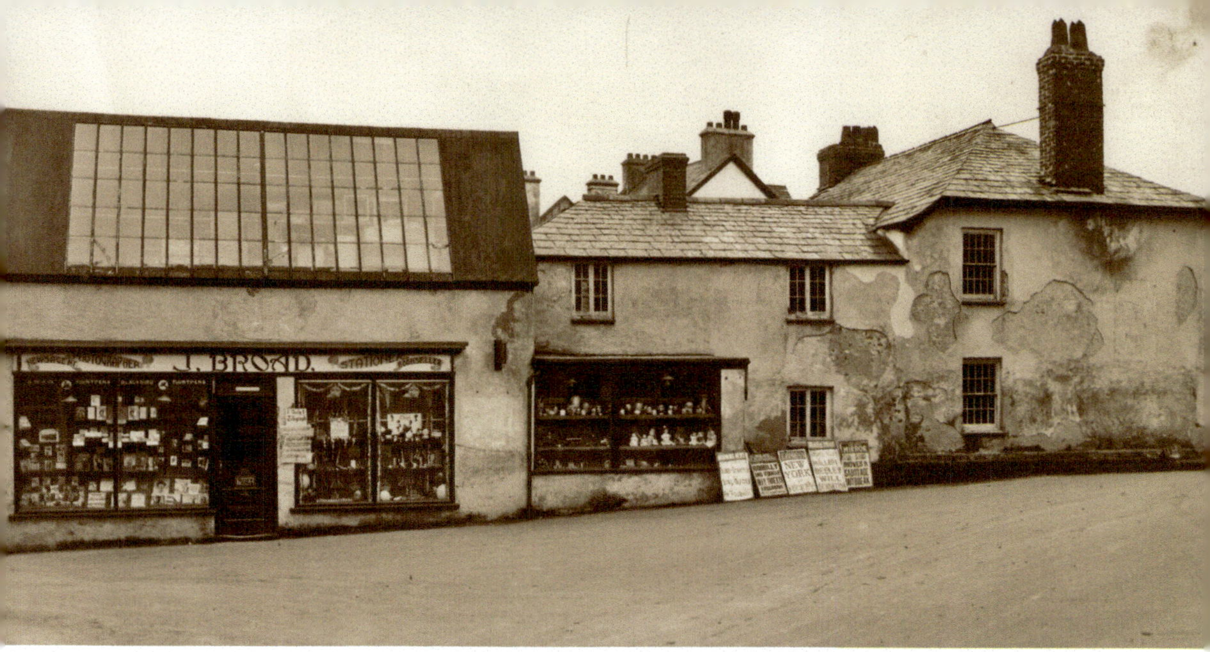

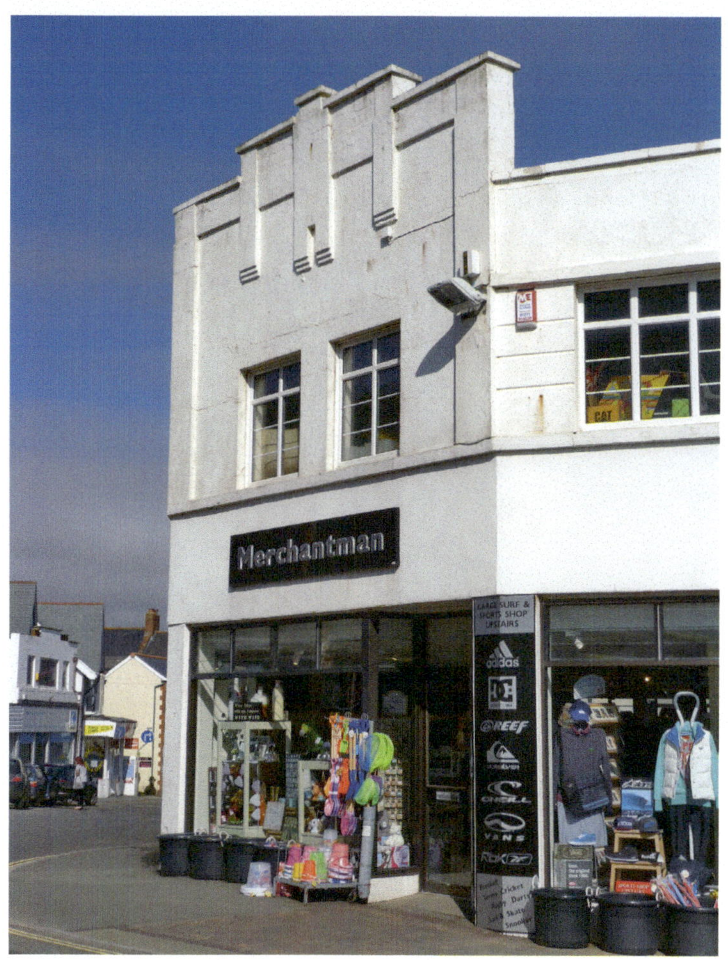

Edward's Shop, 1930s
Edward's Shop at the top of Belle Vue in what is now the town centre. Site of the current Merchantman, Springfield House was partly a cottage and partly Broad's Emporium. It was then rebuilt as Edward's Emporium, then the Co-op (1960s), then Merchantman, which it currently remains. Belle Vue developed into the commercial centre of Bude during the 1960s, and it has remained the prime shopping street in the town, situated on Queen Street.

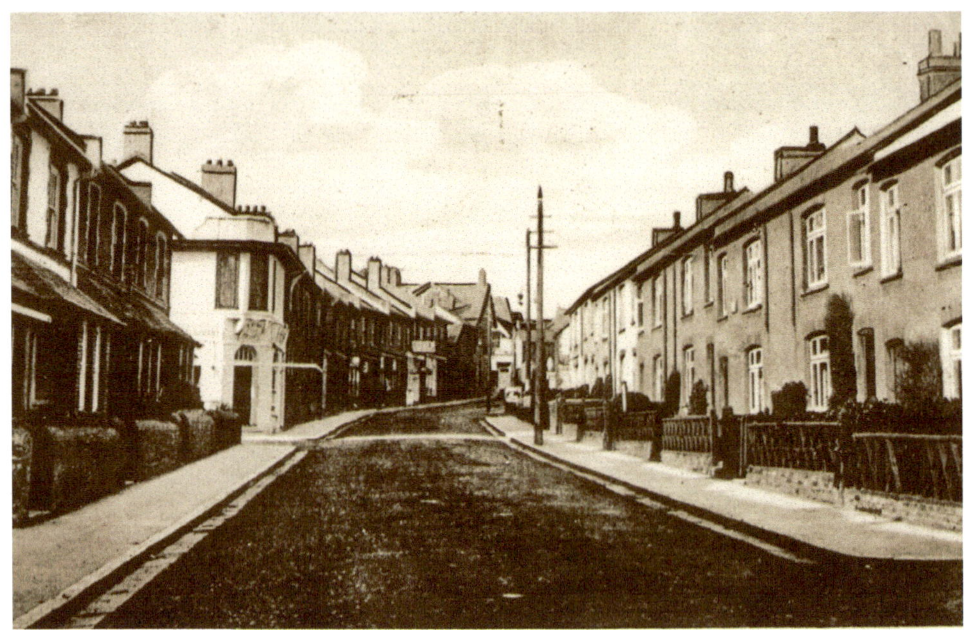

Queen Street, 1910

Back then Queen Street was largely residential, with the occasional shop. Now containing a variety of shops and cafés, it is often the subject of pedestrianisation discussions, and forms part of the current one-way system. The white building on the corner looks to be what is now the popular G's café and diner.

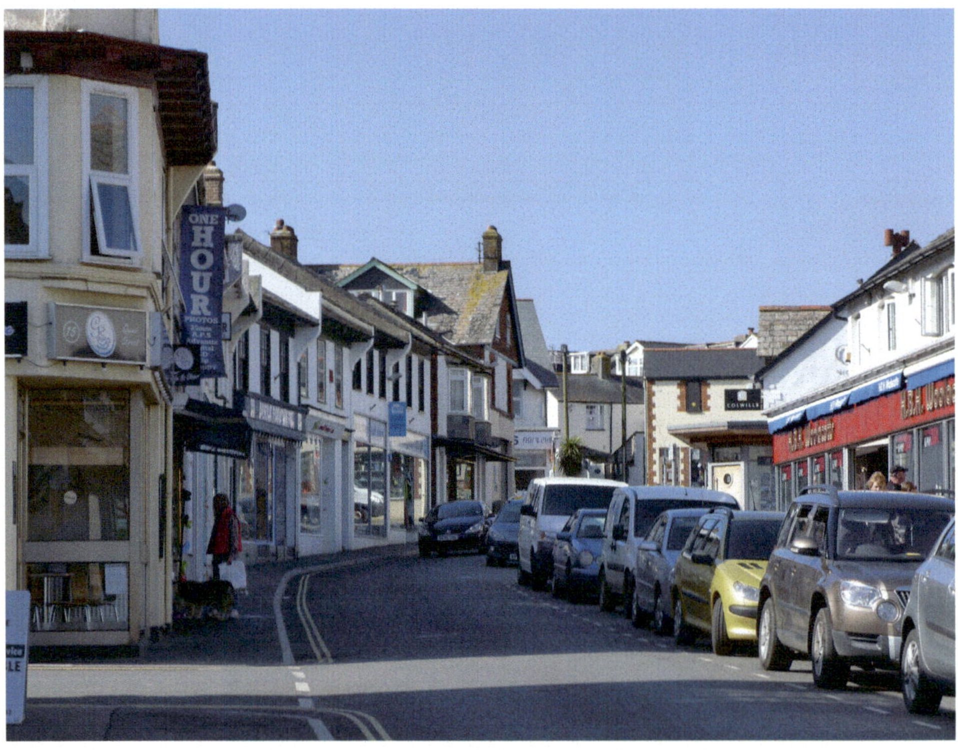

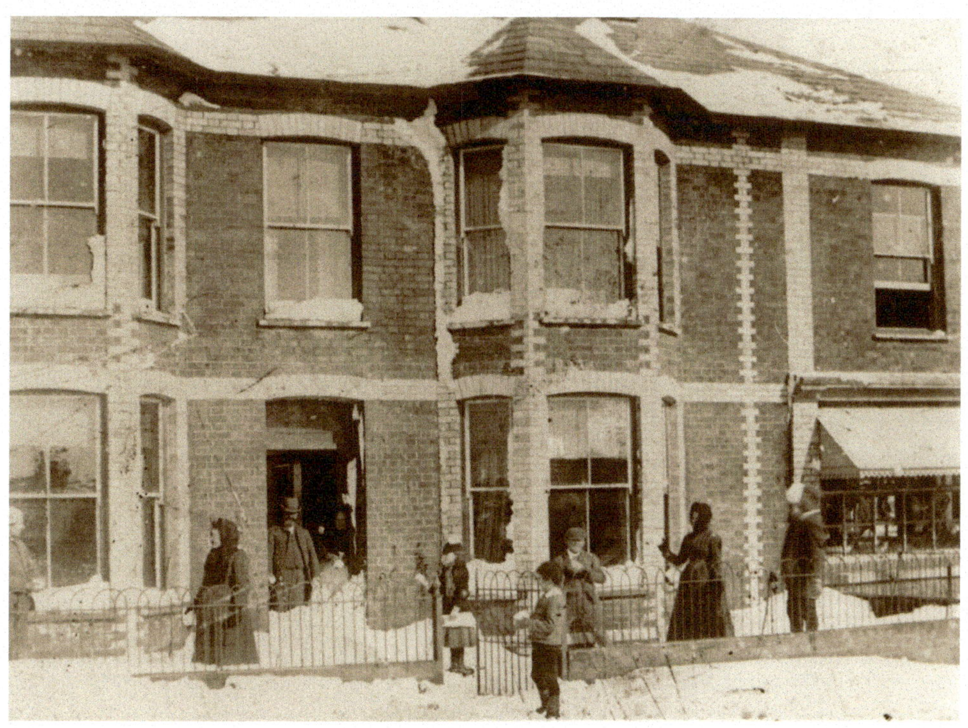

Morwenna Terrace

Morwenna Terrace was at the heart of nineteenth-century shopping in Bude. Here, it is shown with Bude Meat Supply on the corner in the early 1900s. The modern shopfronts are much more obvious.

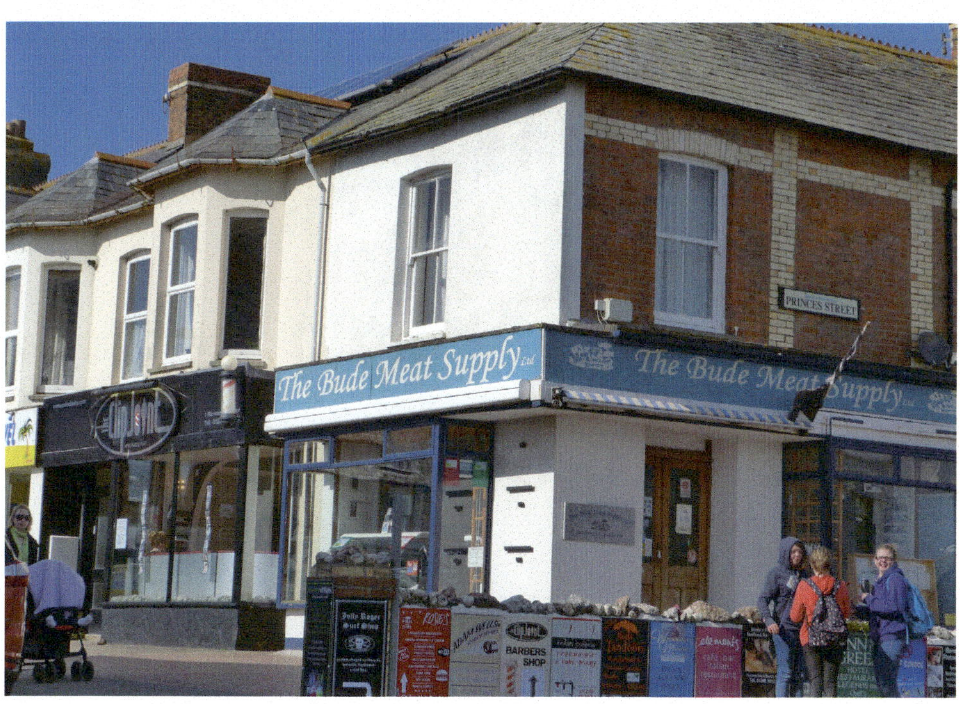

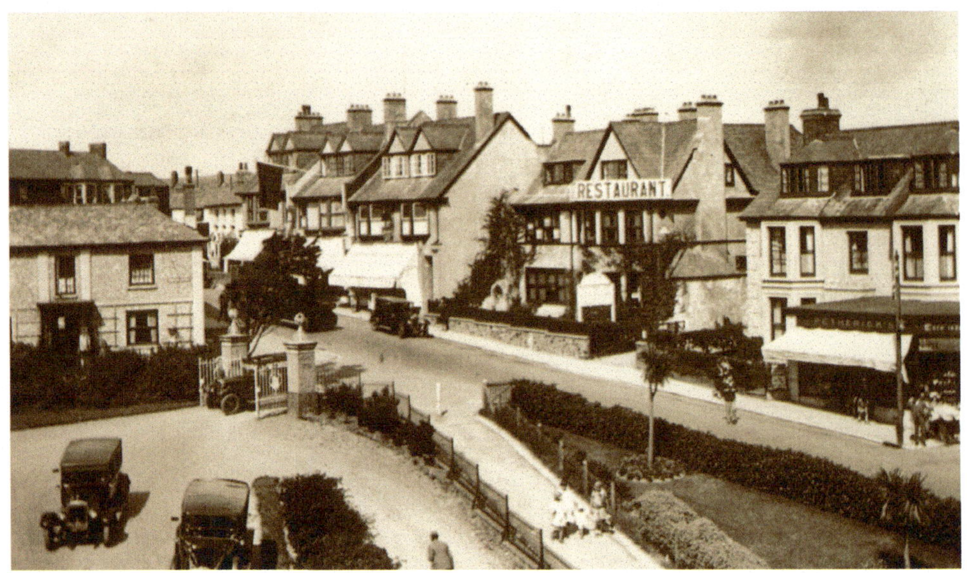

Belle Vue, 1929

A Francis Frith original picture taken from the Grenville, this shows the top of Belle Vue with Dr King's residence, which became a restaurant and is now Time & Tide, and Pethericks china and book shop on the corner where Boots now stands. Despite the influx of some chains, Bude is very fortunate to maintain a high number of independent shops, thereby maintaining its character. The side street near the aforementioned Boots is now looking rather dull by comparison.

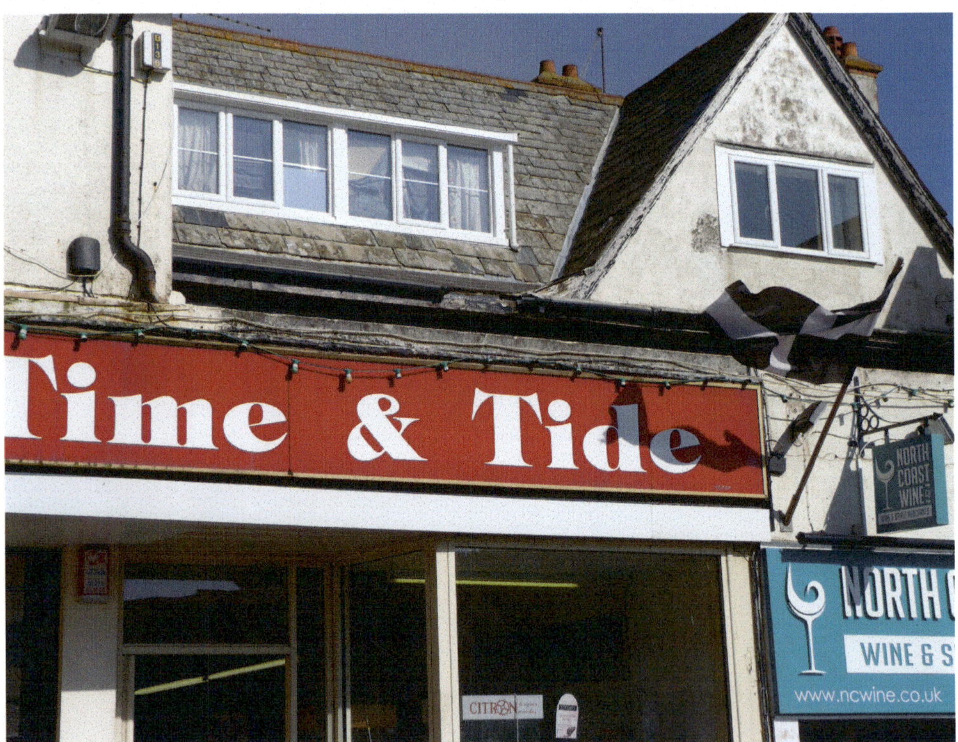

Waterspout, 1940s

A stunning waterspout seen (and captured on film) above Hawkings (now Truscott's) shop in Lansdown Road. These tend to be associated with thunderstorms, but no one seems to be sheltering in this photograph, despite the huge dark cloud above them. Below, Truscotts on Lansdown Road is a local hardware and ironmongery business, which has over 100 years' experience, and remains very popular with local people. It is one of the many independent local businesses that help to keep Bude unique.

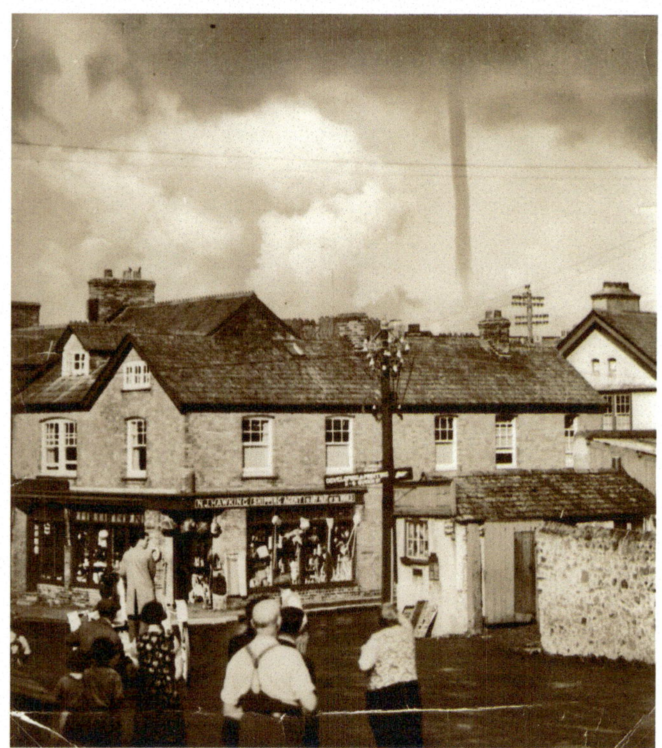

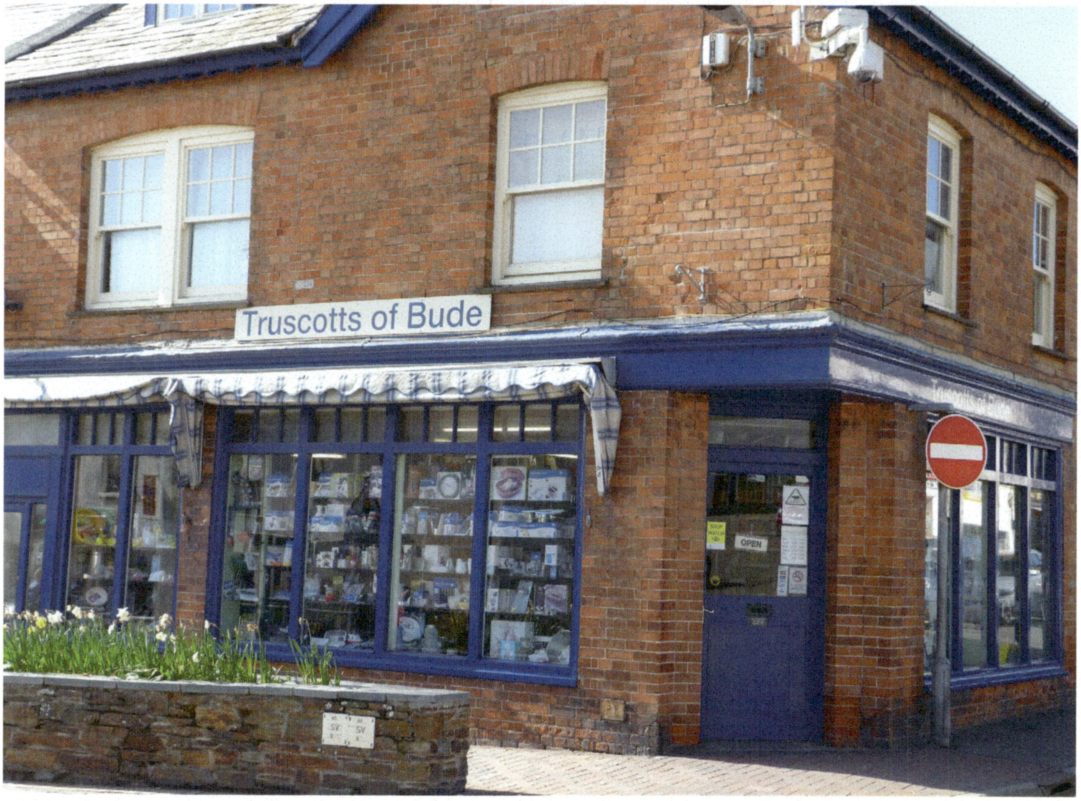

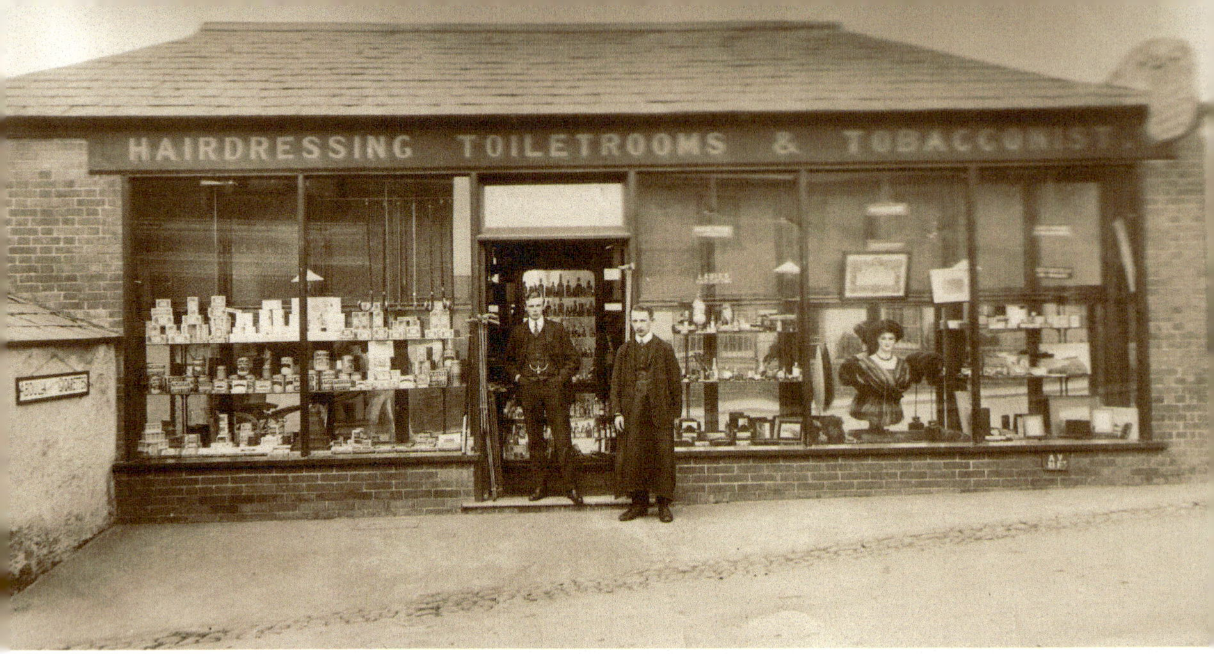

Spencer Thorn

Spencer Thorn's shop, which looks similar in most respects to the present shop (an independent bookshop at the top of Belle Vue). In this incarnation, it was a gent's hairdresser, supplier of toiletries and tobacconist. Today, it remains a beautifully decorated and attractive shop. The business, Spencer Thorn, has been trading in Bude since 1921. The current owners moved from London in 1999 to transform it into the delightful book and gift shop that it is today.

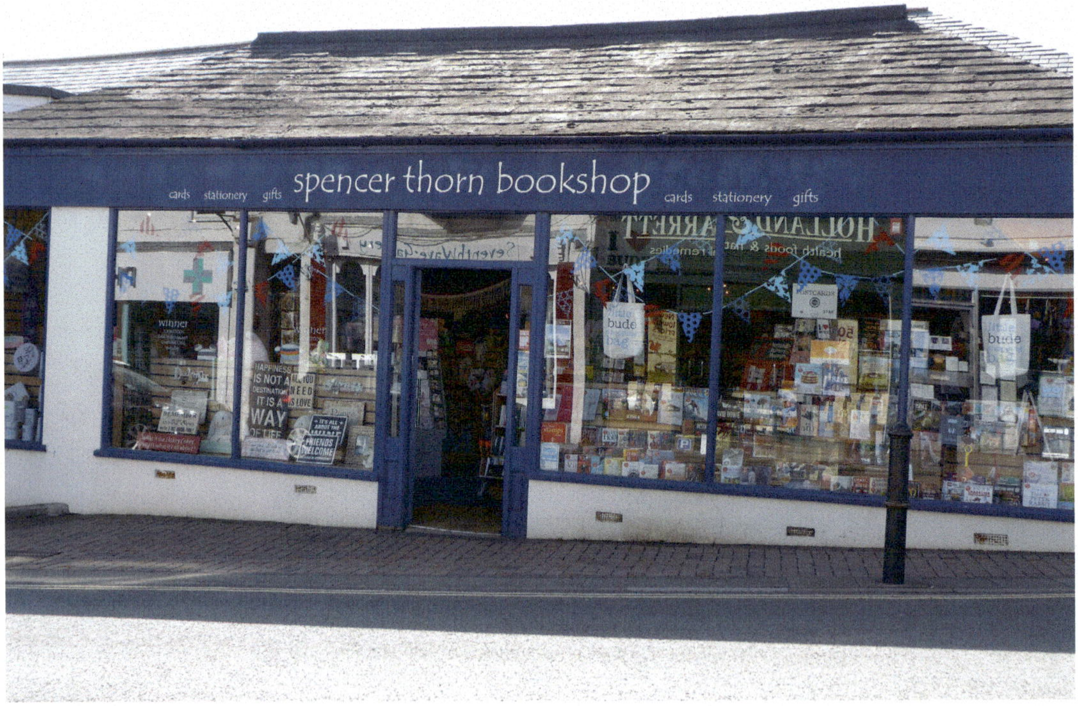

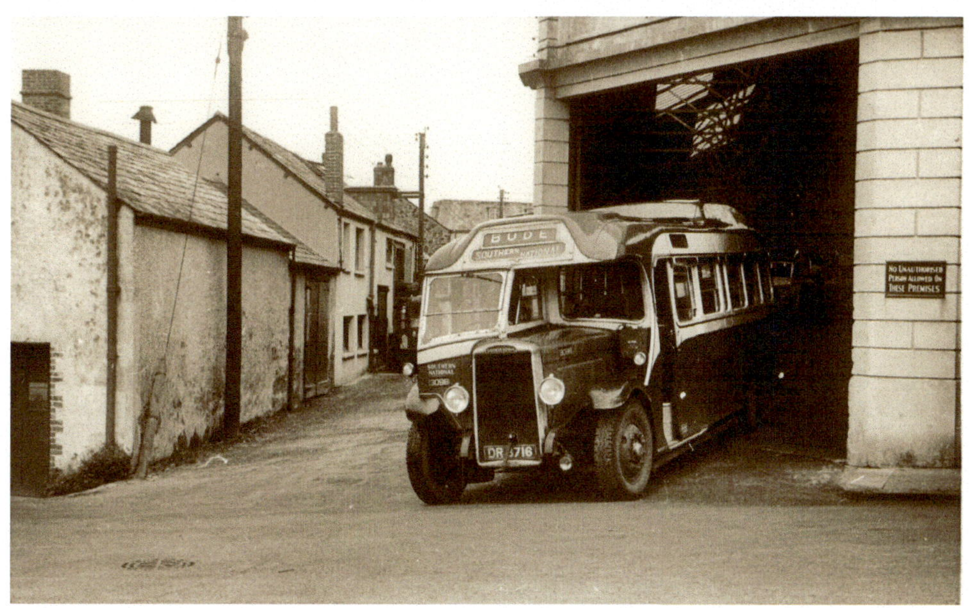

Bus Garage, August 1952

The national bus garage in Lansdown Road – subsequently used for many years by Jennings Bude, due to its railway being the LSWR – had Southern National buses, whereas most of Cornwall had Western National from the Great Western links. The old Art Deco garage and one-time cinema building is now derelict and requiring renovation. There were a few Art Deco buildings in Bude, epitomising the development of the 1920s and 1930s, where the modern merged with traditional.

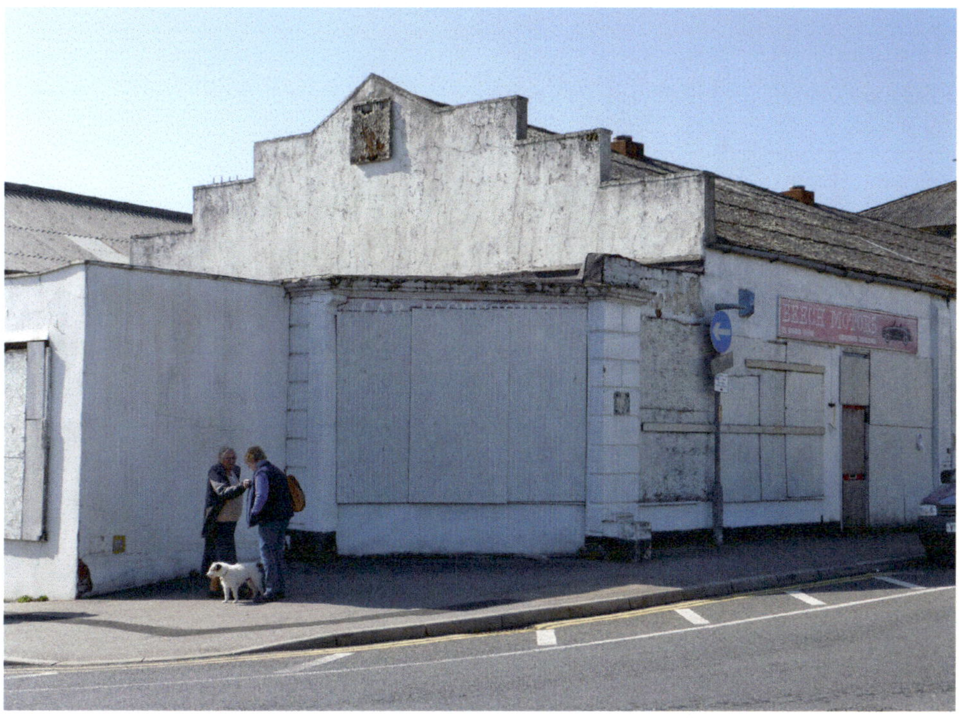

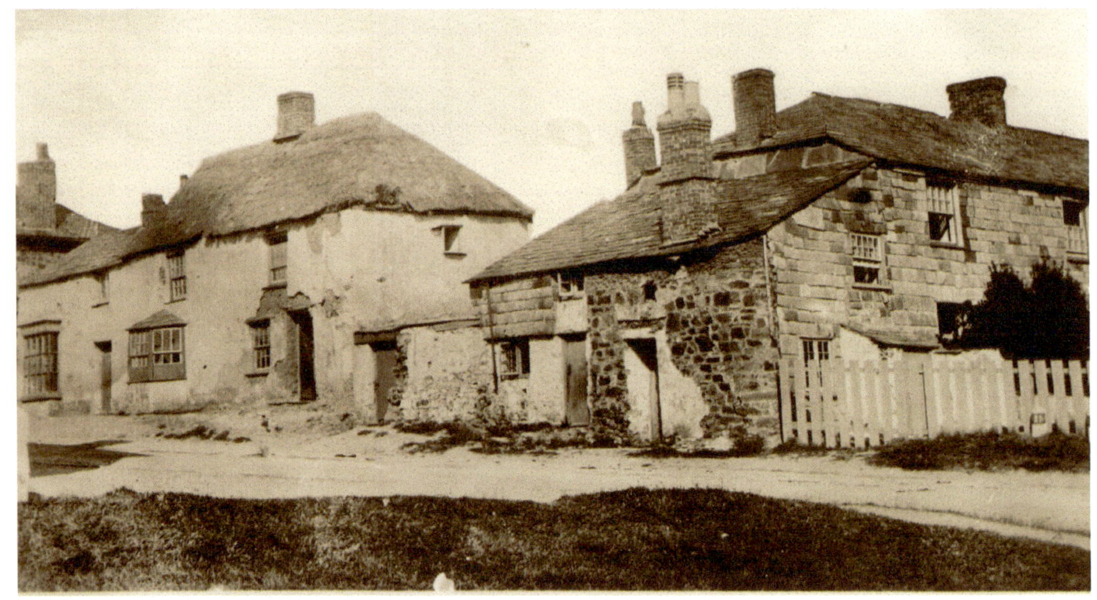

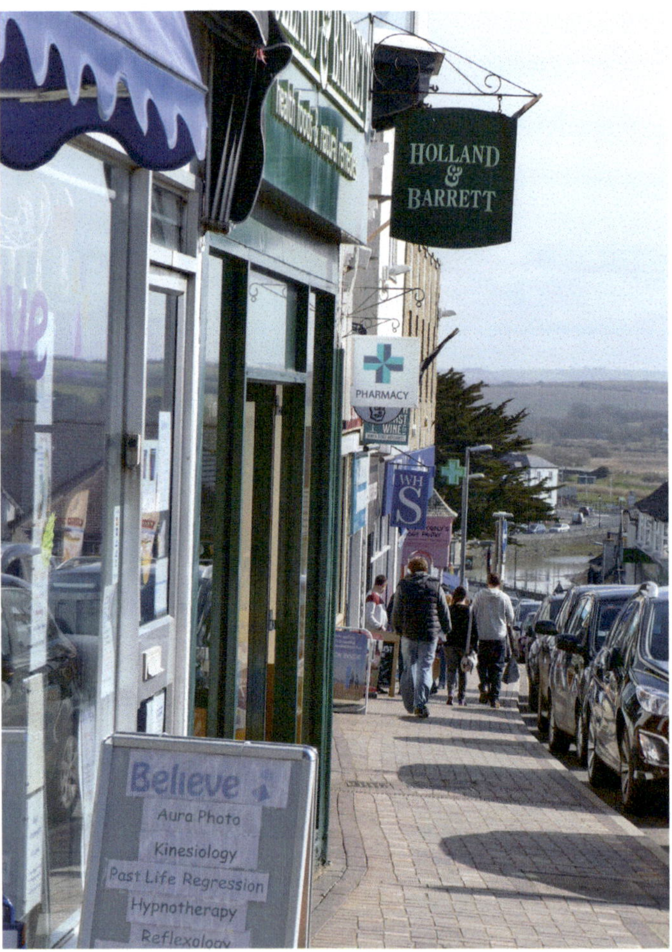

Belle Vue and Othello Terrace

These old cottages and shops at the top of Belle Vue were demolished at the end of the nineteenth century. The bottom building, roughly where Boots is now, is the end of Othello Terrace, which extended opposite Hartland Terrace. Othello Terrace was named after a wreck, but now no longer exists. The *Othello* was wrecked at Morwenstow rocks in 1808, and its figurehead apparently adorned one of the seafront terraces for many years until eroded by weather and salty air. Now things could not be more different on modern Belle Vue, thronged with people, cars and shops on a busy shopping day in the sunshine.

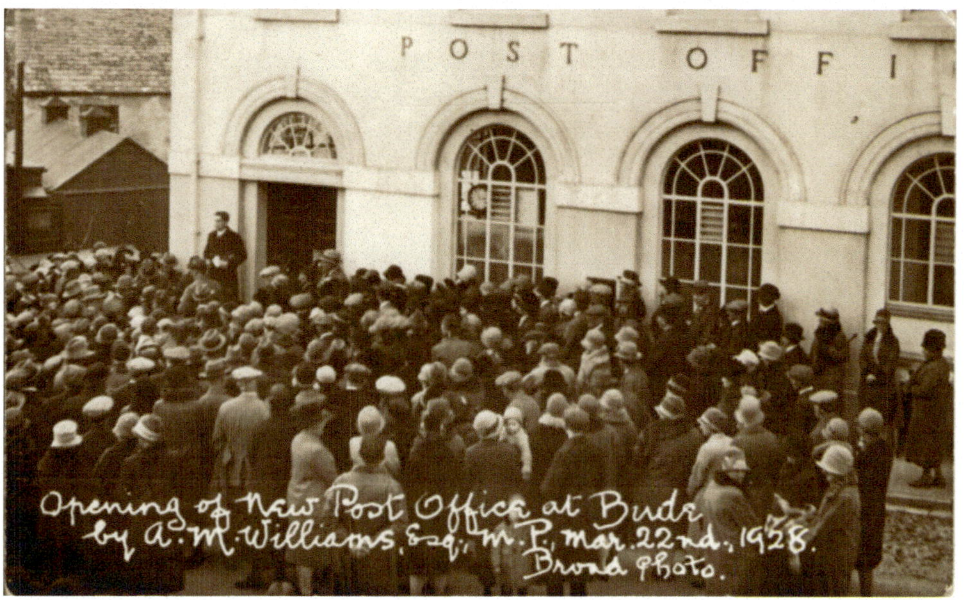

Post Office, 1928

Above, the opening of a new post office at the top end of Belle Vue, which was built on a site originally earmarked for a new parish church. The opening of any major new building brought the crowds out, and this was no exception. The post office has a pagoda roof, and round-headed windows with keystones, so it certainly makes an impact on the area and is still a local landmark.

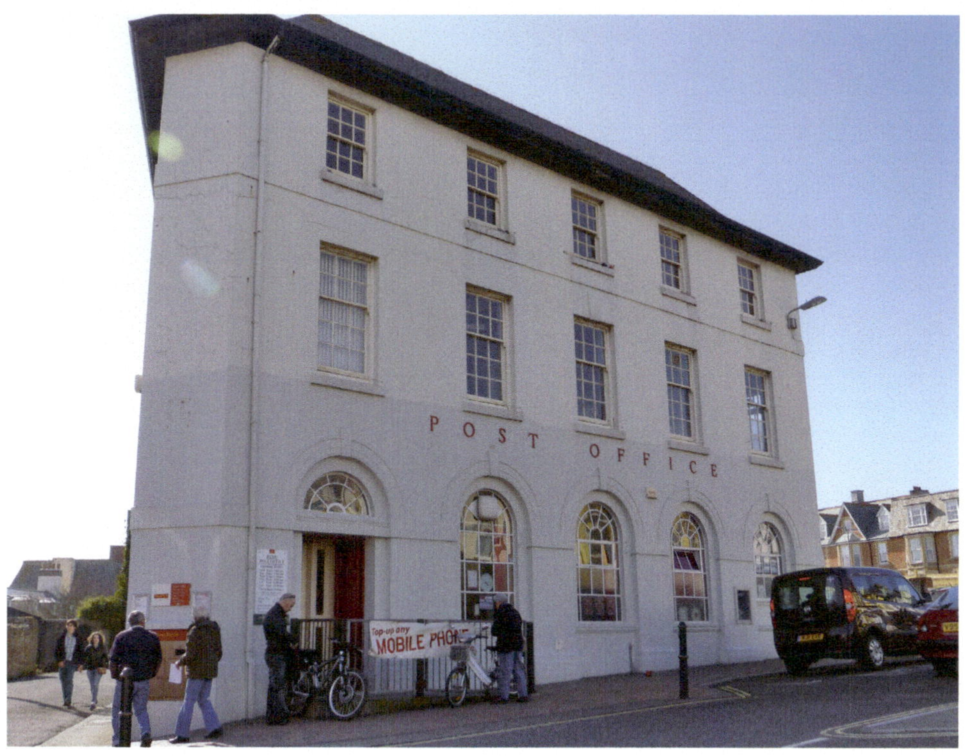

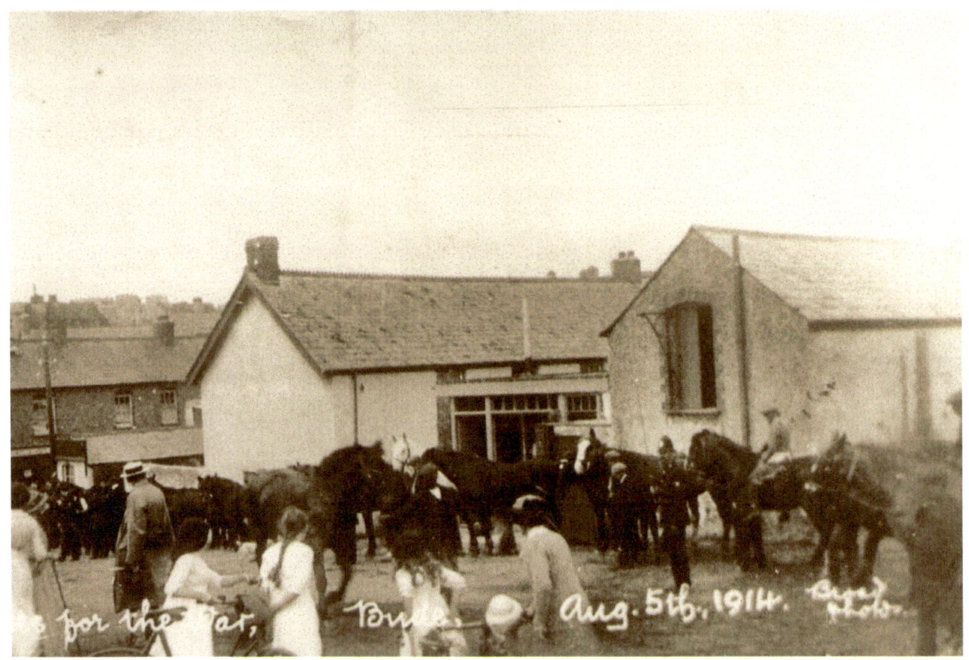

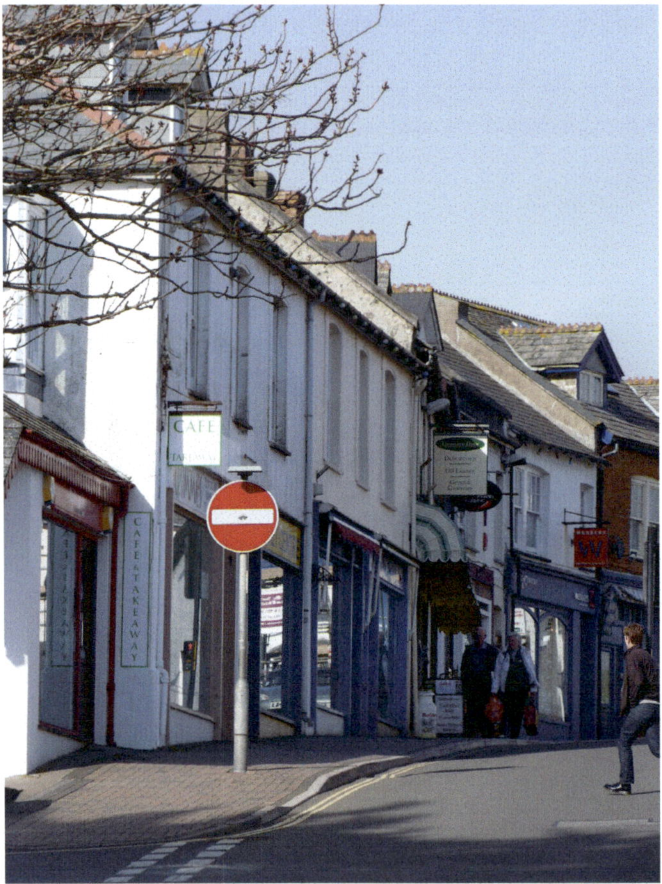

War Horse

Gathering the warhorses for the First World War. Here, horses were being collected for appraisal by War Ministry vets outside Lansdown Mews. Michael Morpurgo's novel *War Horse*, published in 2007, was adapted into a film set in neighbouring Devon and did a great deal to draw attention to the sacrifices made by the million horses sent to France between 1914 and 1918, of which only 62,000 returned. Here, Bude played its part in the war effort, and the unlucky equines were shipped to France. To the right, Lansdown Street today with the locally famous Lansdown Delicatessen and a variety of other shops – and not a horse in sight.

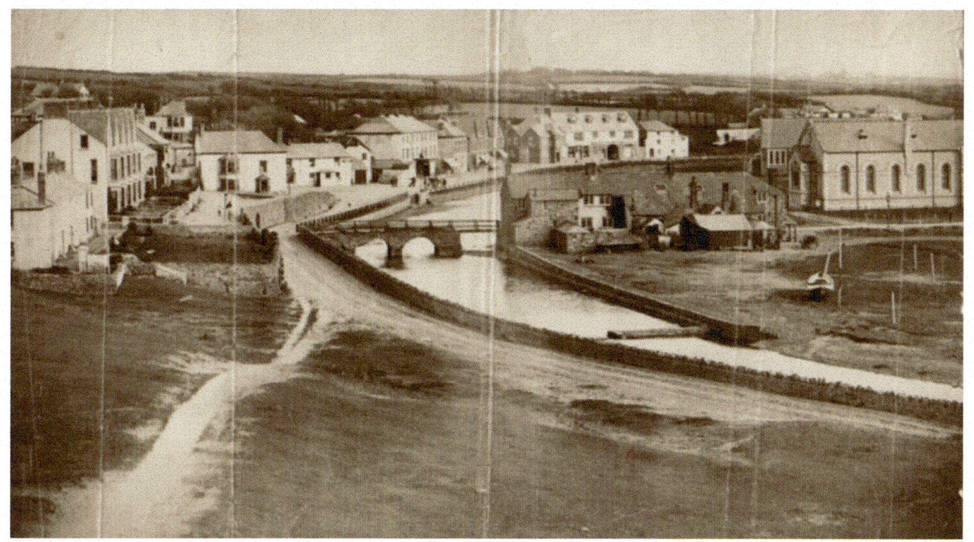

Nanny Moore's Bridge, 1894

To the left is Marine Terrace, demolished to make way for the Grenville (now Adventure International activity centre, attracting large numbers of children to Bude for outdoor pursuits); then the end of the Bude Hotel (previously the Bewd Inn), with the old Globe Hotel (previously the Jolly Sailor, which was popular with sailors and carters) opposite. Early development was mainly at the southern end of the Triangle, on the northern side of the Strand. Next to that is a smithy and, further along, part of one of the old Strand warehouses built on land belonging to the Thynne family. So, Bude is recognisable certainly, due largely to Nanny Moore's bridge and the curve of the Neet, but it is much less densely populated than today, as the modern picture, with its now closed Strand Hotel, shows. The Strand, at the gateway to Bude, has had a chequered history. It most recently reopened in 2011 and closed only a year later, so, once again, needs regenerating as a gateway to Bude.

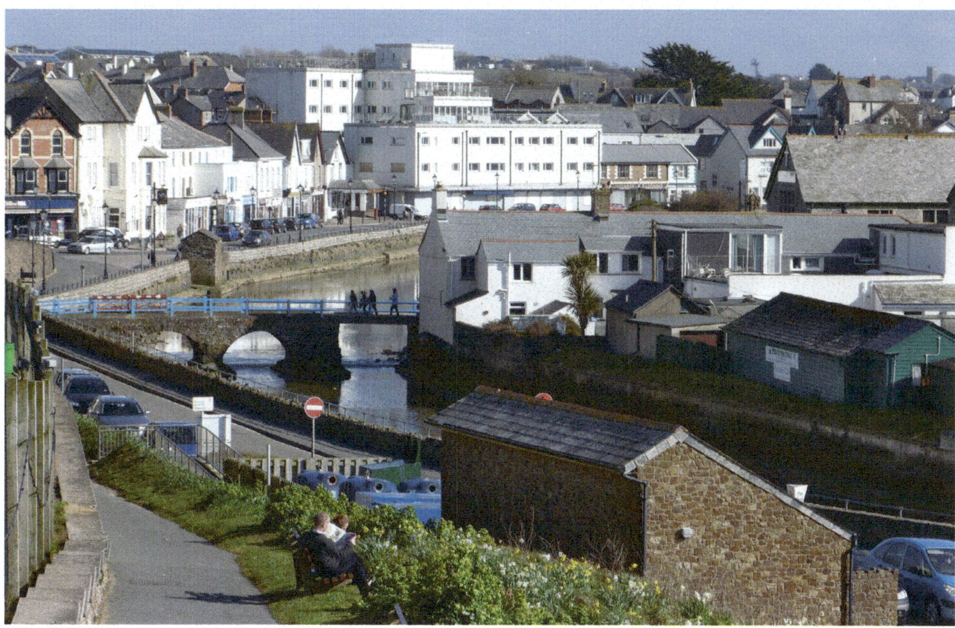

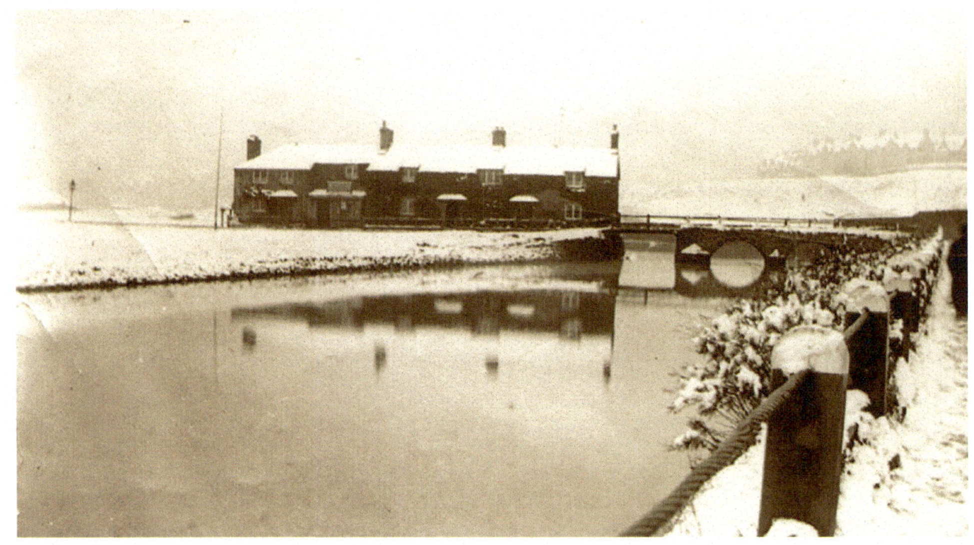

Nanny Moore's Bridge, 1900s

Nanny Moore's three-span, rubble-stone bridge, shown here in snow prior to the building of the recreation ground. The cable between the posts in the foreground is reputed to have come from the wreck of the *Bencoolen,* but it was replaced by the present wall in 1961/62. The bridge is Grade II listed and was originally Bude Bridge, used for packhorses and carts as well as pedestrians; it was renamed after a nearby nineteenth-century 'dipper', Nanny Moore. She was a widow, who lived in one of the cottages next to the bridge (Leven Cottages) in the early to middle part of the nineteenth century. She was a Victorian bathing machine attendant or 'dipper', who assisted the women using them to immerse themselves, especially when the water temperature was cold. She died in 1853 and is buried in St Michael's and All Angels churchyard. Below are Leven Cottages today. In 1933, there were tea rooms here, rather than the houses seen now. However, there are tea rooms further along towards Castle Green.

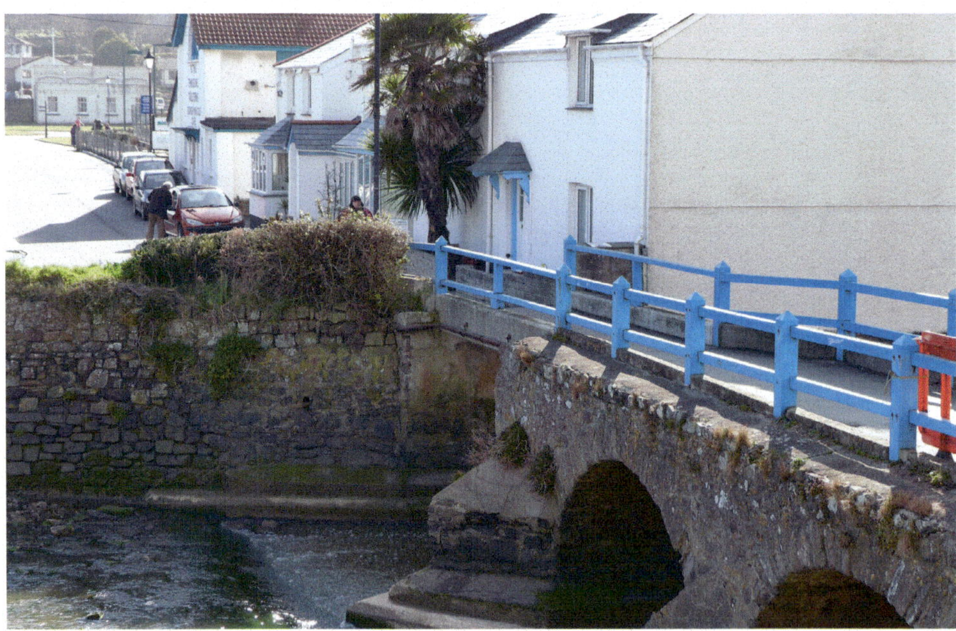

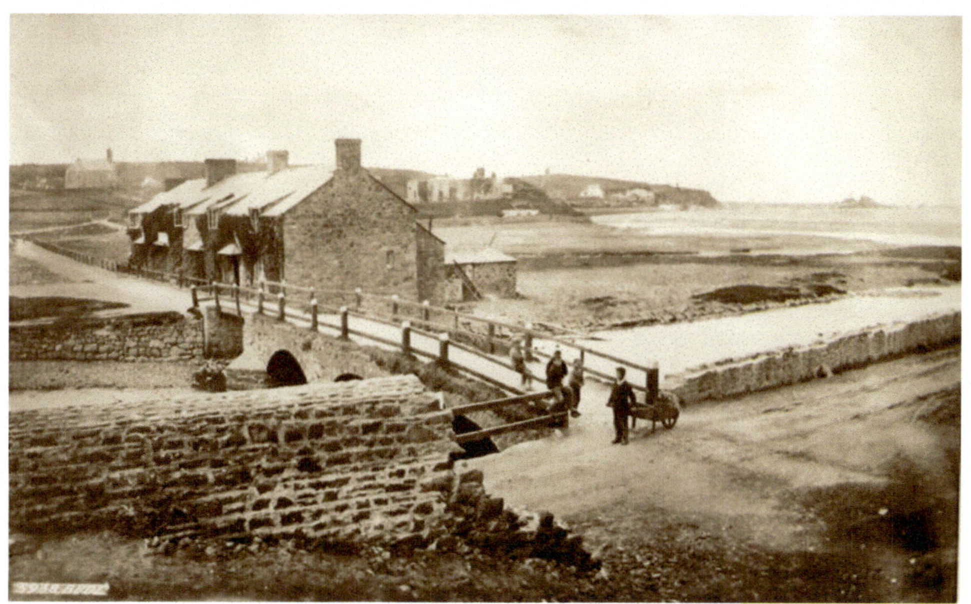

Nanny Moore's, 1870s

Nanny Moore's with Leven Cottages, seen prior to the building of the nearby squash courts, bowling green, tennis courts, putting, and other facilities. Now a pedestrian only bridge, Nanny Moore's was built around 1589, with the neighbouring quay built in 1577. The rather neat but elegant Quay Cottage, the oldest house in Bude, still exists on the town side of Nanny Moore's Bridge and contains an inscription stone 'AJA 1589', standing for Anne and John Arundell.

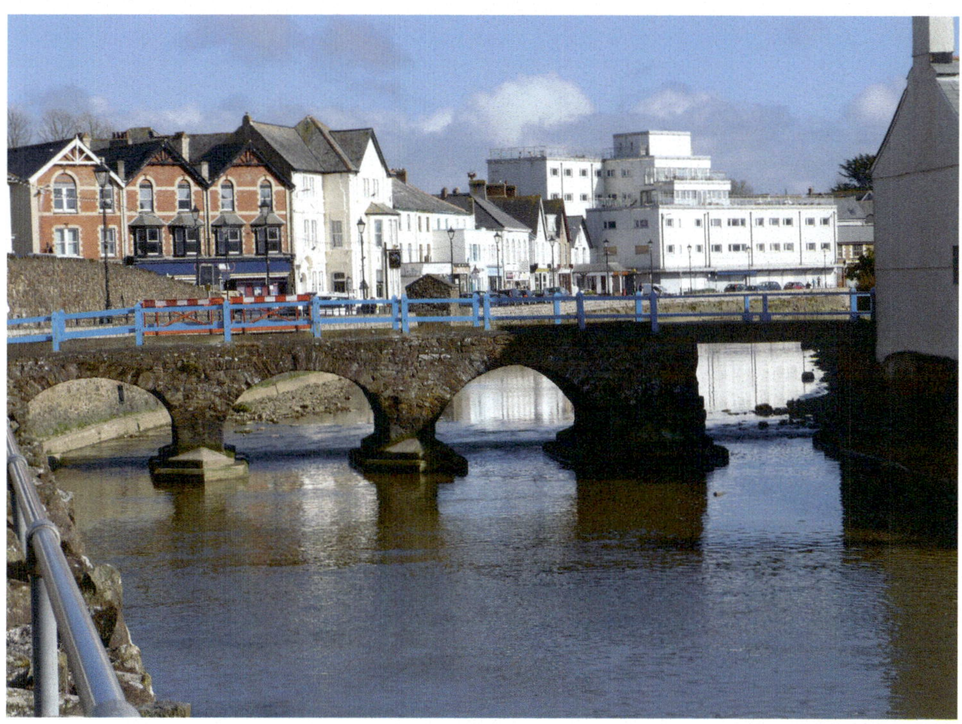

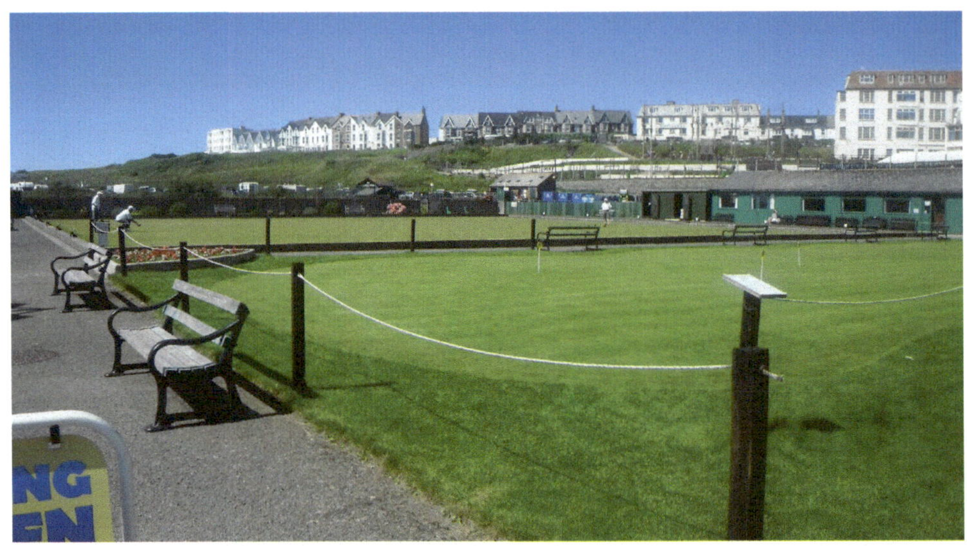

Leisure Centre and Tennis Courts

Looking towards Summerleaze car park provides a popular outdoor leisure centre that attracts locals and tourists. Behind Nanny Moore's Bridge, the pink climbing wall of Adventure International, the old Grenville Hotel, stands out as a town landmark.

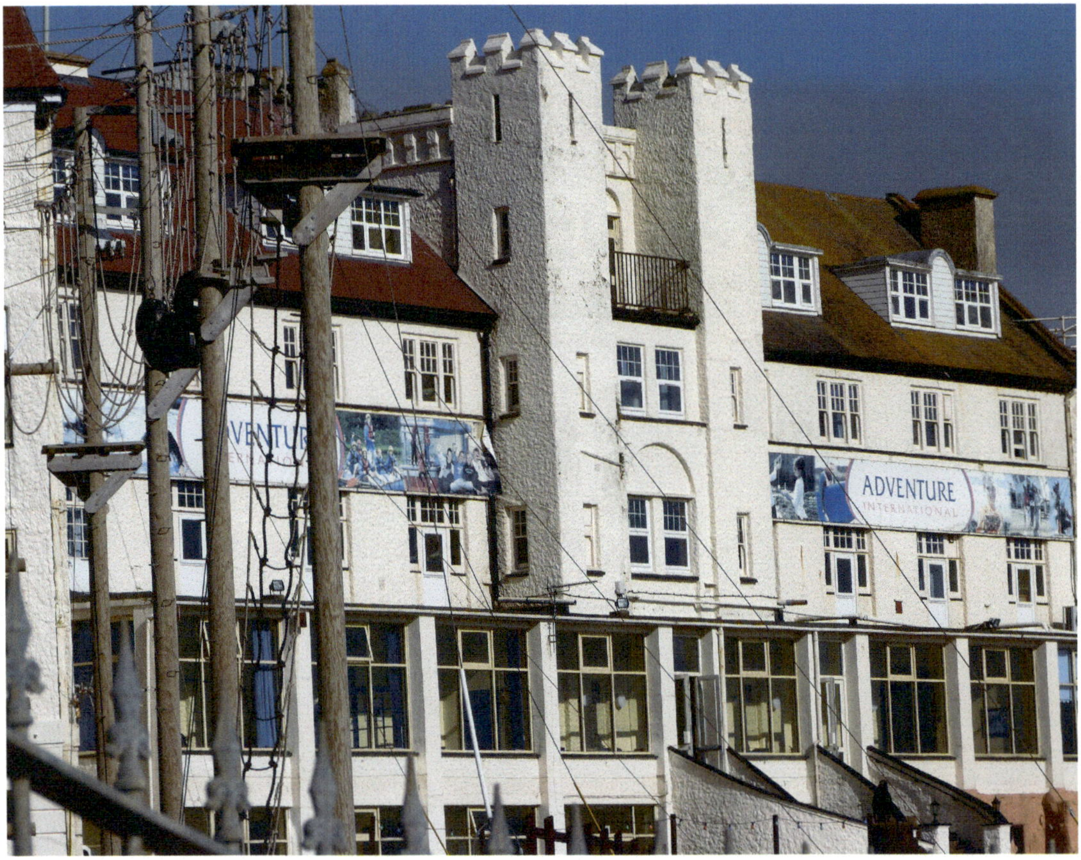

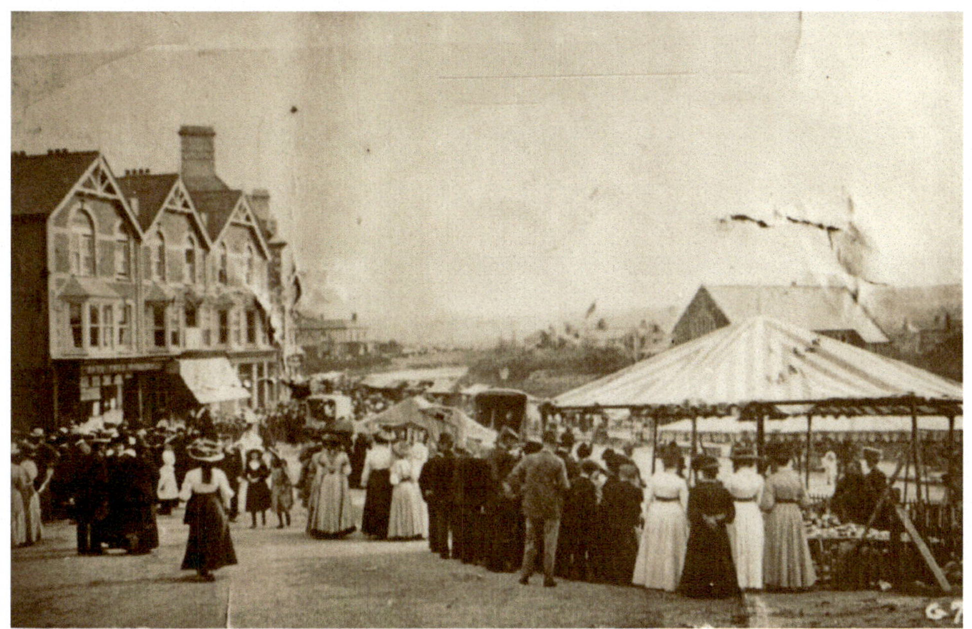

Bude Fair

Bude Fair was a popular event, the fair day was held annually on 22 September. This photograph was taken between 1895 and 1902, but probably around 1897. Now the travelling fair comes to Bude (most recently Summerleaze car park) annually. Bude Hotel is still in existence in this picture, where Lloyds TSB is now. During Carnival, people still line the Strand's pavements and populate the Triangle. The modern-day Strand maintains its shops and remains the gateway to Bude town centre.

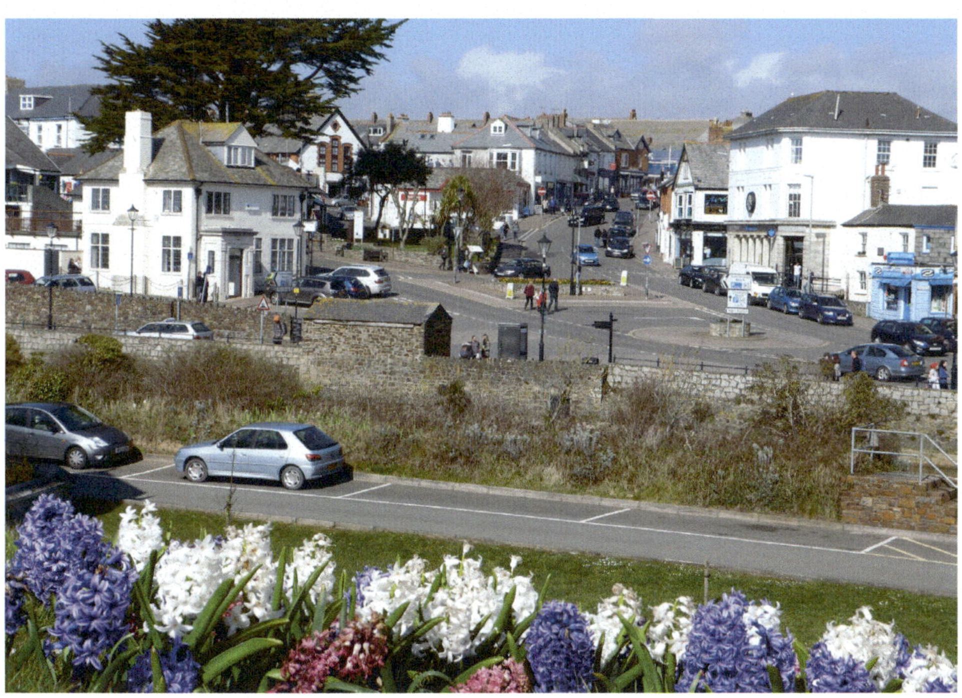

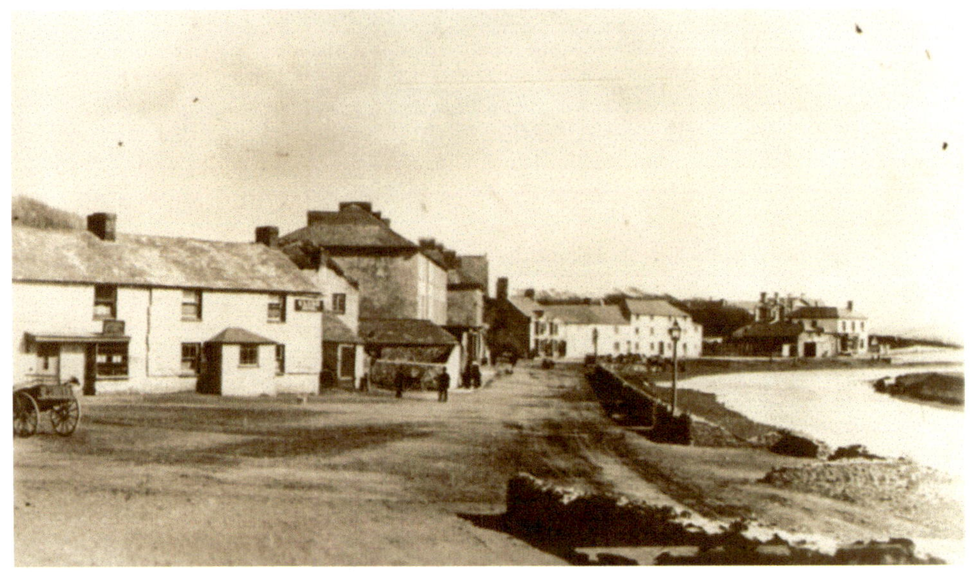

The Globe and the Strand, 1882

An early view of the Strand, with the old Globe, the Hockin & Hooper corn stores, and a river without defined banks. The Globe was built in Edwardian Baroque style by one of Cornwall's most renowned nineteenth-century architects, Silvanus Trevail. 'Tre' is popular in Cornish names, meaning 'homestead'. It is said that 'by tre, pol and pen, shall you know all Cornishmen'. If you look at the Globe, and the adjacent William Hill bookmaker's, you will see that they are all built in a similar style, designed again by Silvanus Trevail. Despite his many public successes both professionally and in Cornish politics, Trevail had a history of depression. He committed suicide by shooting himself in a train as it entered Brownqueen Tunnel near Bodmin station.

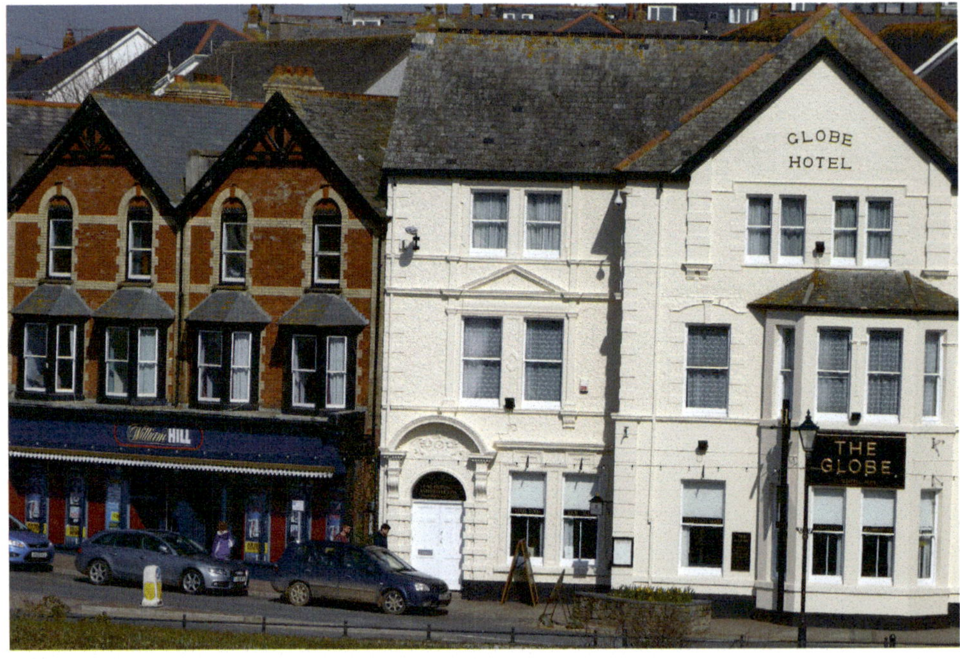

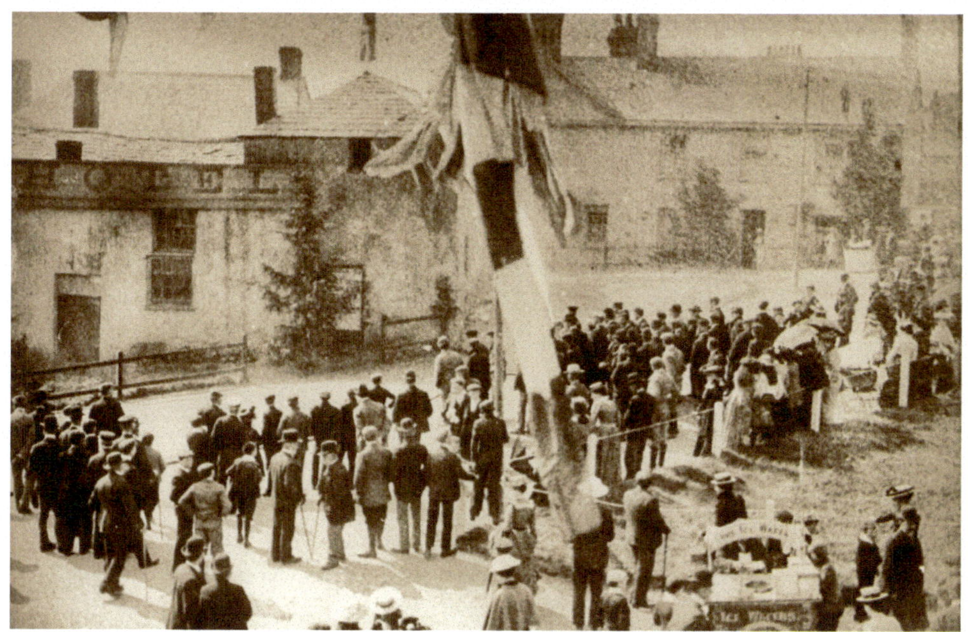

The Triangle

By the Triangle, with the old Bude Hotel opposite, General Redvers Buller – after who the Bullers Arms was named – turned on the first mains water supply for Bude in 1903. This replaced the water pump in the Shute Triangle. The Bude Hotel is now the Lloyds TSB bank, built Lutyens-style with some eclectic Art Nouveau influences. Sir Edwin Lutyens (1869–1944) was a great British architect, who designed country houses, commercial buildings and even the Viceroy's House in New Delhi. Below, a different kind of crowd, on Lifeboat Day 2011, with people listening to the band playing at Bude Light. Lifeboat Day is a very popular local day and a massive local fundraiser for the highly respected RNLI.

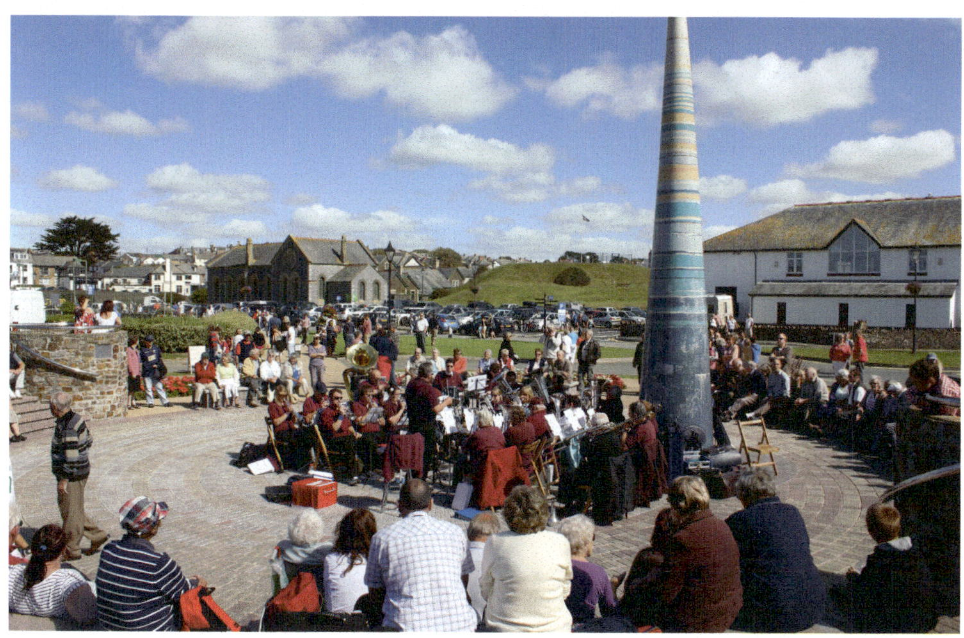

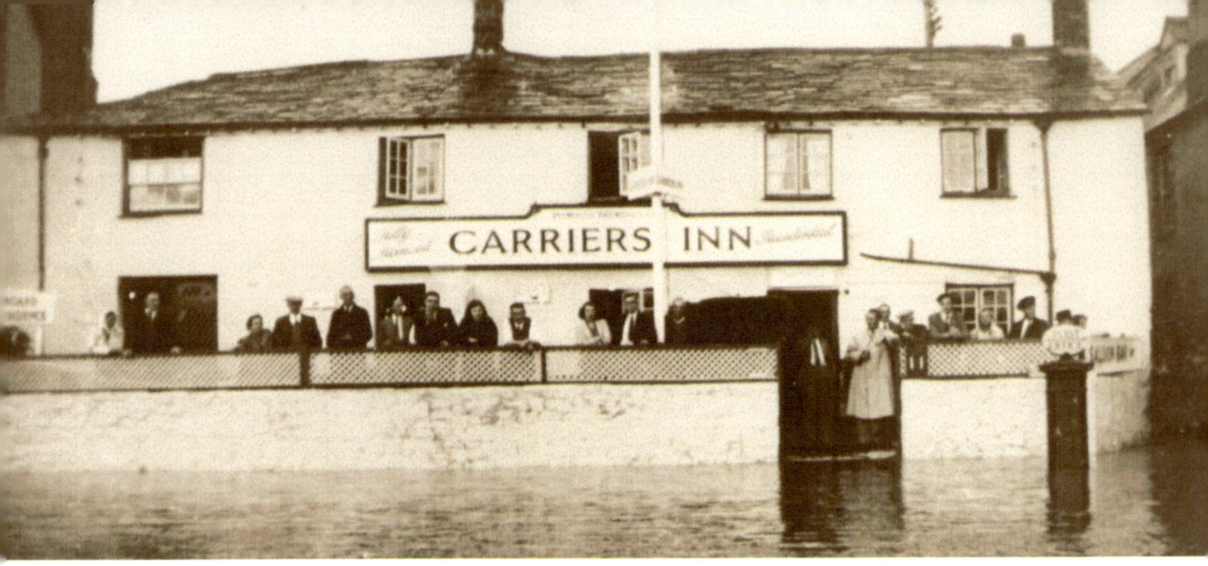

River Neet

It is the 1950s and the River Neet is in flood, but people seemed happy enough looking on from the Carriers Inn on the Strand. In recent years, the Carriers, in the heart of Bude, has had many changes of ownership and management, but it remains the oldest pub in town and a fine place to sit out on a summery day. The Neet is a tributary of the Strat, neither of which are very long but which respond quickly to rainfall, making flooding a problem. This means that extensive flood defence schemes are in place at Bude and out to Helebridge. The river catchment is largely agricultural land, which has led to some erosion of the riverbanks from cattle and sediment issues. The Neet meets the sea at Bude.

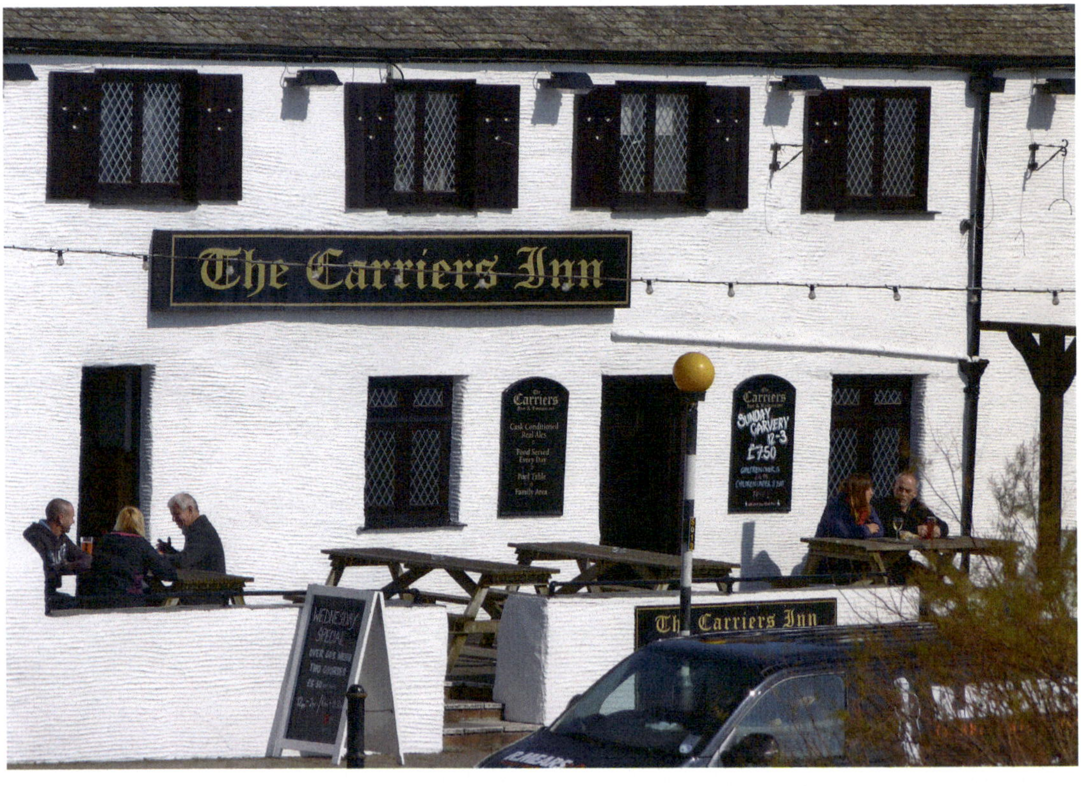

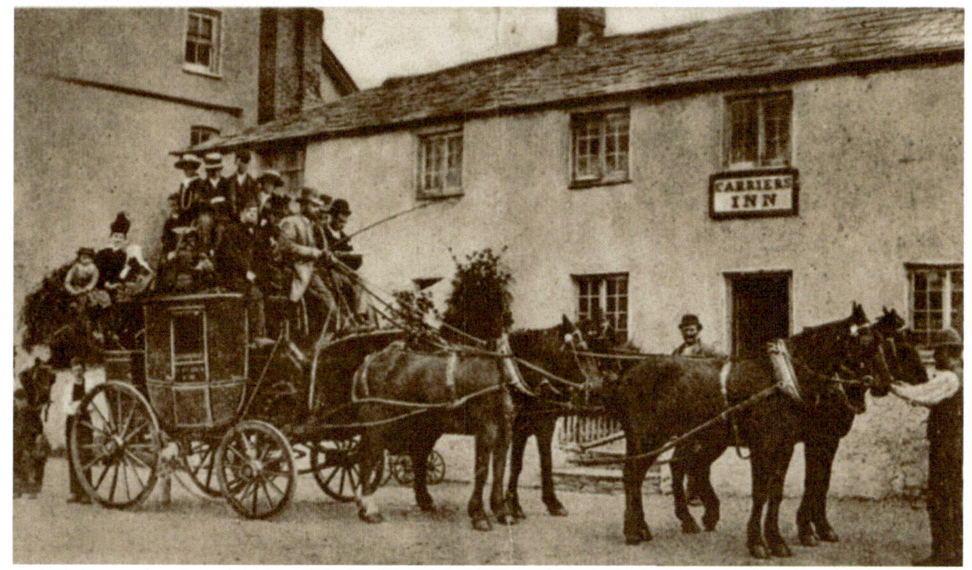

The Carrier's Inn, 1900s

The proprietress of the Carrier's Inn at this time was a Miss Cobbledick. The Carriers was originally a farmhouse owned by the Cobbledick family, who were successful horse-drawn coach operators. There are twelve people on top of the coach. How the horse-drawn coaches would have managed the floods is a mystery, but the No. 135 to Plymouth, via Stratton, Launceston and Tavistock, was doing well making its way along the Strand in the 1950s following a flooding of the River Neet.

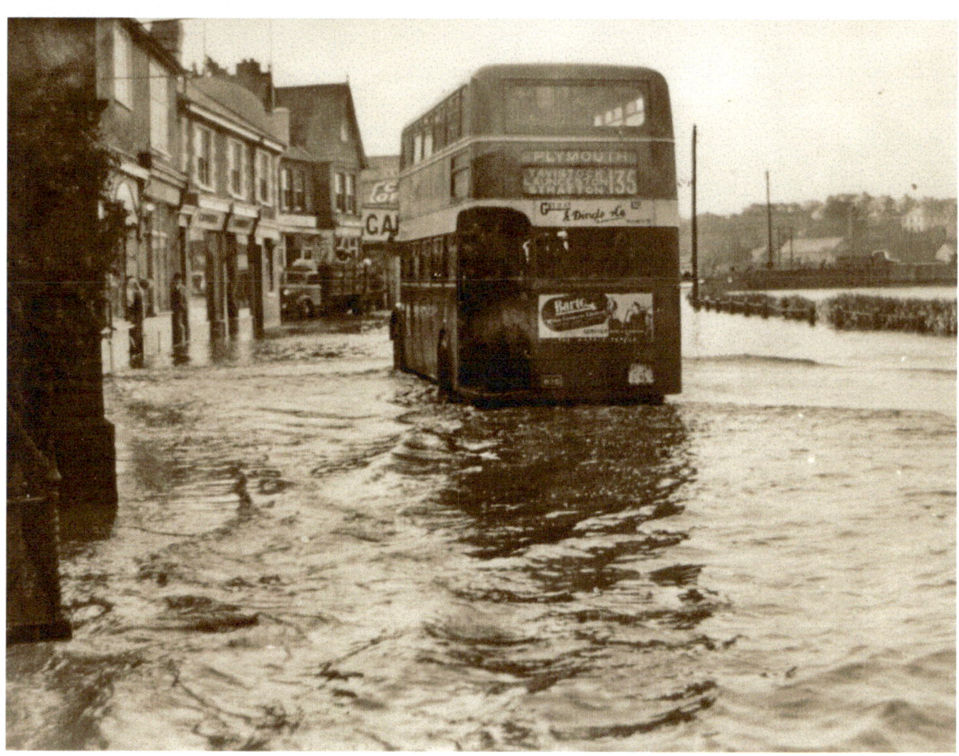

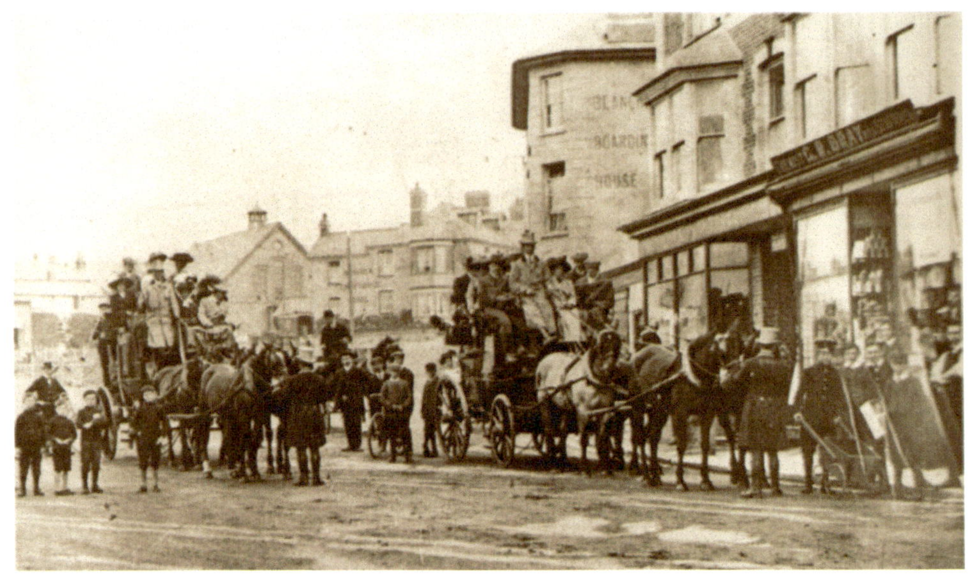

Coaches at the Triangle, 1895

It is amazing how many people could get on top of a coach. In the background are the parish hall, built in 1894, and the Norfolk Temperance Hotel, with Blanchminster Boarding House also noticeable to the right. Below, the Triangle today. The Triangle is a popular meeting point and is used as a focal point on Remembrance Day and during Carnival. The Blanchminster Building is now Barclays Bank. The Triangle was once Blanchminster Square.

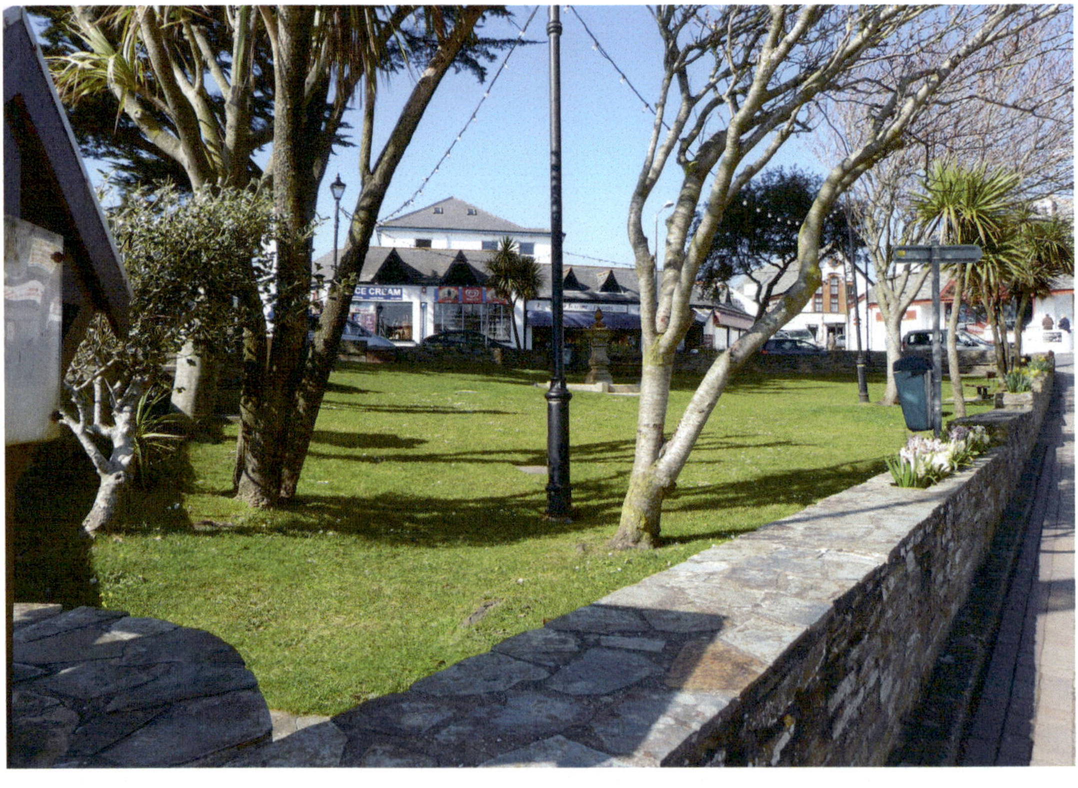

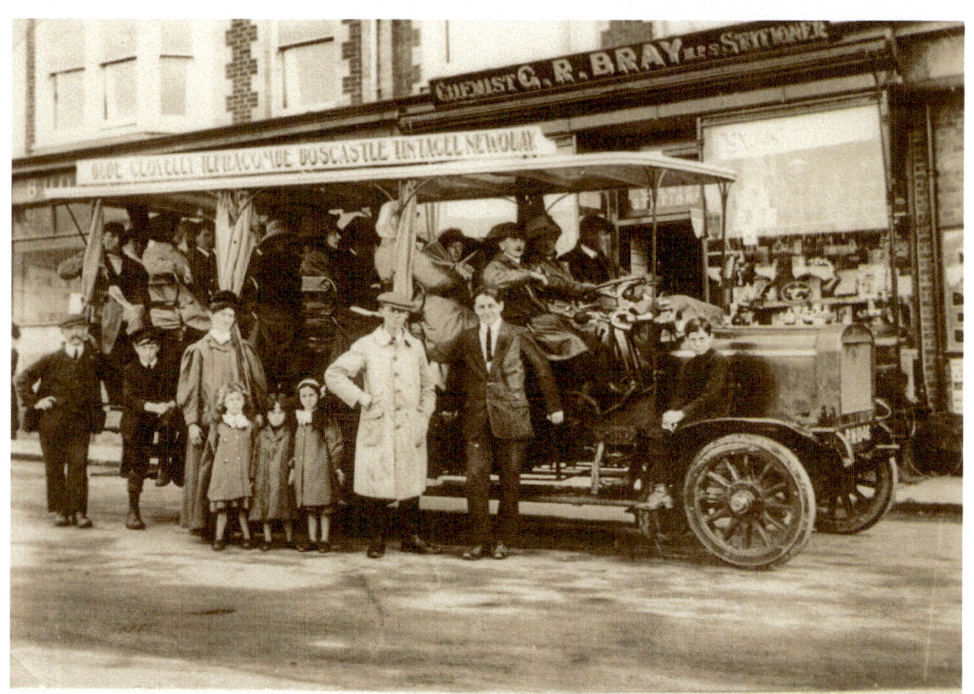

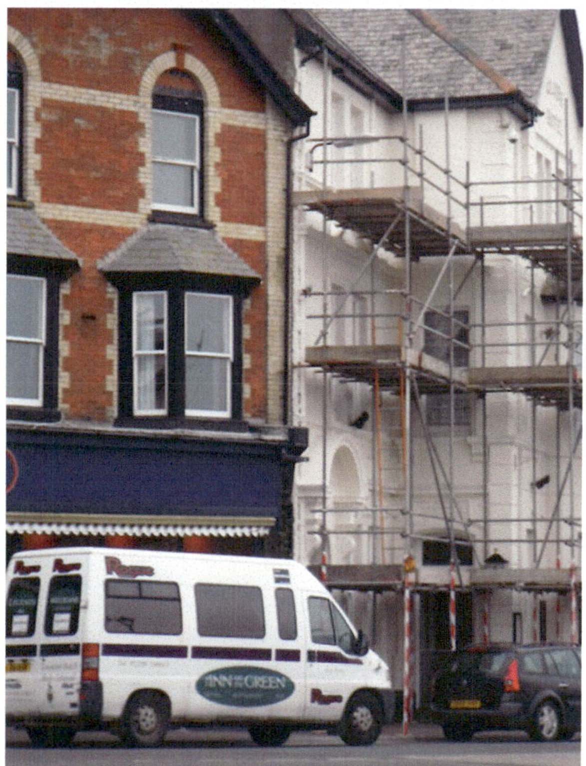

Coach Outside the Old Post Office, *c.* 1920.

This is a charabanc run by the Petvin family, outside what is now the bookmaker's opposite Lloyds Bank. Next door is the Bude post office of its day, immediate predecessor to the present one. The building on the left of the image to the right is the bookmaker. The white building is the Globe.

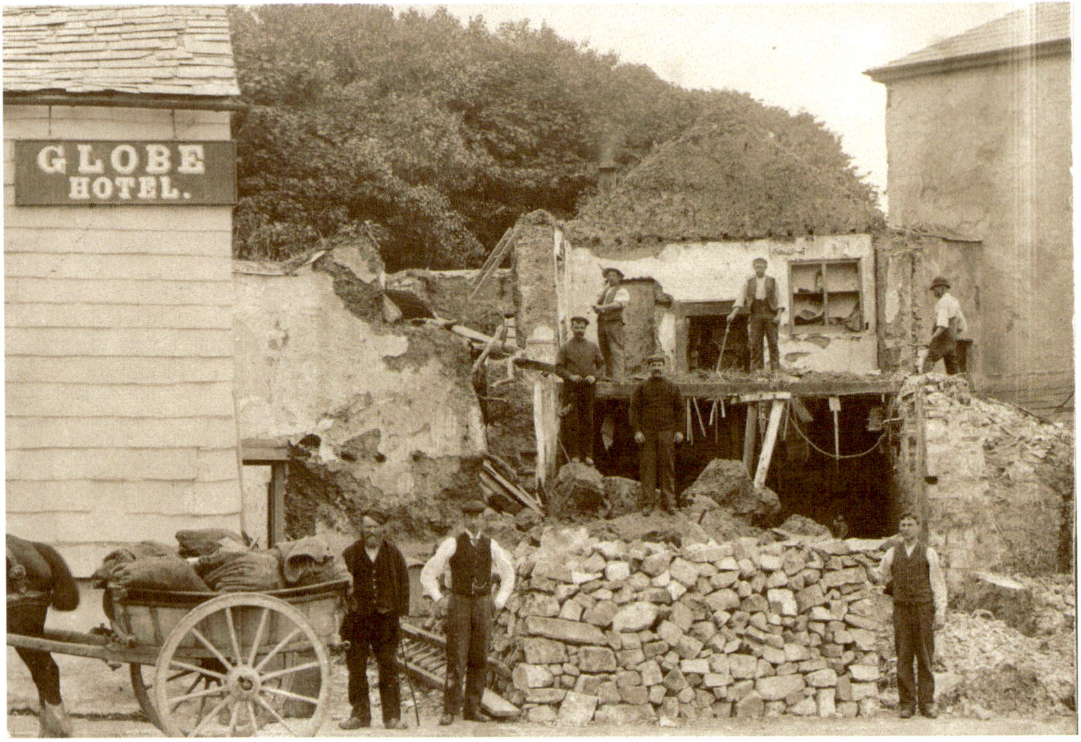

The Globe and Strand Hotels

Demolishing the old blacksmith's shop next to the original Globe Hotel, before the building of the present Globe, and the building that now houses the bookmaker's. In 2011, the Strand Hotel reopened. Here, people were out on the rooftop terrace watching the Bude Carnival procession pass by. Sadly, the Strand is now, once again, closed.

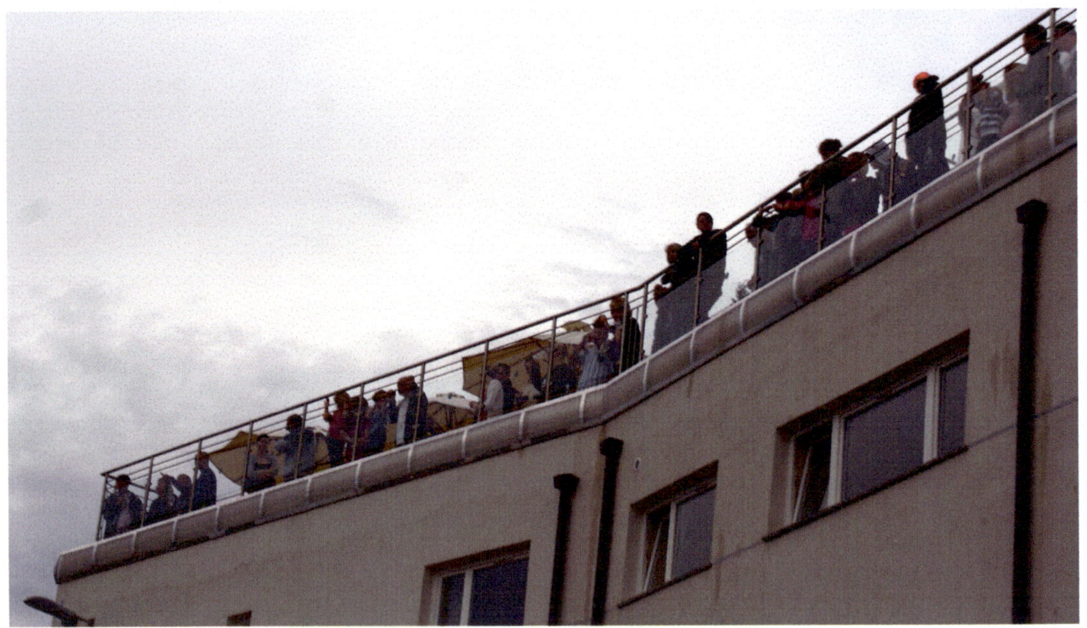

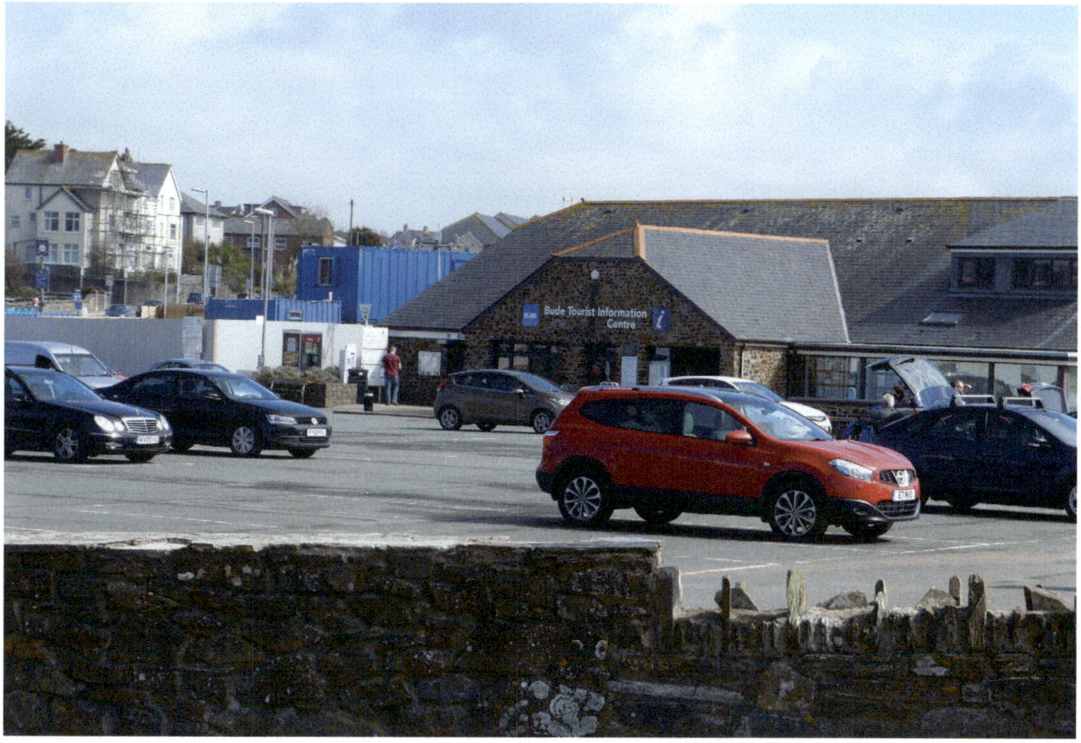

Bude Fair, 1911

Rides and sideshows in what is today's Crescent and Visitors' Centre car park, rather more characterful than the modern-day view. A great space, but usually full of cars during the summer and certainly no fairground any more, as these now tend to be held at Summerleaze car park or the Castle Green.

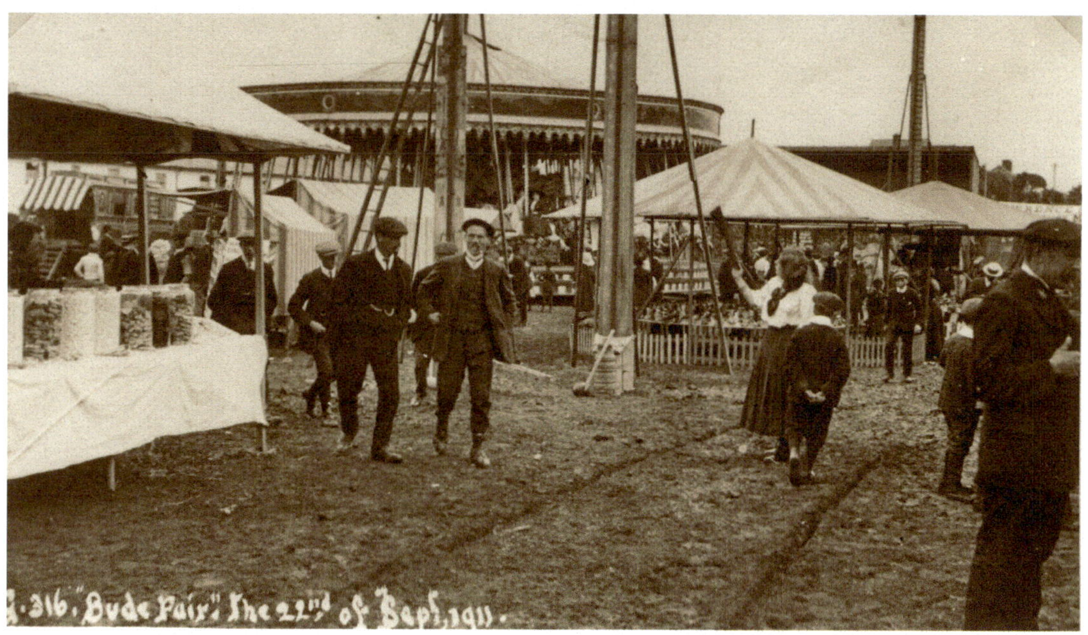

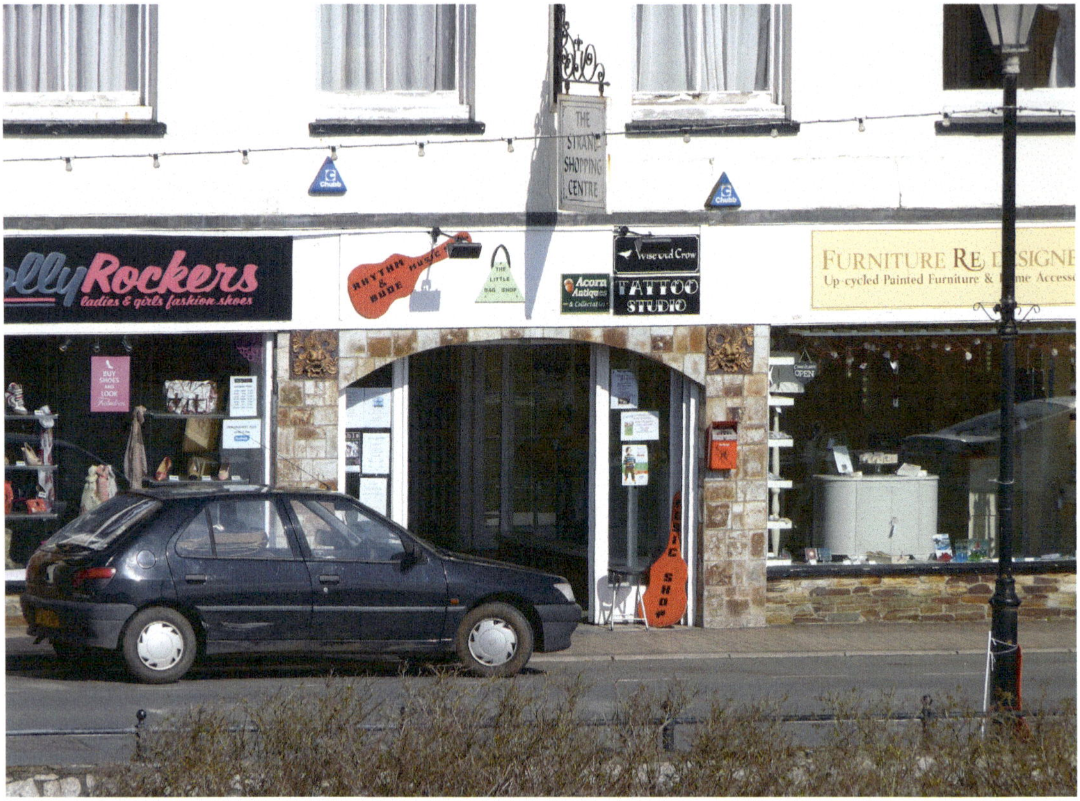

The Strand

The northern part of the Strand in 1910 looks much as it does today. Next to the Globe is Tapson's Terrace, built in the 1840s, followed by Julia's Arcade, showing a solid façade. Nearer the camera are the remains of the old warehouses. These were finally demolished in 1928. Locals still often call the Strand shopping centre Julia's Arcade, or Julia's Place.

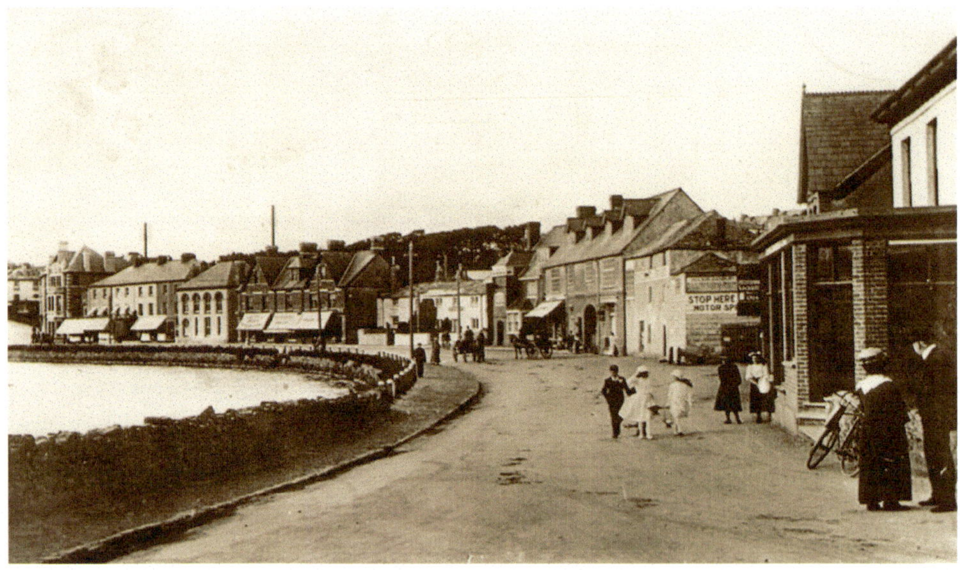

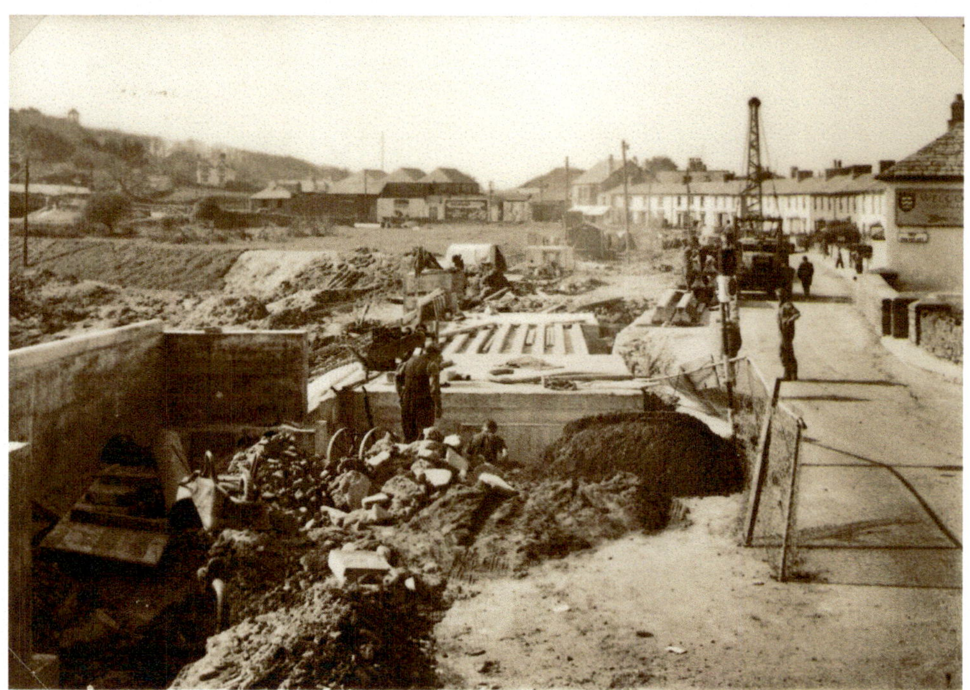

Bencoolen Bridge

Above, the old Bencoolen Bridge being demolished in 1961 and the present bridge – currently itself being removed – being built. Just over the bridge lies the rather desolate looking Crescent Visitors' Centre and car park, which is rather full in summer. Little changes, as the Bencoolen Bridge is once again undergoing works in 2013 (*below*). The Bencoolen Road Bridge carries the coastal traffic between Bude and Widemouth Bay over the River Neet. The bridge was built in 1957 and also forms a flood defence. Due to it being regularly flooded with seawater, and subject to coastal waves, the bridge supports were in poor condition, so the bridge is currently (2013) being replaced.

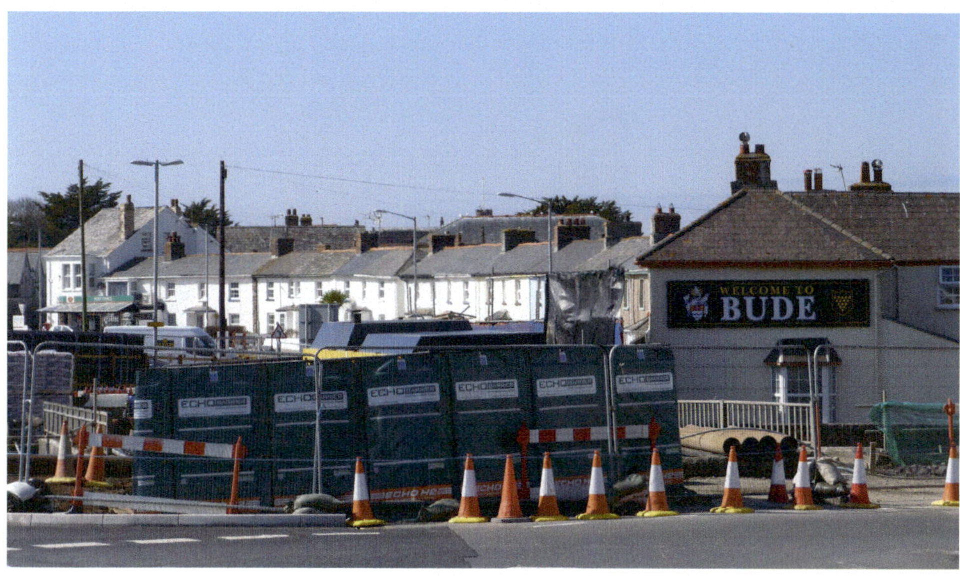

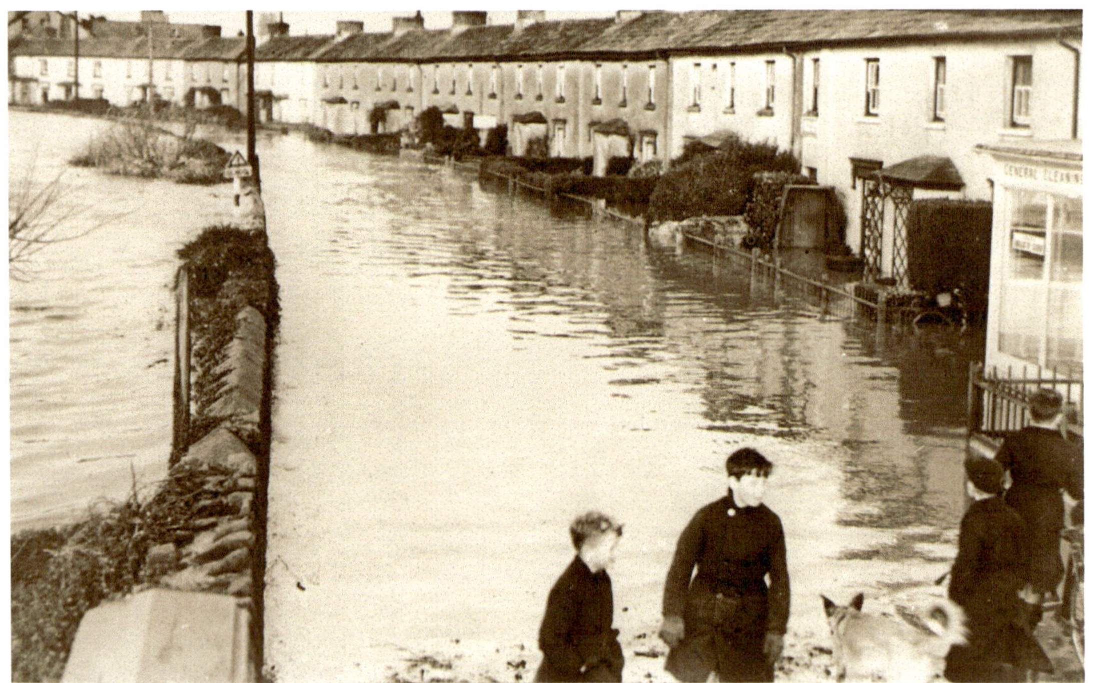

Floods

One of the regular flooding events along the Crescent in the 1950s. The low garden walls along the Crescent are constructed largely from slate stone. More recently, the image below shows people being rescued from the 1990 floods in the Crescent.

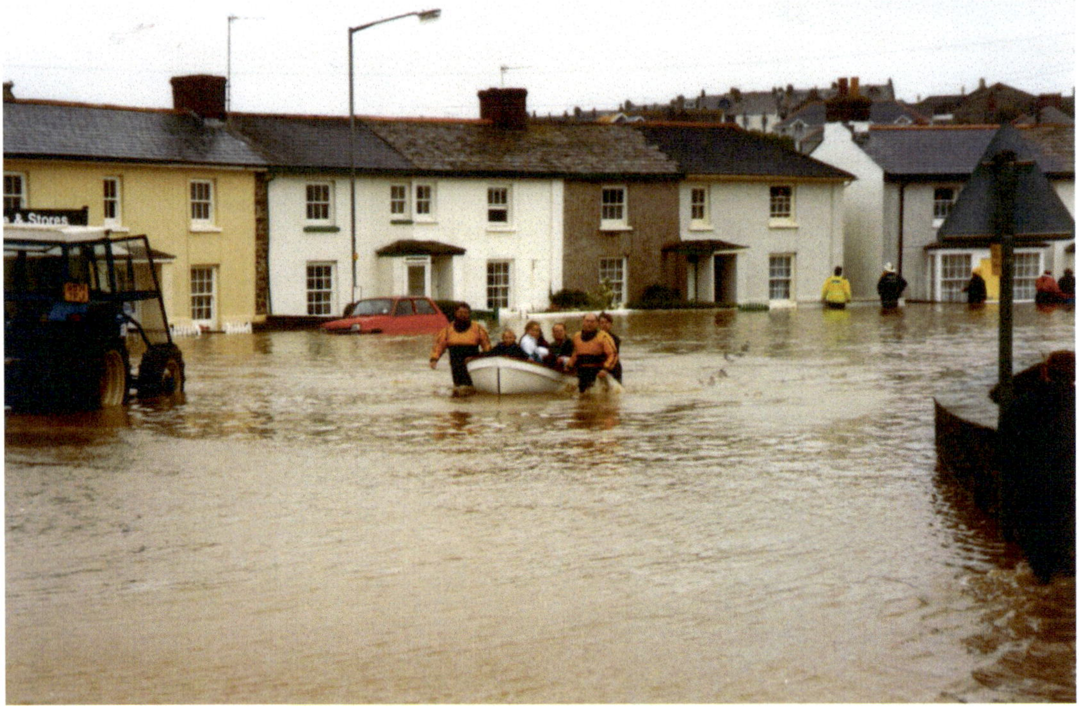

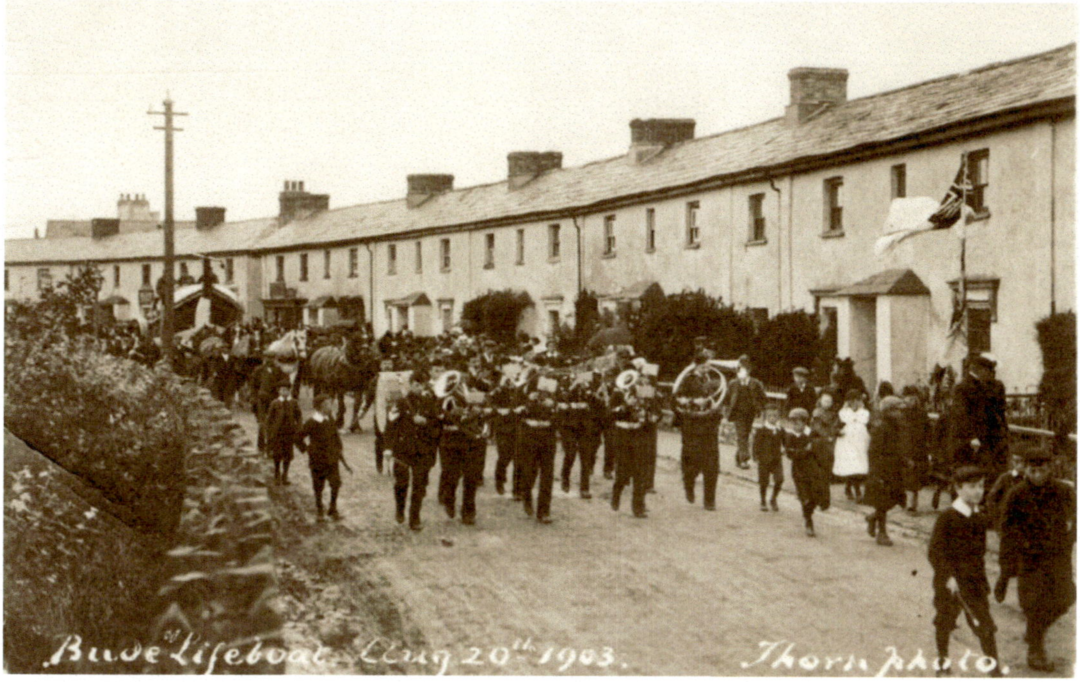

Lifeboat Day, 1903

One of the early annual celebrations of Lifeboat Day. Most processions now seem to start at Bude Light and journey past the Parkhouse Centre, along the Crescent, then the Strand and up into town. Bude also now has an annual Jazz Festival procession, too. People are as excited as ever by processions and carnivals, and turn out in their droves to watch the spectacle. This is the Triangle at the bottom of Belle Vue.

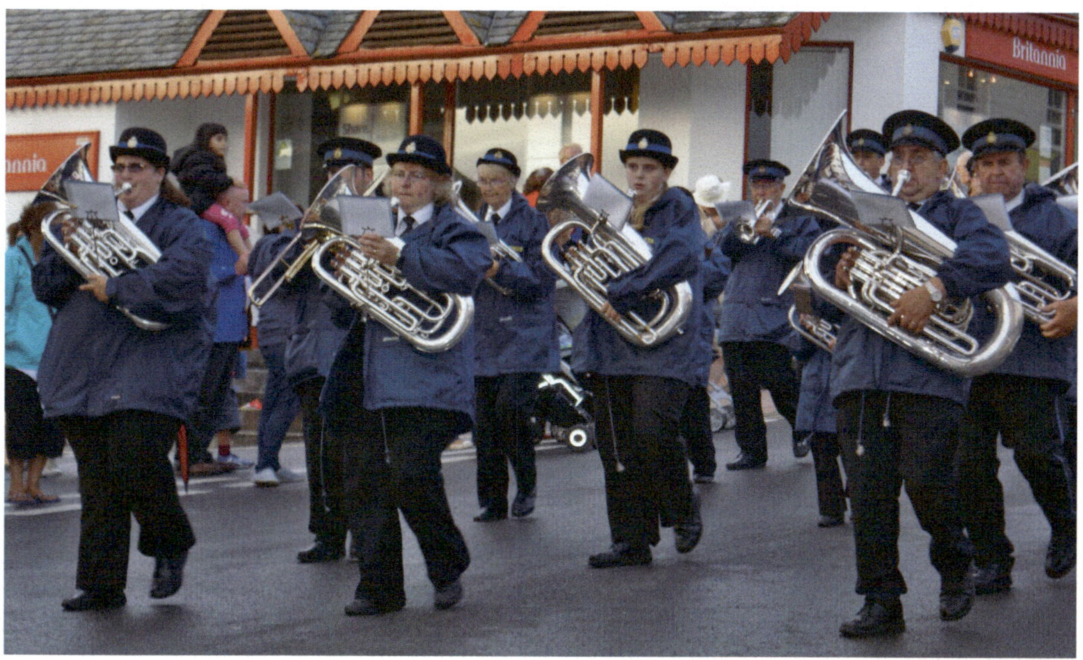

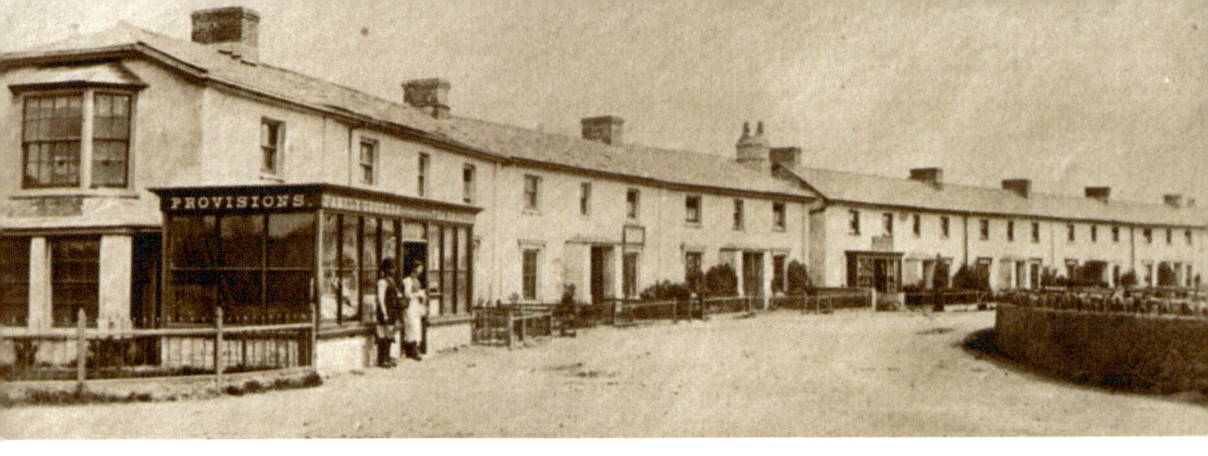

Crescent, 1900s

Including the now popular and busy local post office, previously a provisions store. In 1870–72, John Marius Wilson, in his *Gazetteer of England and Wales,* described Bude as below: 'BUDE, or Budehaven, a village and a chapelry in Stratton parish, Cornwall. The village stands on a small bay of Bristol Channel, at the mouth of the Bude canal, 1½ mile west of Stratton. It has a post office, of the name of Bude, North Devon, and a hotel; is frequented as a bathing place; and carries on a great trade in the deportation of shell sand as manure. A fair is held at it on 22 Sept. The tract around it includes drifted sand hills, a grand coast, brilliant view points, and the house of Mr Gurney, the inventor of the Bude light. The chapelry includes the village; and was constituted in 1836. Pop. 766. Houses, 163.' What is interesting is that it is noted for its post office, but also that the size of the population is still very small, and there seems to be a confusion that Bude is in North Devon (which still happens among visitors today). Built from the 1820s, these were originally cottages for the navvies building the canal. It has had several names: Southern Terrace, Shalder Terrace and even Frying Pan Row! Originally, several of the cottages also housed shops. This is now the busy post office situated at The Crescent, Bude.

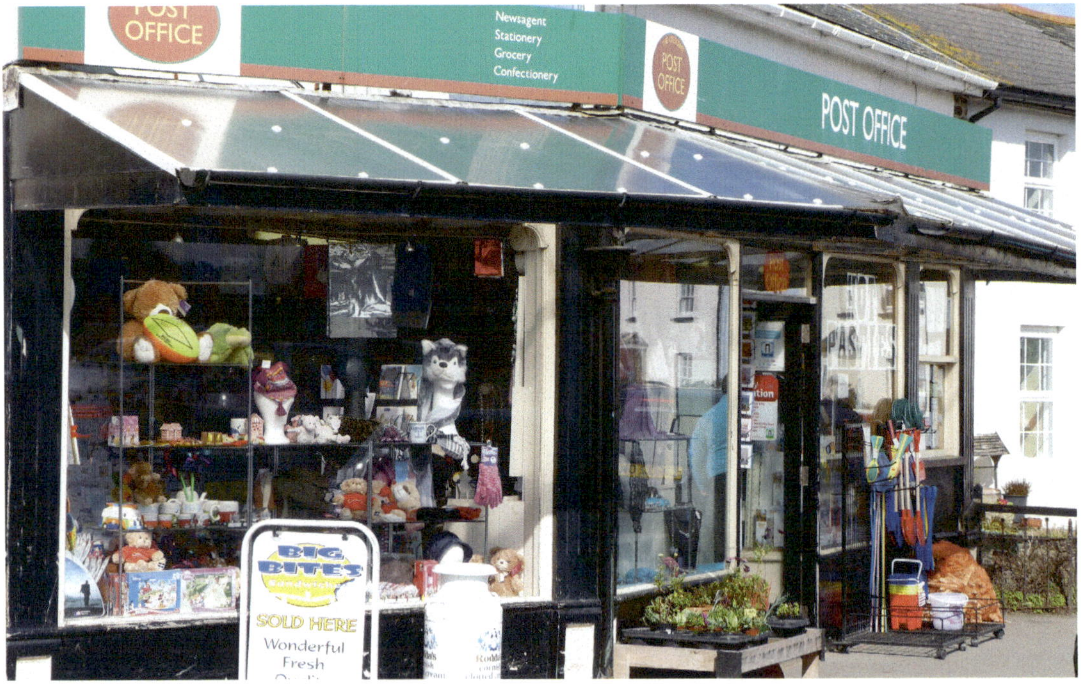

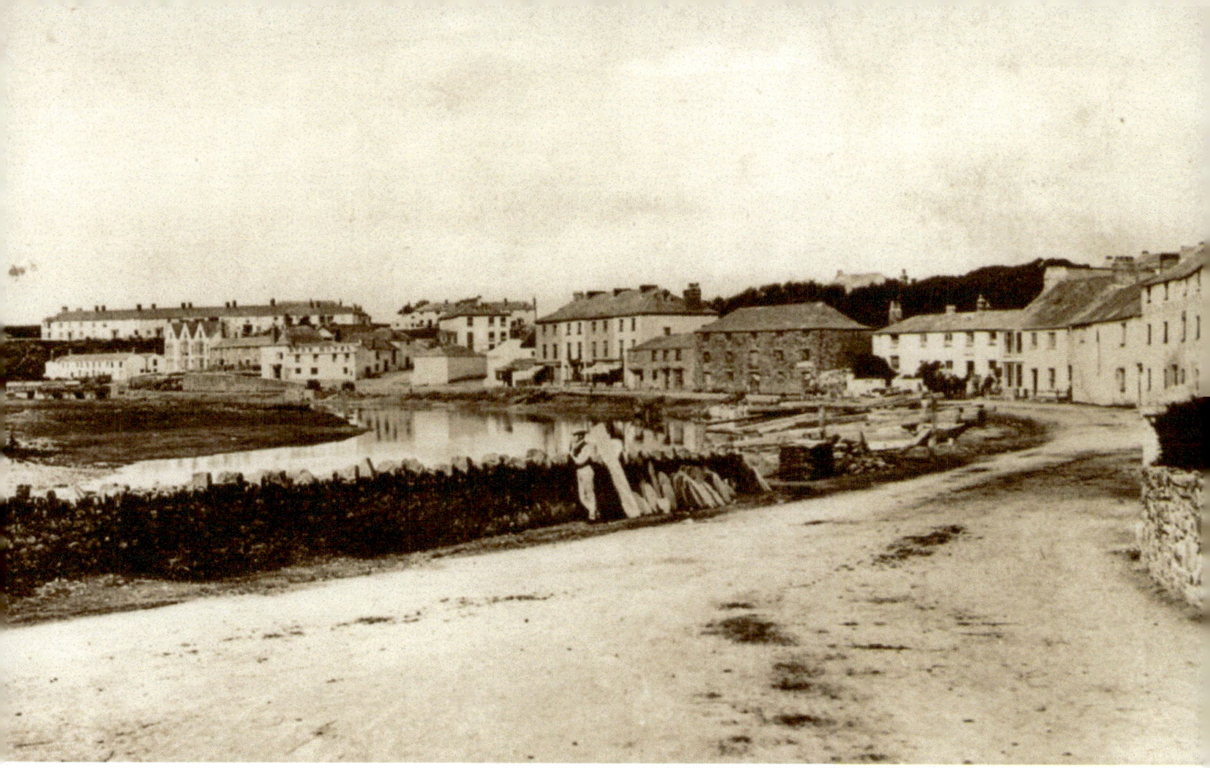

Flooding, Again

Above is the Strand in 1875, where the riverbanks are shored up by wood and the buildings were still mainly warehouses, though the Bude Hotel is clearly seen in the distance. Below, a half-submerged car can be seen just above the waterline on a flooded Strand.

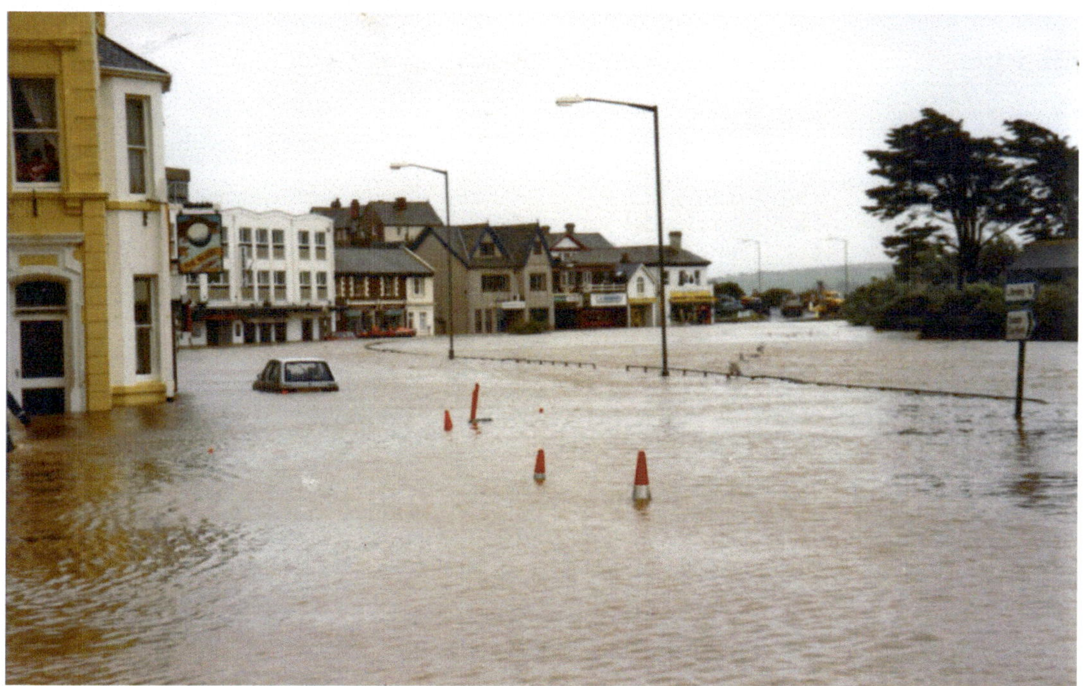

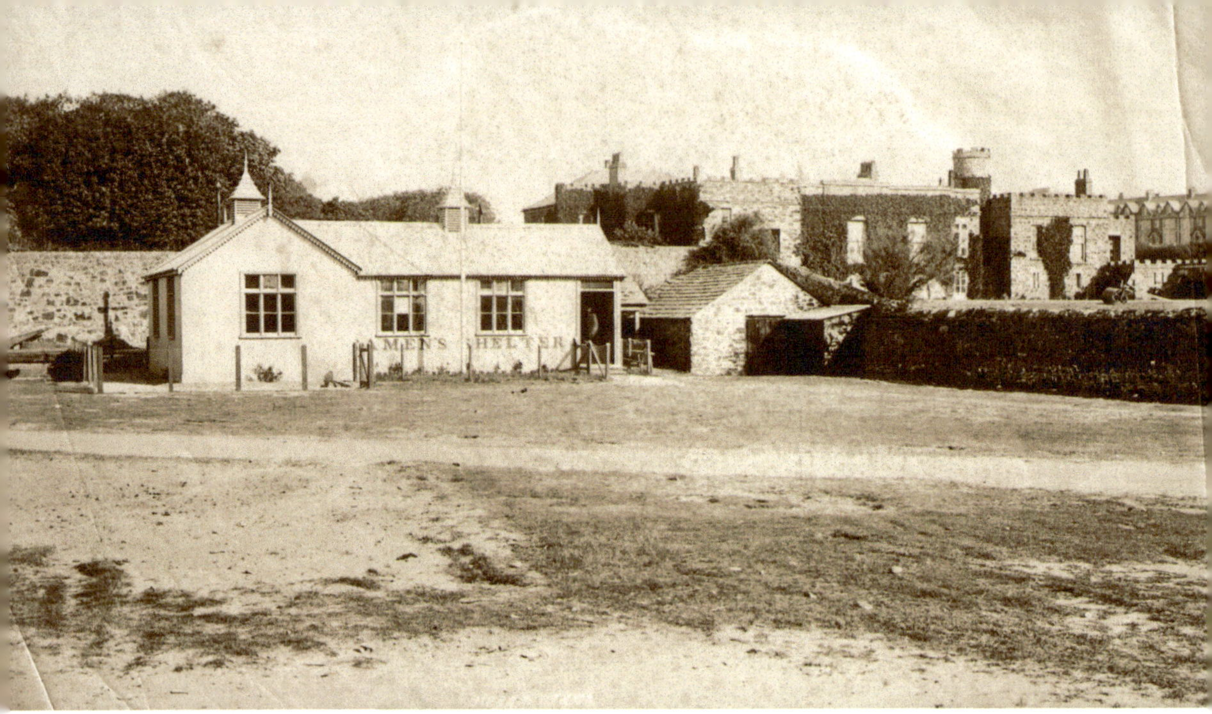

Scout Hut, 1893

The Scout Hut, now demolished, was originally built as a sailors' shelter. The building next to the hut was the morgue, near what is now the Canal Wharf car park (pay and display) with its Castle Tea Room. The tea rooms have large plank doors, in keeping with the previous industrial character of the building. Today, the car park is the site of the local library, One Stop Shop, and the Castle Tea Room.

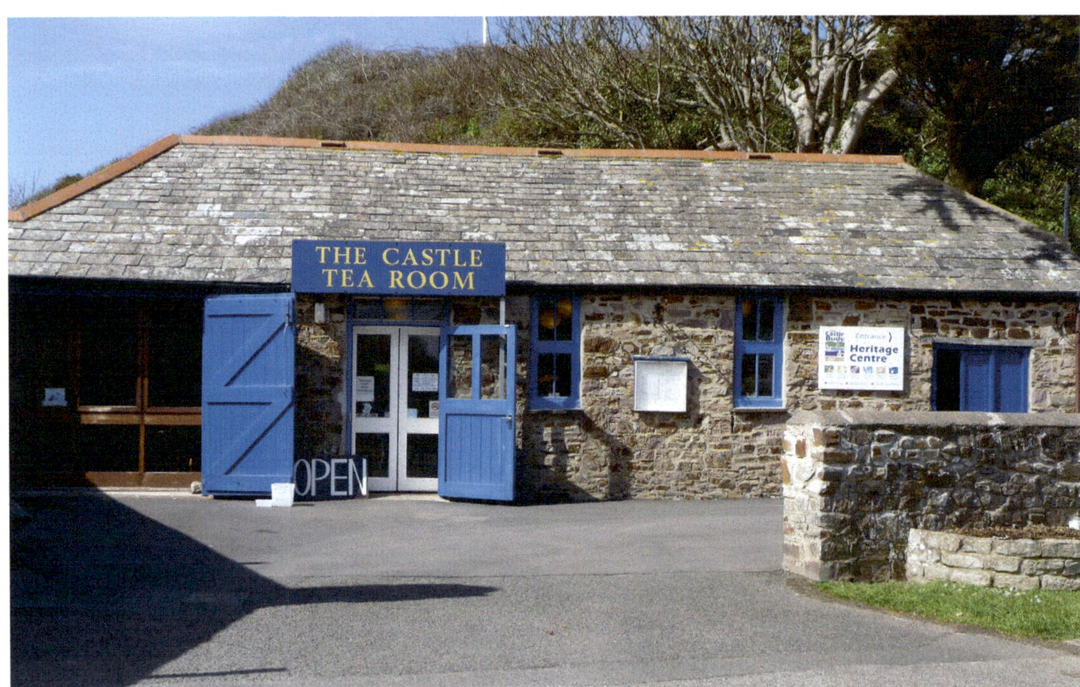

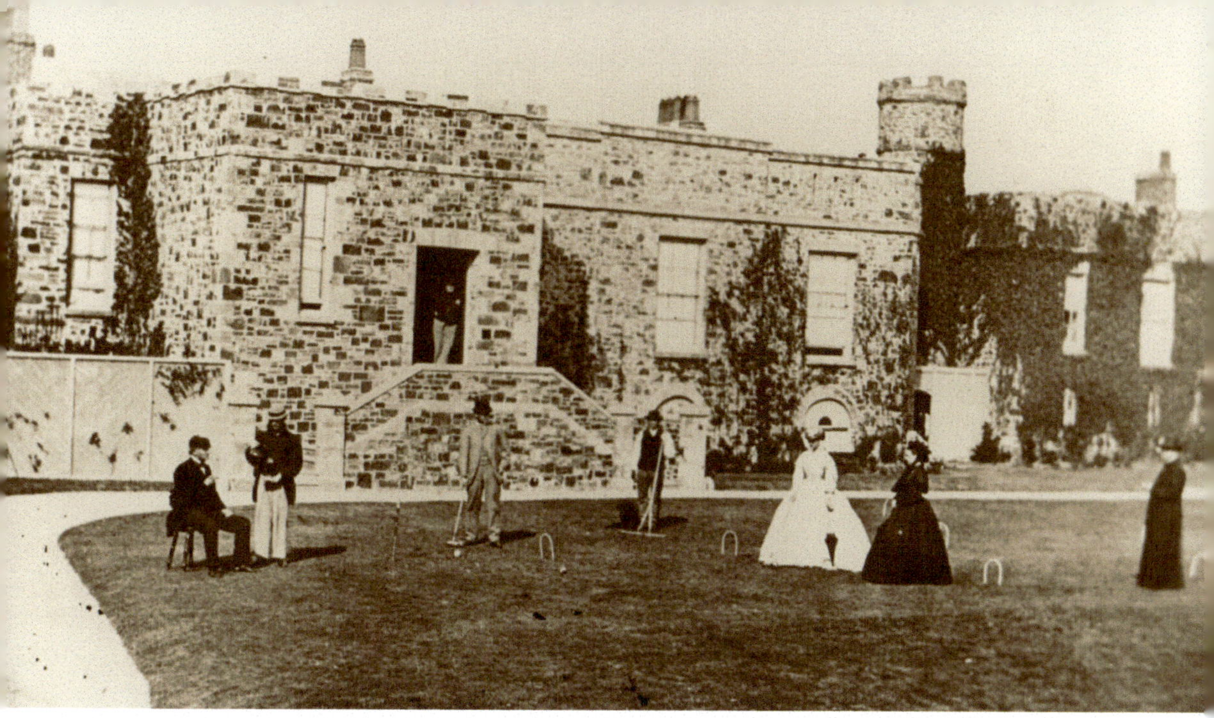

Castle Green Lawns

Genteel croquet on the Castle Green lawns, around 1890. Not much change to the present, except the rather attractive ivy is gone, and the grass is no longer generally used for croquet, though the idea has again been mooted in the Bude Partnership Plan. The lower windows to the right of the steps were, for many years, the town library run by a Mrs Full. The library is now situated at the Wharf car park. As private buildings go, this one was actually rather public, because of Gurney's desire to demonstrate his engineering skills on a difficult site. Gurney was quite the inventor, one of his ideas being a 'steam coach' before the arrival of the railways. The council used to be situated in the castle, but it is now used as a Heritage Centre. It looks a little bare without the ivy.

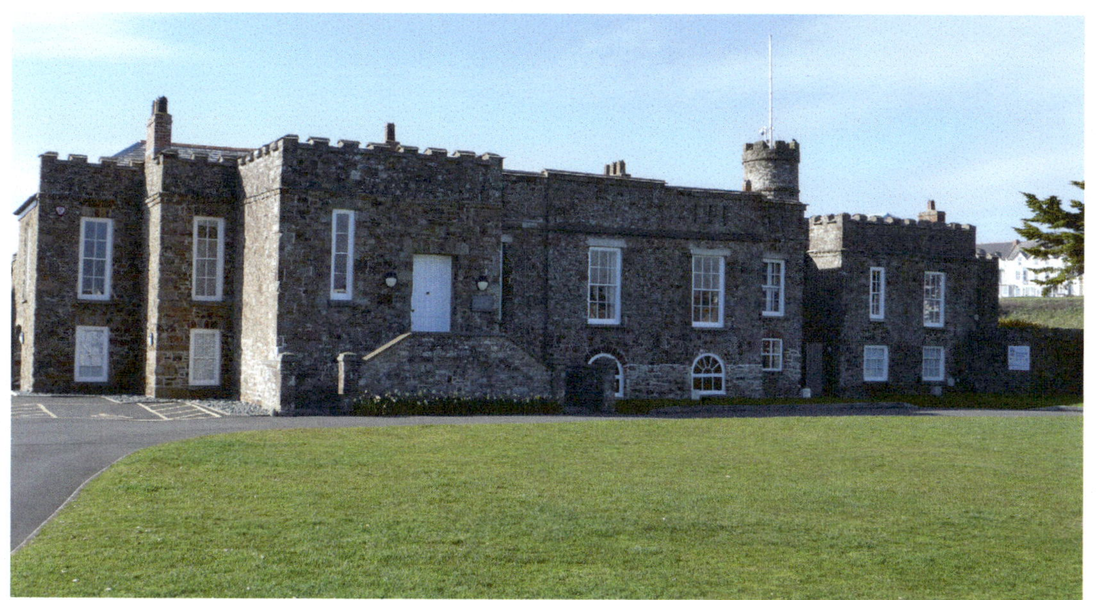

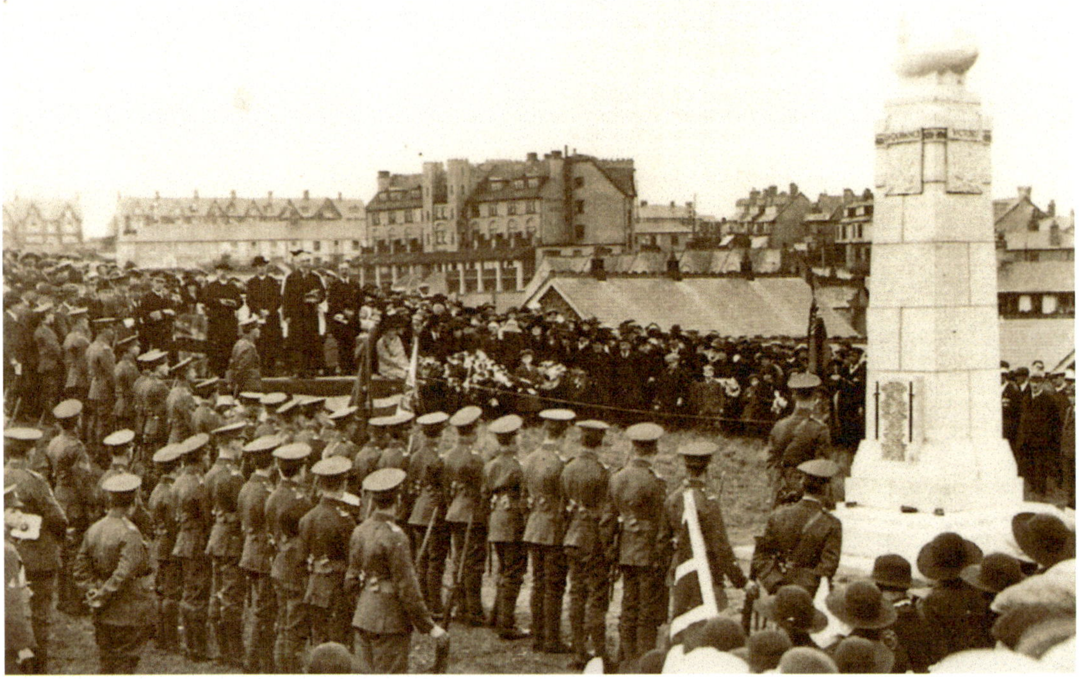

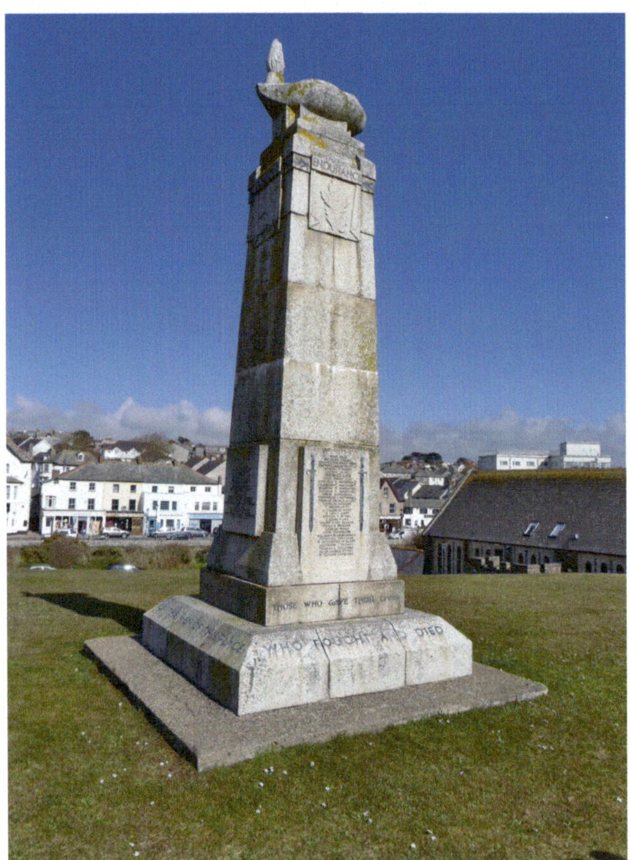

War Memorial

The unveiling of the granite Bude war memorial on 11 November 1922, at Shalder Hill, by the Lord Lieutenant of Cornwall. It was designed in the form of a Greco-Roman rostral column, generally used to commemorate sea victories. Beautifully clean when built, the memorial was inscribed with sixty-four names from the First World War and thirty-eight from the Second World War. Left, looking much more austere now, the war memorial in Bude. Shalder Hill is a man-made structure that housed the original town reservoir and now offers panoramic views across town and to the sea, giving you a whole new perspective on Bude. It also overlooks the Nonconformist chapels across the River Neet from The Strand.

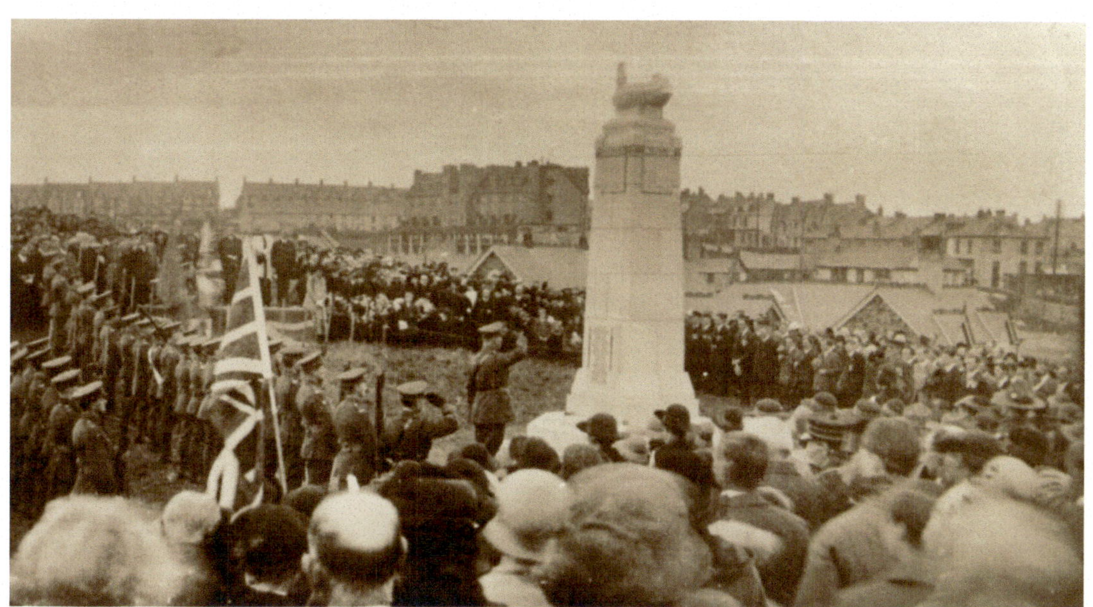

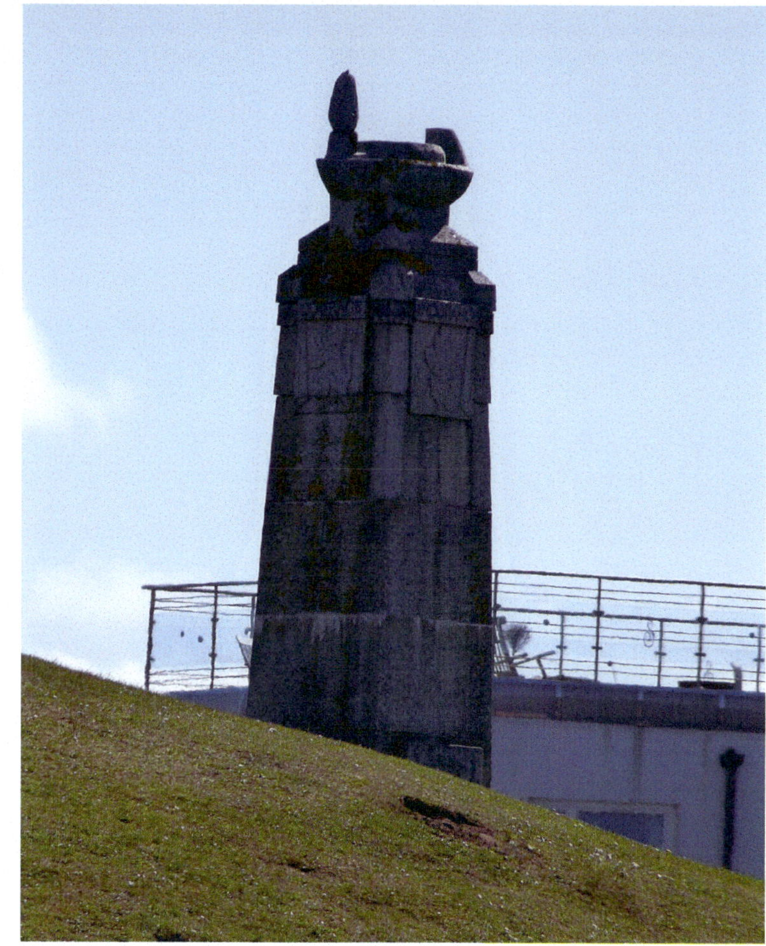

Remembrance Day
Above, Remembrance Day, 1922, at Shalder Hill, with a dedication to the war memorial. To the right, in 2013, the memorial is still thought provoking, with its list of war dead. A Lancashire sculptor, Walter Marsden, worked on the memorial. The stone is a tapered square stone pillar on a single step. It contains representations of the TOC H lamp (used for soldiers operating on the Ypres salient) and a stone flame and sword of sacrifice on each side of the inscriptions, better seen in the modern picture.

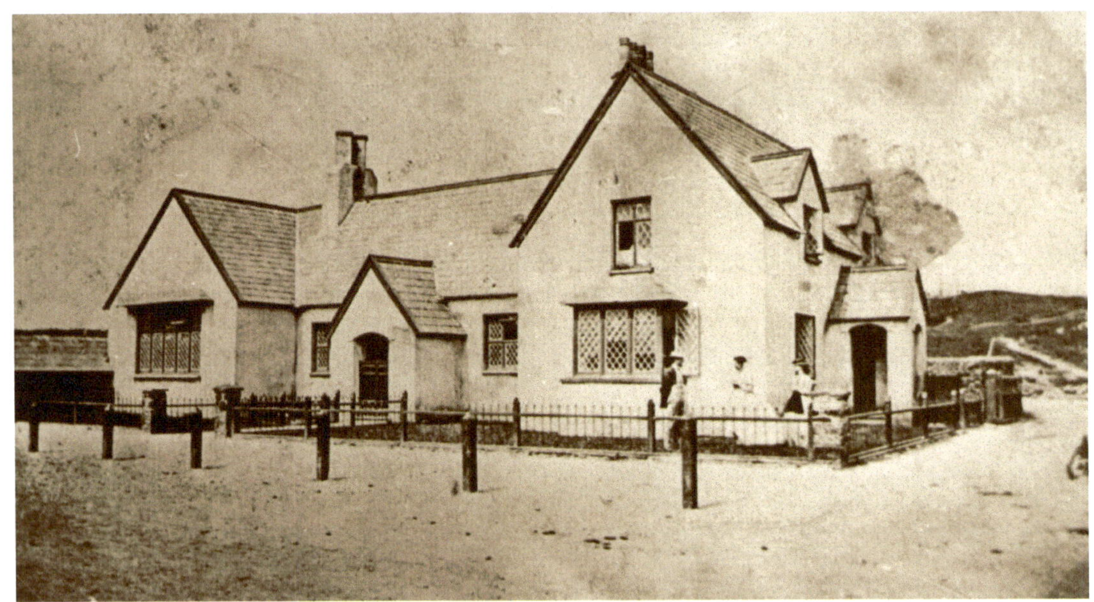

Primary School, 1890s

Now part of the Parkhouse Centre, this was originally Bude's charity school and later the primary school; it was built in 1851 by Sir Thomas Acland for the poor of the town. The section to the right is the schoolmaster's house. As new housing was built towards Stratton, the school moved to Stratton in 1985 and the old school buildings were revamped into a community hall known as the Parkhouse Centre. The building now houses the Bude-Stratton Town Council, previously situated in Bude Castle. The modern photograph shows to the right the early to mid-nineteenth-century east wing of the former school.

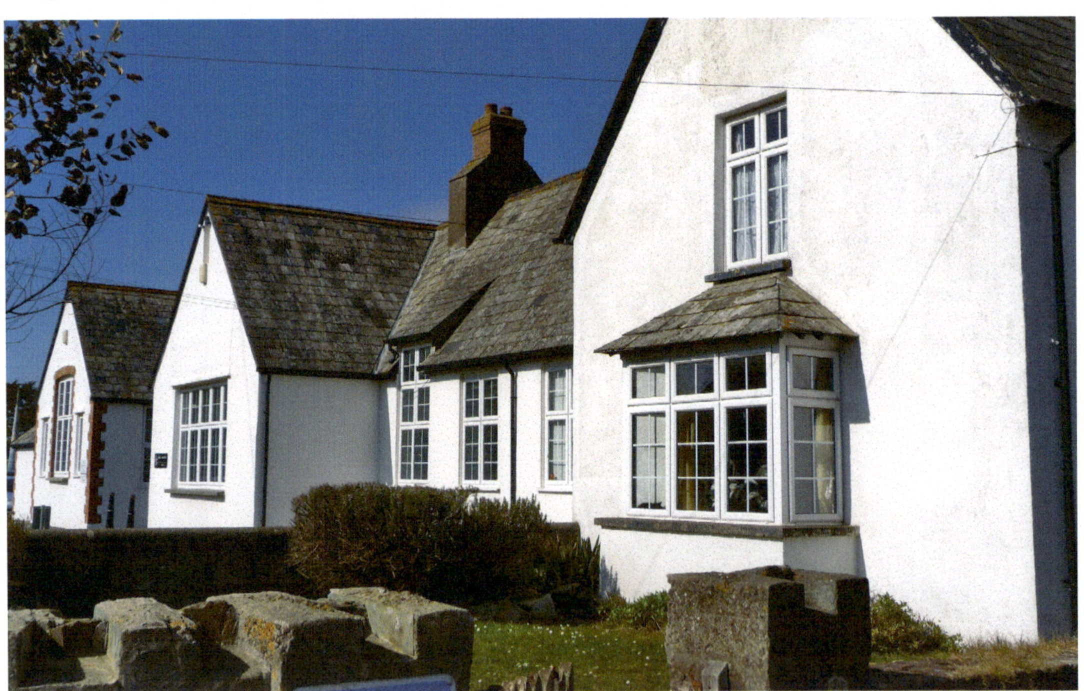

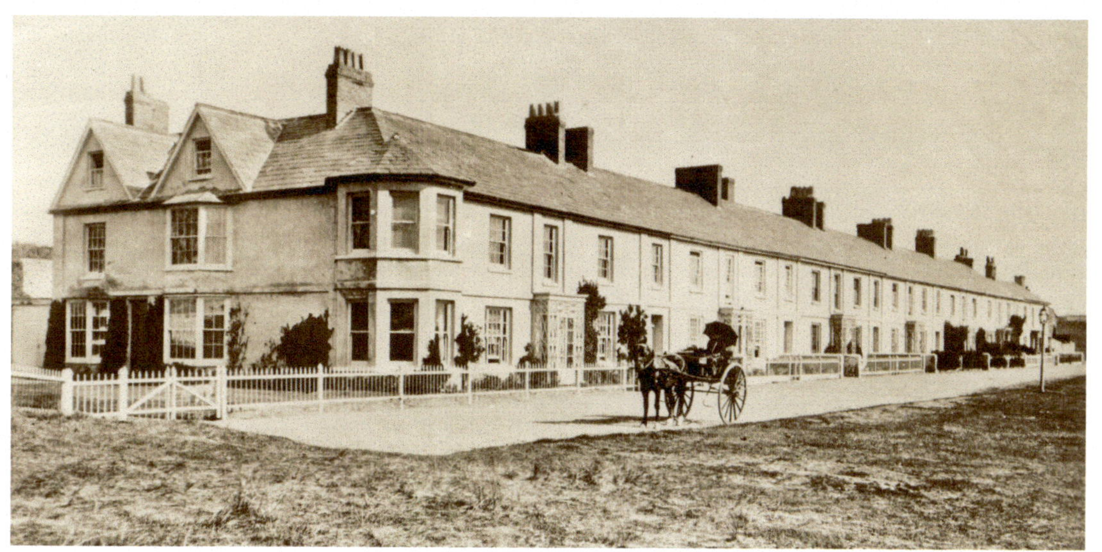

Hartland Terrace, 1890

An original Francis Frith photograph. Built in the 1850s–60s, Hartland House was converted to Hartland Hotel in 1934/35. Originally, Hartland House with its mansard roof stood alone on the cliff, but as the town expanded Hartland Terrace was built to provide homes for wealthy ship owners. The house was later purchased by a Fry's chocolate magnate as a holiday home. The family stayed in Bude for thirty years of holidays, travelling by their yacht the *Fireflash* – which they moored on Bude Canal – from Bristol to Bude. During the Second World War, it was requisitioned by the government to provide accommodation for officers from the nearby Cleeve Camp and boarding school accommodation for evacuees from Clifton College, Bristol. Now it is a private road, with the hotel based at the seaward end 200 yards from the beach.

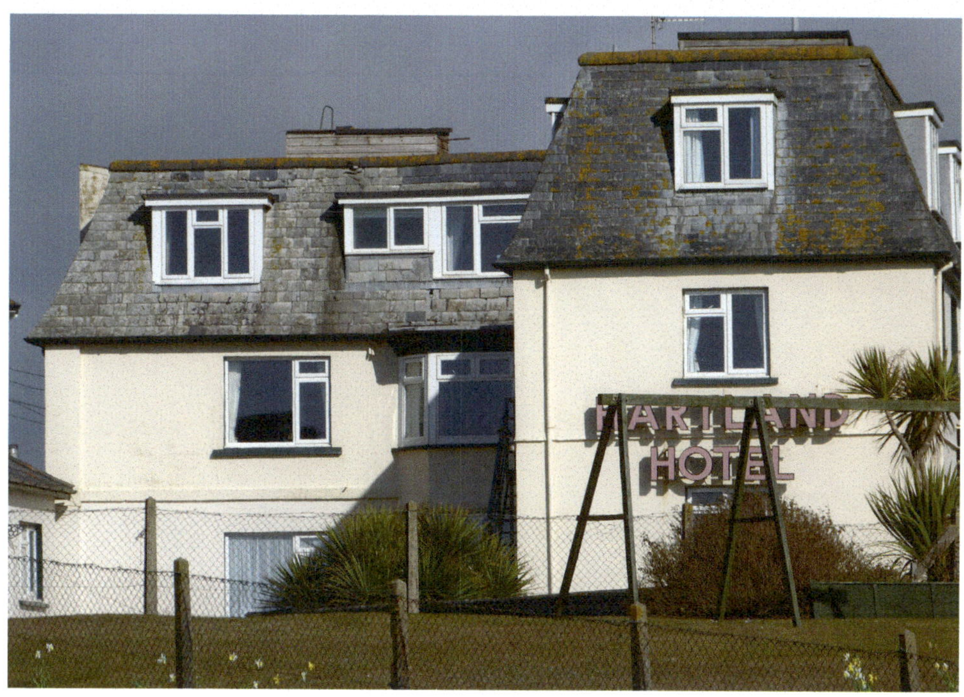

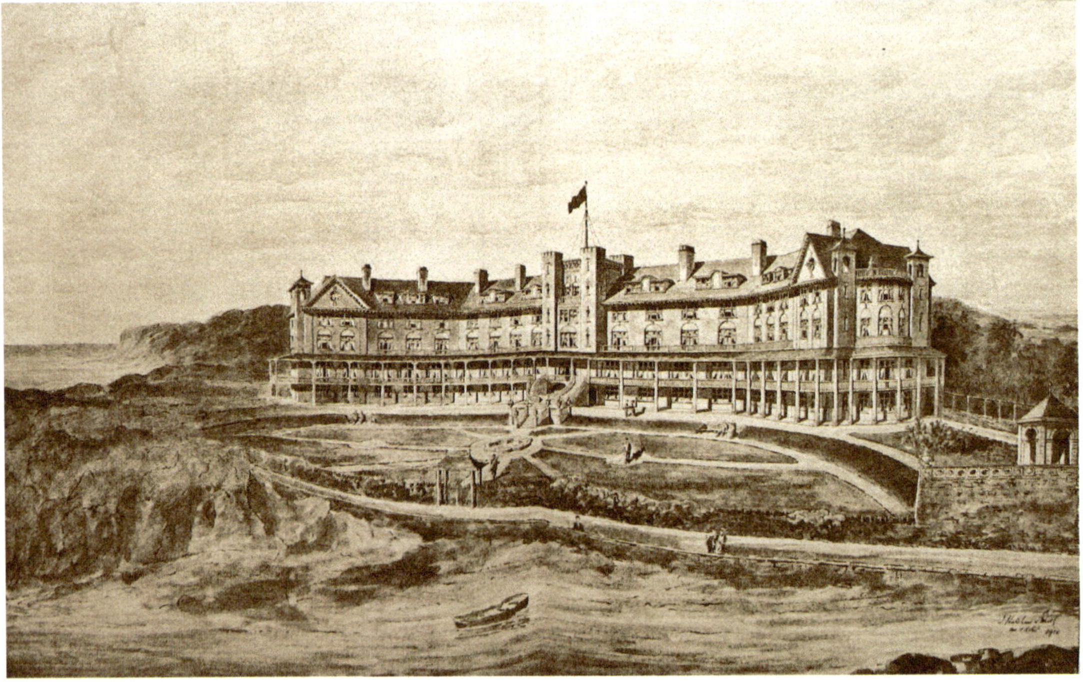

The Grenville

Above, the Grenville depicted in an advertisement from the *Architect* magazine in 1912. It shows the Grenville as it would have looked in its heyday, newly built, with few buildings nearby – rather chateau-like. At five storeys high, it really did dominate the landscape and still plays a major role as it may be seen from all over Bude.

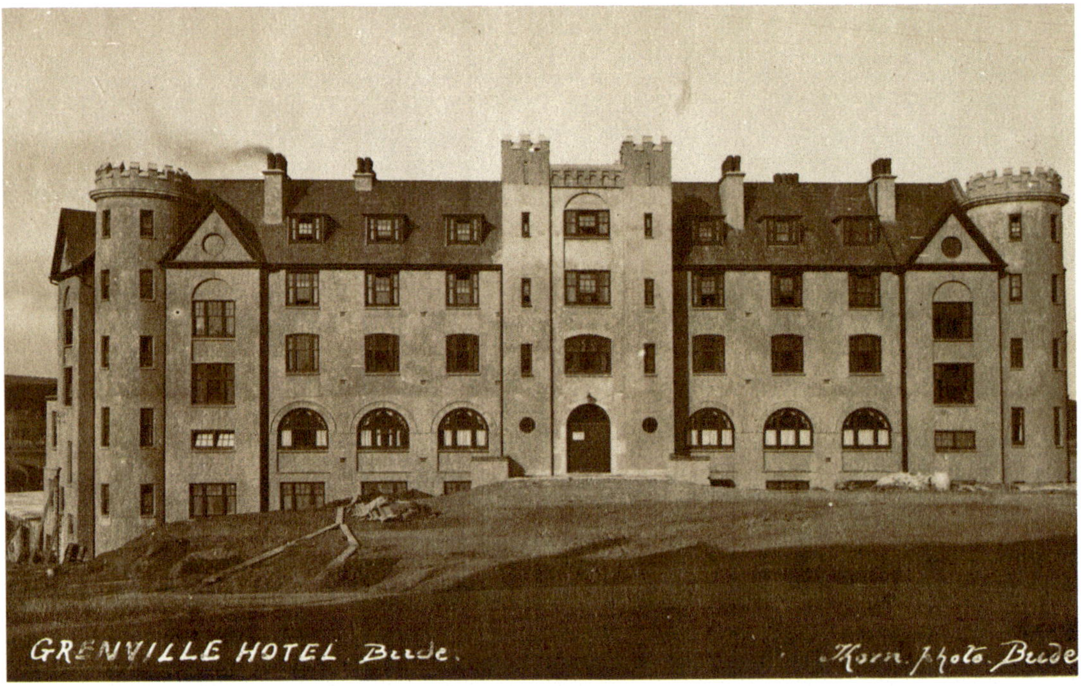

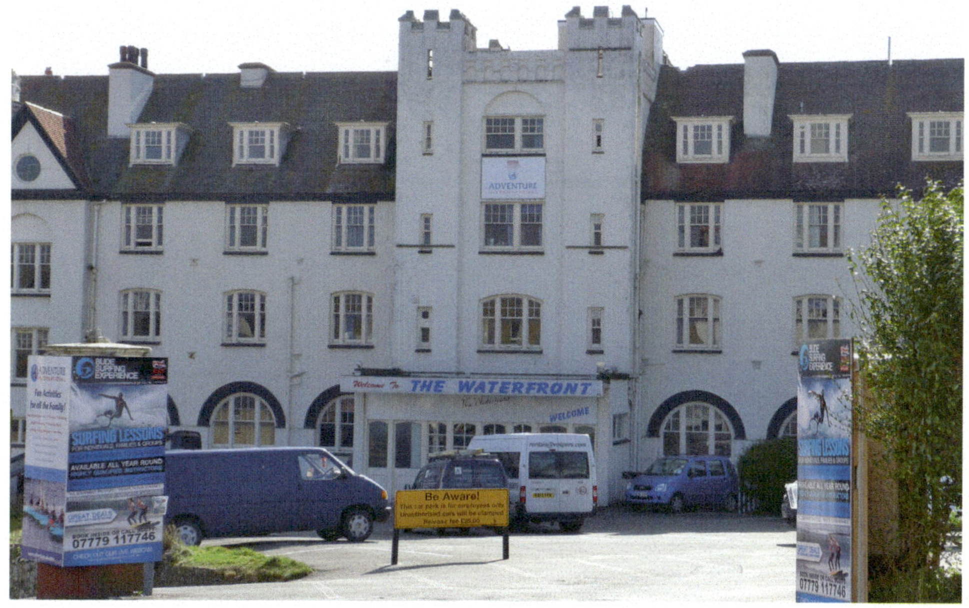

The Grenville Hotel

The front of the current Waterfront/Adventure International from Belle Vue. The Grenville Hotel, April 1910. The Grenville is built into the hillside below Hartland terrace. The castellated five-storey structure made it an iconic symbol of Bude, dominating the local landscape. Yet somehow it always looks a little too eclectic; with its *oeil de boeuf* ('bulls-eye'), Diocletian (large semi-circular) windows and mansard (sloped French-style) roof, the intention was rather 'French chateau' in style, though I am not sure how well it works. The Grenville originally opened all year along with the Falcon. Adventure International now brings in young visitors on activity holidays for much of the year. The Grenville has been home to Adventure International since 1979. Built in 1909, it occupied a stunning central position in Bude. Now it is one of the largest activity centres in the country.

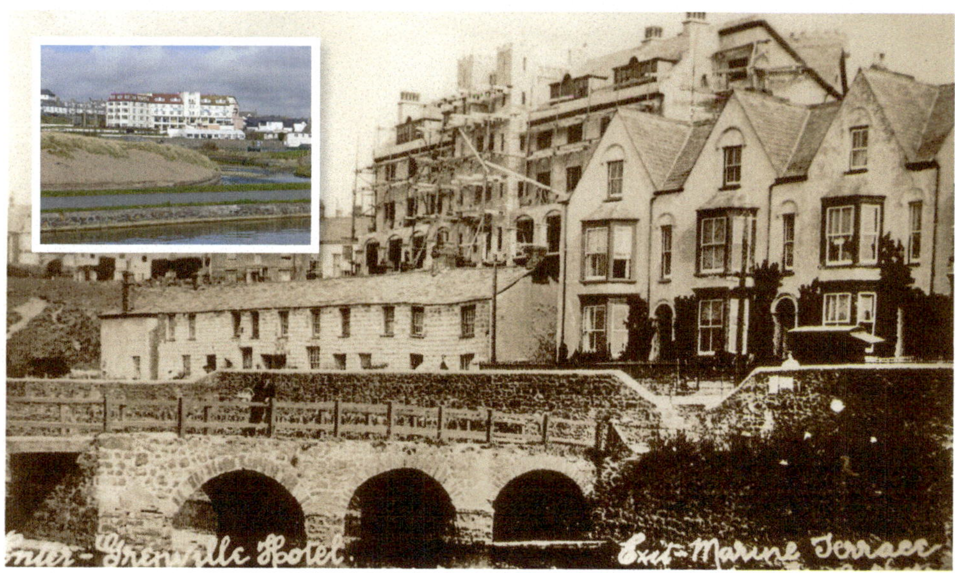

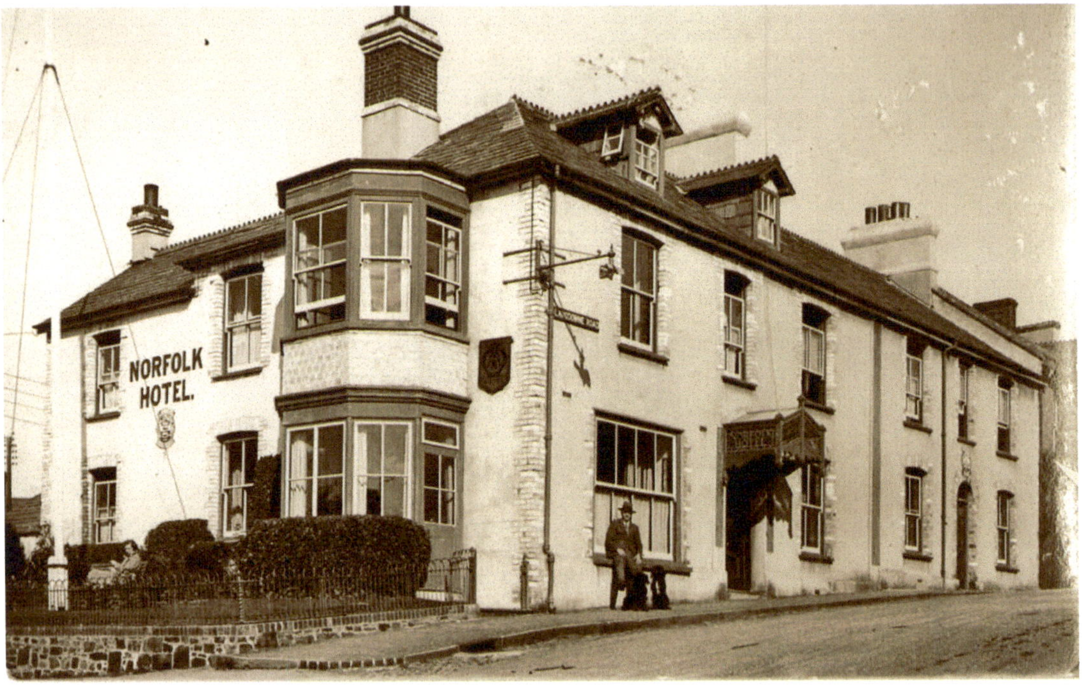

Lansdown Road

Another major hotel was the Norfolk. A temperance hotel, it was situated at the bottom of Lansdown Road. Now, it is the financial services office, craft shop and fish shop. That part of Lansdown Road used to be called Garden Terrace. Below, Lansdown Road, after the Great Blizzard of 1891. Some suggest that the blizzard was over-exaggerated, but certainly images seem to suggest not. There is, for example, a stunning image of a train stuck in a huge snow drift near Princetown at Dartmoor.

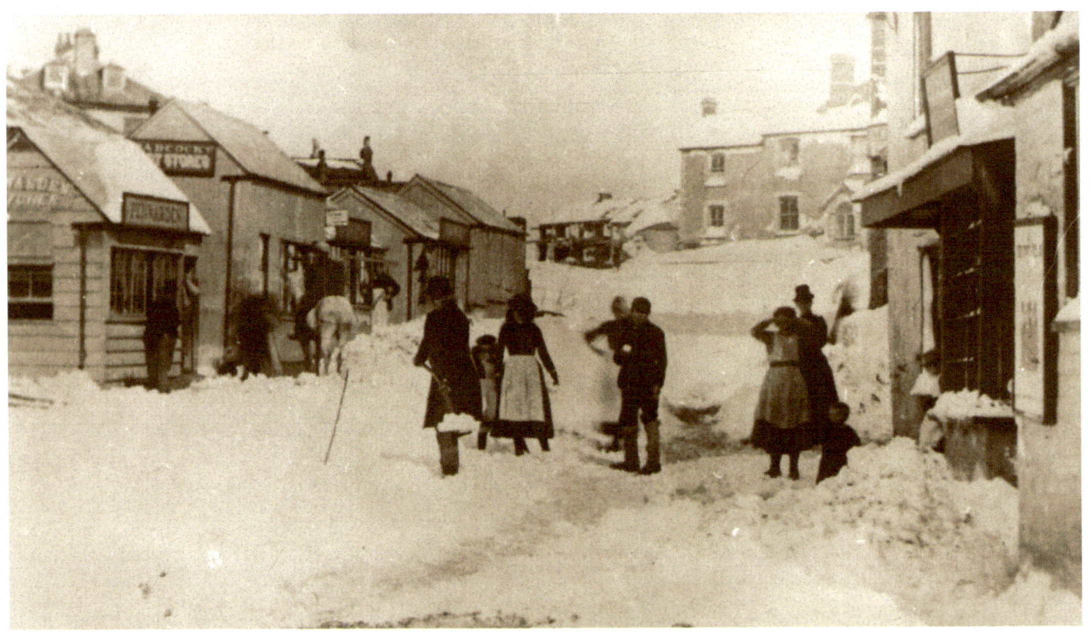

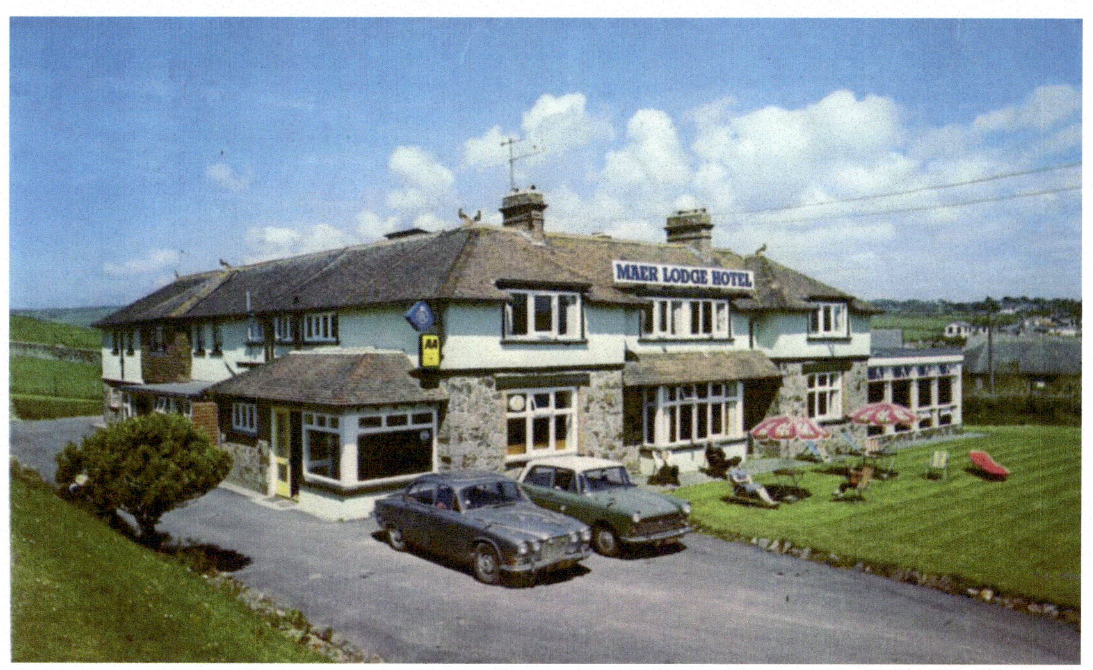

Maer Lodge Hotel, 1960s

Built in the 1930s, the hotel was recently replaced by flats. The flats are very pleasant inside but do not quite have the same allure as the hotel.

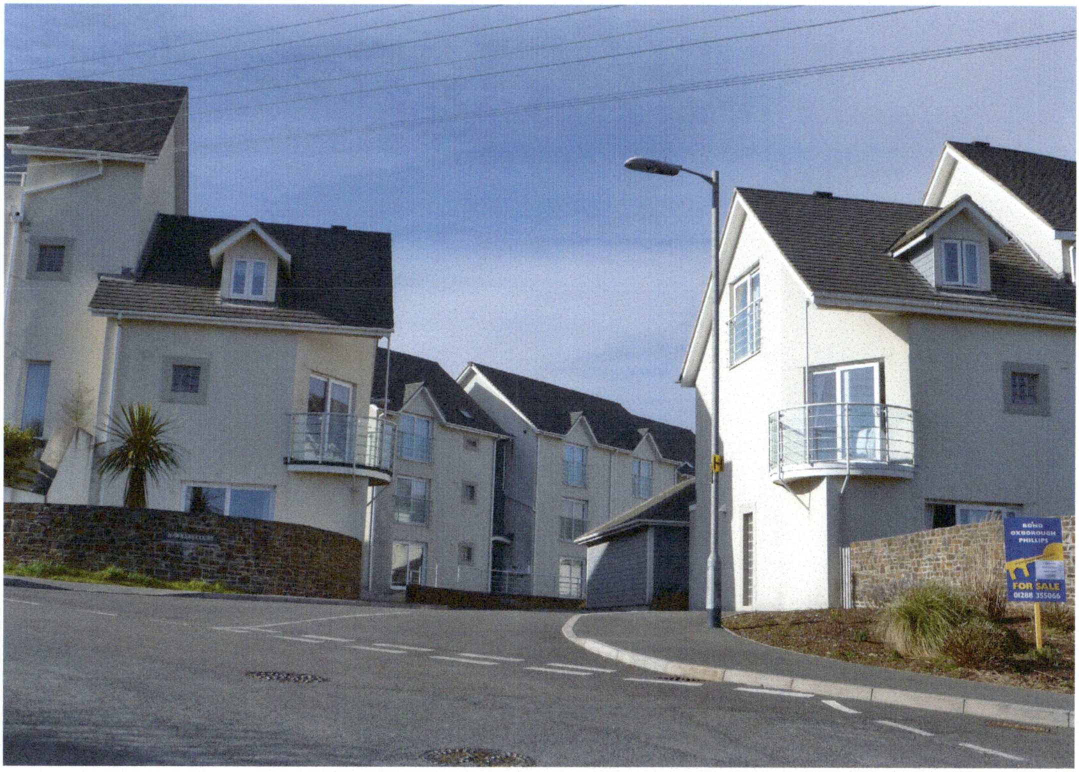

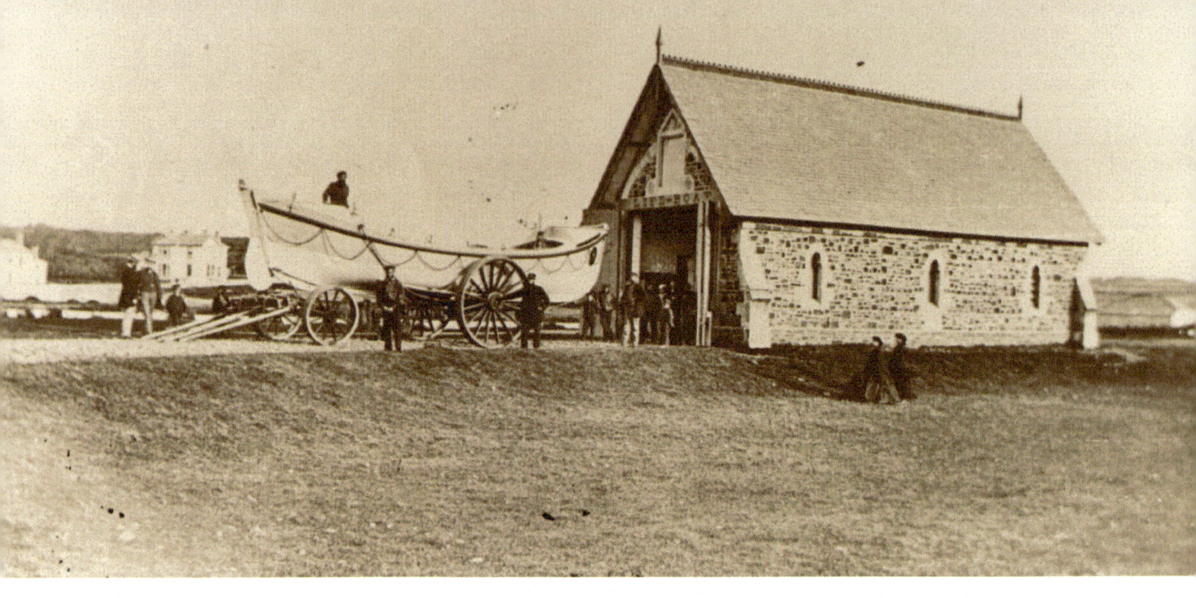

Lifeboat at the Boathouse, 1890s

Elizabeth Moore Garden can be seen outside the old lifeboat house. Built on Acland land, the lifeboat house is now a converted holiday cottage in the car park of the Brendon Arms, opposite the Falcon Hotel, with the Bude Canal pleasantly situated to one side. The RNLI lifeboat house, housing the inshore lifeboat suitable for rescues around the rocky coves, is now situated on the car park at Summerleaze Beach, from where the lifeboat is launched, thereby bypassing the canal. Bude had three lifeboats called *Elizabeth Moore Garden*: one from 1863, one from 1886 and the last from 1911, all with ten oars, and growing increasingly longer, ranging from 33 to 35 feet. To the side (now private land) Gothic elements are incorporated into the old lifeboat house, such as pointed arches and trefoil-headed windows. The Garden family, not directly connected with Bude, gave it its original lifeboat house and its three successive lifeboats. Elizabeth Moore Garden was the wife of Robert Theolophilus Garden, and their surviving children donated the lifeboat house in her memory.

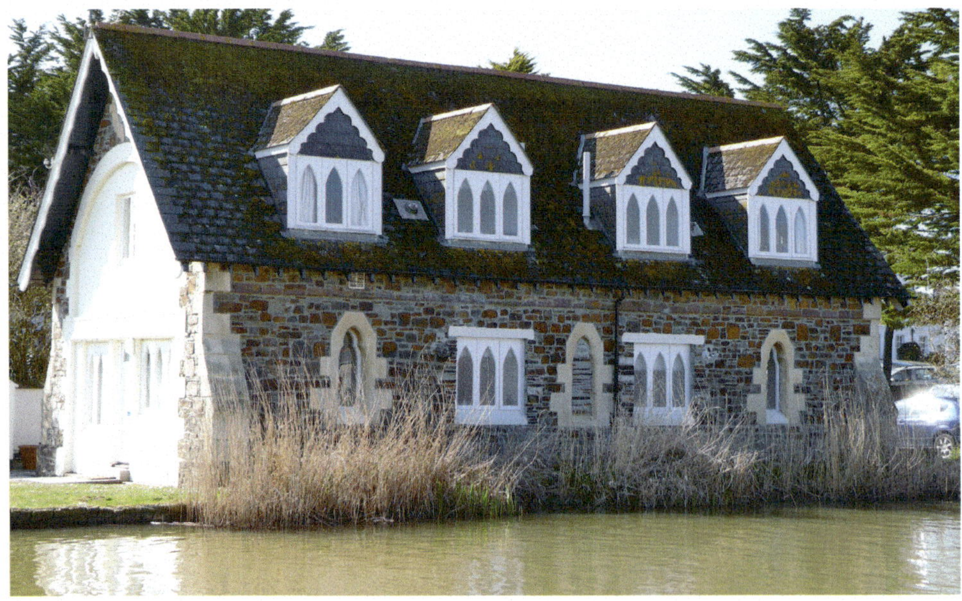

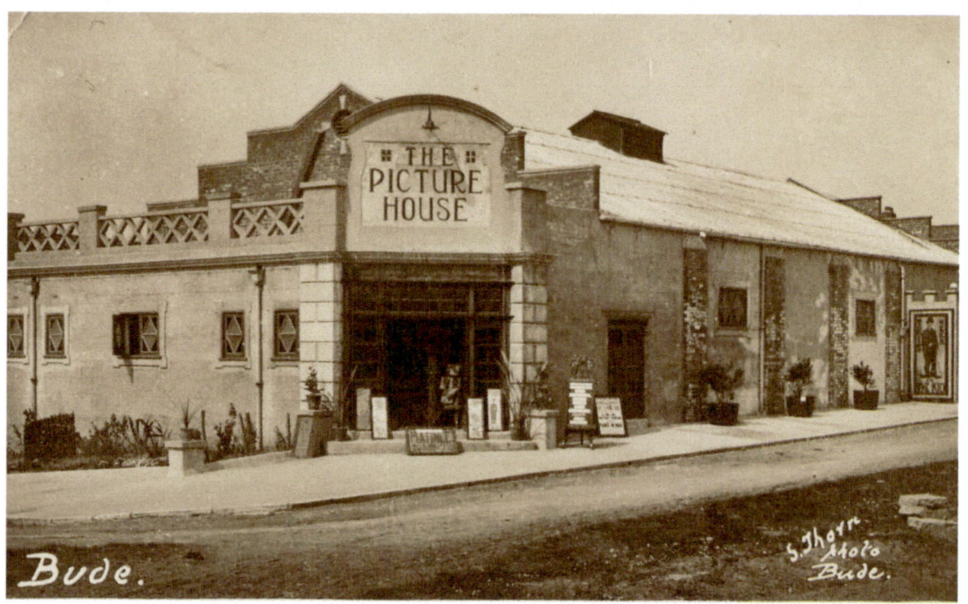

Picture House, Burn View, 1921

Robert Edgar Booth opened the cinema in 1922, seating around 500. The advertised film is *The Kid,* starring Charlie Chaplin (produced 1921). Early programmes carried the slogan 'to amuse and entertain is good, to do both and instruct is better'. Now there are merely the remains of a garage and old cinema, visible from the Co-op. In 1936, the new Art Deco Picture House opened. By 1941, the cinema was allowed to open on Sundays for local troops (mainly Americans).

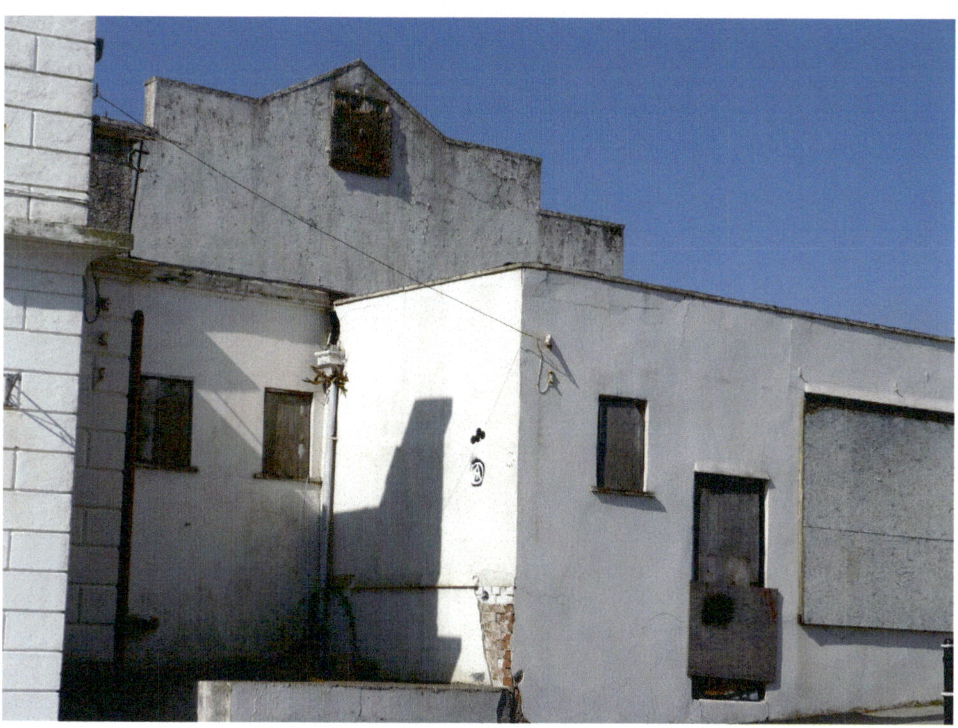

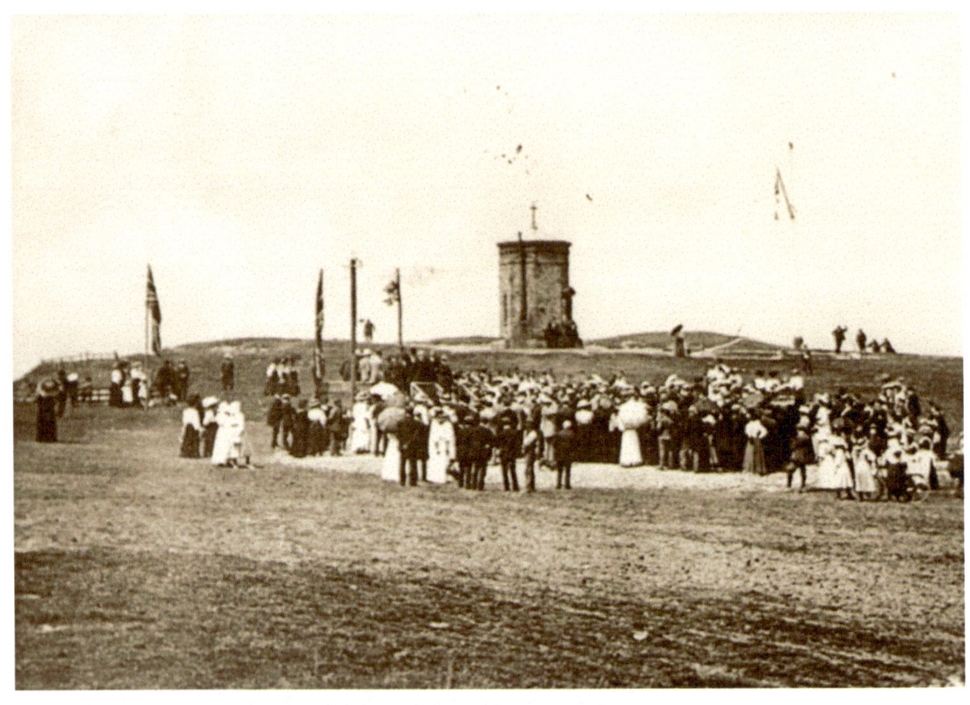

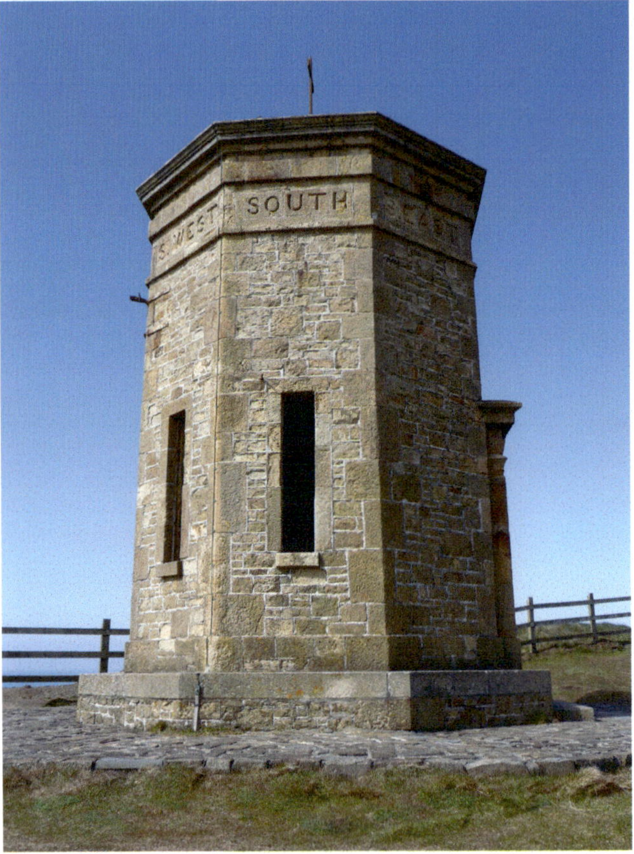

The Pepperpot

Above, the opening of the new sewage works, 1909. A tunnel down through the cliff leads to the beach below, so the sewage was released out to sea at every high tide. To the rear, you can see the compass point storm tower. This was commissioned by Sir Thomas Acland in 1835, built in 1840, and designed by the architect George Wightwick as a rather elegant sandstone refuge or look out for the coastguard and an 'eye-catcher'. It is based on the Temple of Winds in Athens, an octagon with compass points carved in. It was later repositioned away from the cliff edge in 1880, and is known by most people locally as 'the pepperpot'. To the left, the pepperpot as it looks today.

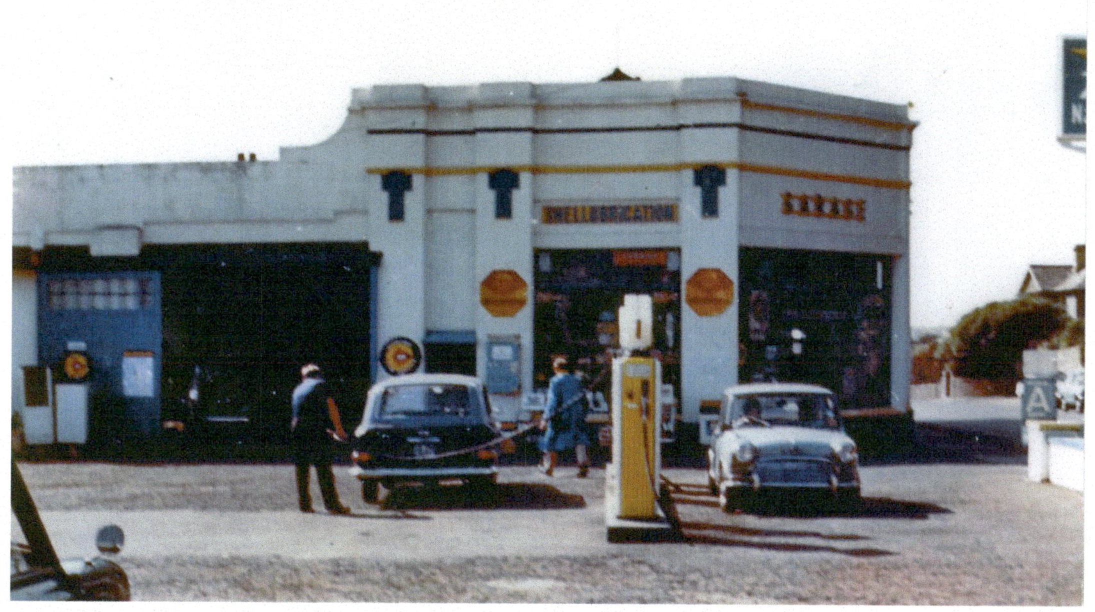

Old Ambulance Station

Maynards Garage in Bencoolen Road in the 1960s; just down from this was the old ambulance station, which was replaced in 2000 by Swallow Close housing association properties (*see below*).

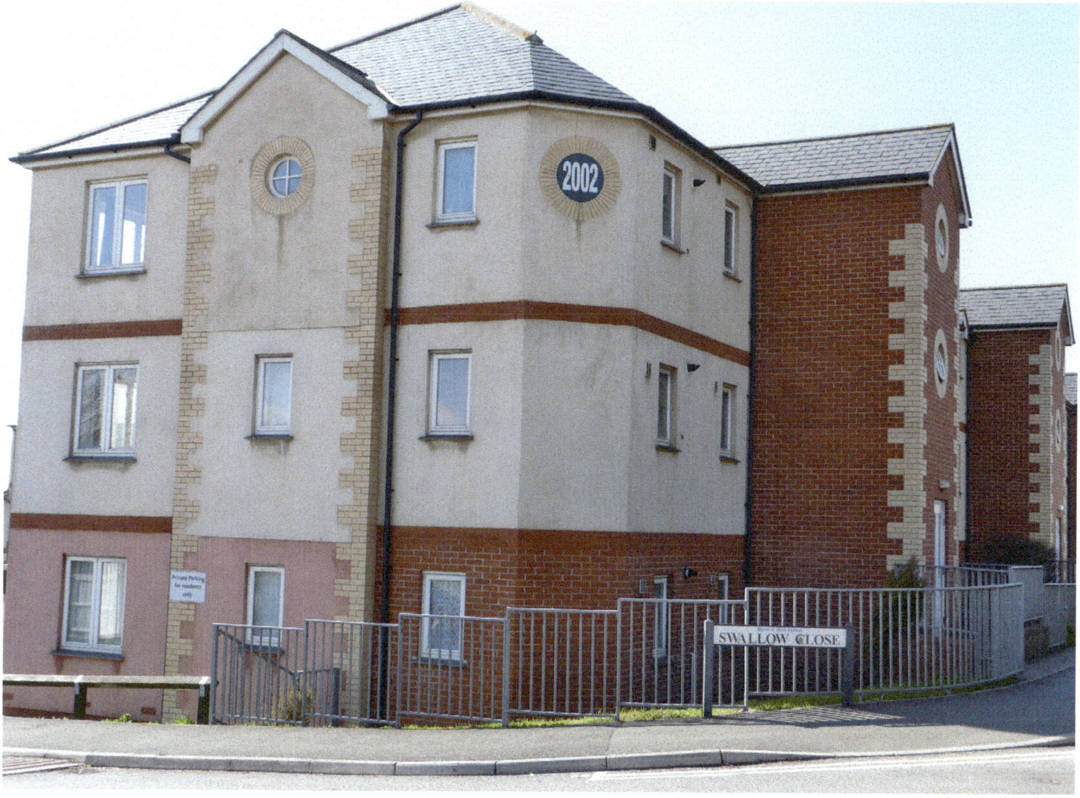

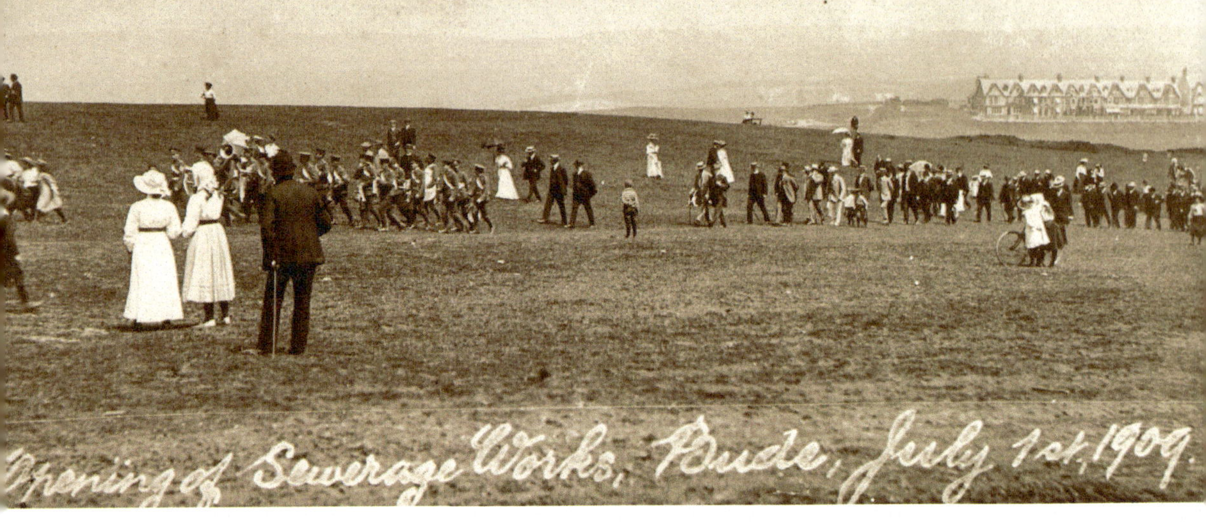

Sewage Day Parade

Above, the opening of the new sewage works, 1909. It is hard to imagine people traipsing across the downs to see a new sewage works. Originally, sewage was discharged without treatment off Compass Point into the sea, but at least it was one up on earth closets in the garden. The ceremony was held on Efford Downs, at what was effectively a trap door! Today, there is no parade to the sewage works, but the 5 March – or the nearest Sunday – sees the St Piran's Day march in Bude and the rest of Cornwall. This celebration of Cornish heritage has grown in popularity over the years. St Piran is the patron saint of Cornwall, and a holiday is a tradition that started amongst tinners in West Cornwall. Perrantide involved the consumption of a great deal of food and drink among the miners, who worked very hard. St Piran's Day has grown popular among those trying to revive the Celtic culture.

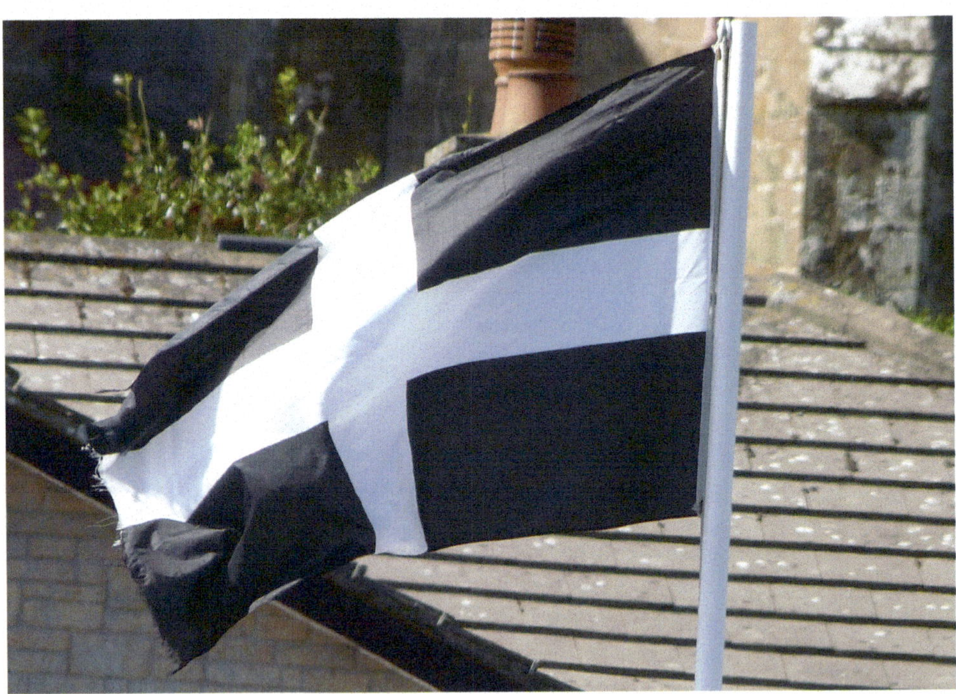

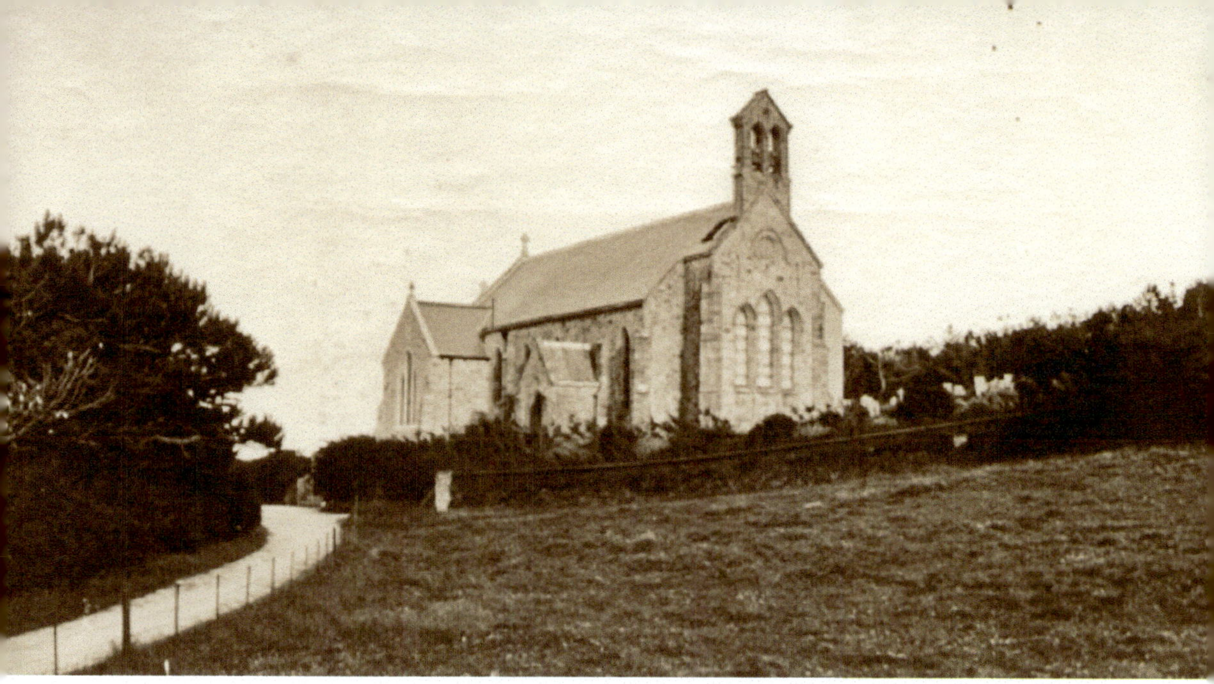

St Michael's Church

St Michael's church meant that local people no longer had to travel to Stratton for church services. It was commissioned by Sir Thomas Acland and built to the Early English Gothic design of Wightwick in 1834 using stone, unsurprisingly, from Trerice. It has a gabled belfry. The chapel started as a chapel of ease, but became the parish church when Bude became an ecclesiastical parish in 1836. It was enlarged in 1878, the work commissioned from the architect Edward Ashworth. However, nonconformity also grew in Bude. Pamela Colman-Smith, designer of tarot cards, died penniless in Bude in 1951 and was buried in this churchyard.

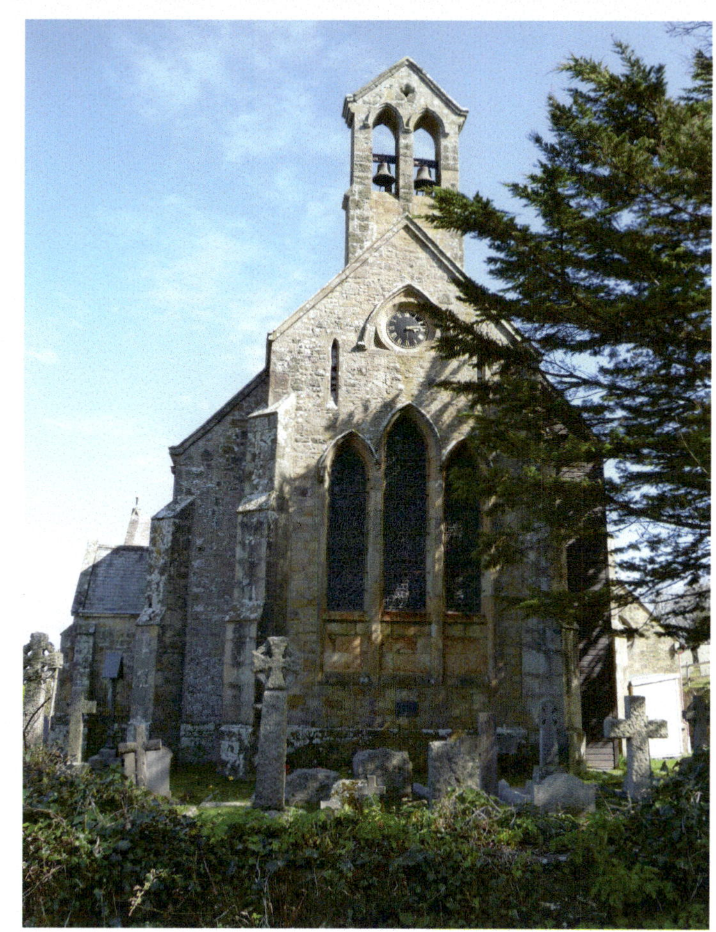

Printed and bound by CPI Group (UK) Ltd, Croydon, CR0 4YY

11/07/2026

02158879-0010